INSIDERS' GUIDE®

OFF THE BEATEN PATH® SERIES

Off the Beaten Path®

SIXTH EDITION

alaska

A GUIDE TO UNIQUE PLACES

MELISSA DeVAUGHN

Revised and updated by

DEB VANASSE

D1052179

INSIDERS' GUIDE®

GUILFORD, CONNECTICUT

AN IMPRINT OF THE GLOBE PEQUOT PRESS

The prices, rates, and hours listed in this guidebook were confirmed at press time. We recommend, however, that you call establishments to obtain current information before traveling.

To buy books in quantity for corporate use or incentives, call **(800) 962–0973** or e-mail **premiums@GlobePequot.com.**

INSIDERS' GUIDE®

Copyright © 1996, 1999, 2002, 2004, 2005, 2008 Morris Book Publishing, LLC

Text design by Linda R. Loiewski
Maps by Equator Graphics © 2008 Morris Book Publishing, LLC
Illustrations by Carole Drong
Spot photography throughout © Ron Niebrugge/wildnatureimages

ISSN 1537-050X
ISBN 978-0-7627-4534-0

Printed in the United States of America
10 9 8 7 6 5 4 3 2 1

To Andy and Roan,

my two Alaska boys,

and to Reilly,

my very special little Alaska girl

—Melissa DeVaughn

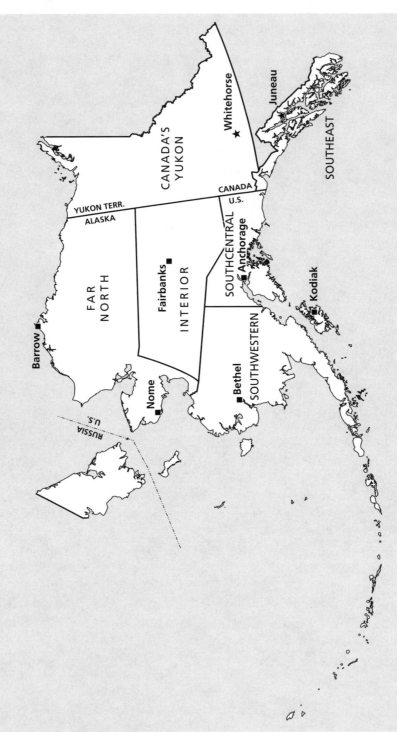

ALASKA

Contents

Introduction

Chances are, if you stay here long enough, someone's going to ask you this: "So, what made you move to Alaska?"

I can't tell you how many times I have been asked that question since I crossed the border into Alaska and settled into my first home here, along the shores of Cook Inlet on the Kenai Peninsula, and now, in the friendly community of Eagle River, just north of Anchorage. It seems as if people see Alaska as a wonderful place to visit, but to live here—to live way out here—who would do such a thing?

Truth is, living in Alaska is easy. I'll tell you why.

My plan—like many people who move this far north—was to experience the wilderness and the wonder of Alaska for a year or two, maybe three, then head back east, to the rural Virginia community in which I was raised. My family's there. My friends are there. It was what I knew and what was comfortable to me. Problem is, Alaska grew on me, too, in a comfortable, unexpected way. Before I knew it I had my own friends and family here (my husband, Andy, was born and raised in Alaska). I see the same faces at the grocery store. I have my own Alaska dentist and doctor, and I've found a mechanic who can't be beat. It's ten years later, and now *I'm* the one who is stopped on the streets and asked for directions.

The landscape, too, has grown on me. The mountains that at first seemed so impenetrable now welcome me, much like the Appalachian Mountains welcomed me as a child. The winters—cold and dark and hunkered down my first winter—are fun now, and getting out means getting on: mushing my dogs, skiing with my husband, tying on snowshoes and exploring a hillside with my son or daughter. The cold doesn't hold me back now; rather, it draws me in.

And the summers. The endless sunshine, the liquid blue skies that wrap around the mountains, and the abundant wildlife that walks through my yard—right past the front door—well, who *wouldn't* stay?

If you're visiting Alaska for the first time, welcome to my home. If you're returning—because no matter how much you had planned to take a vacation to a place other than Alaska again, you just couldn't stay away—well, welcome back. I don't blame you.

You see, Alaska is an easy place to visit, too. No matter what your interests, you can satisfy them here. And no matter what your interests, it's all pretty much off the beaten path. Think about it. Fewer than 700,000 people occupy this state, the largest in the country, with the most wildlands of just about any place on earth. When you arrive in Alaska, you're not just off the beaten path—you're frequently not even on a path at all!

Yet Alaska is an accessible place, no matter how you choose to explore it. I've explored this state by plane, train, automobile, boat, bicycle, dogsled, skis, snowshoes, and even, a few times, by snow machine. My preference is on foot or by dogsled. It is conceivable, traveling by my own power or that supplied by my dogs, to explore places that perhaps no human has ever seen. Once, sitting atop a ridge in Denali National Park and Preserve, I glanced down and saw a grizzly bear paw print deeply mashed into the ground. I wondered, *Are we the only two creatures to have stepped foot here?* Probably not, but it sure feels good to consider such a possibility in this ever-more-crowded world.

With my dogs it is just magical to see winter as they do, full of opportunity and fun—they love to run so—not as the cold, bleak time most people think it must be.

But maybe you prefer a less strenuous way to view this beautiful state. Not a problem. Even if you're seated in a luxury motor coach with plush seats and full meals, just gaze out the window; wherever you look, the view is bound to be breathtaking. Glaciers are within walking distance, bears and moose will likely amble right across the road, and mountain vistas will fill more than your camera lens can capture. Believe me, you won't be disappointed.

Be careful, though. Like me, you may come seeking adventure and realize you've found home.

A Very Small Sketch of a Very Big State

All of Alaska, of course, is located north and west of what geographers call "the contiguous states" of the United States. The Canadian province of British Columbia lies between. Consider this: If Alaska were laid atop a map of the contiguous United States, its size would be one-fifth of the country. It is larger than the three other largest states in the country combined, and it boasts some of the tallest mountains and longest rivers in the world.

In fact, when traveling from one end of the state to the other, you'll encounter varying climates and vastly different landscapes. It's as if Alaska is several countries within itself.

That's why it's best to break Alaska into five generally categorized geographic regions. The southernmost of Alaska's five regions, and closest to the Lower Forty-eight, as Alaskans call these sister states, is **Southeast Alaska.** It's a place of thousands of forested islands plus a long sliver of mainland abutting northern British Columbia. **Southcentral Alaska** forms an arch around the top of the Gulf of Alaska and extends inland roughly to the Alaska Range of mountains, a towering wall of peaks and masses that separates Southcentral from

Interior Alaska. Interior, in turn, forms the huge middle of the state, bordering Canada's Yukon Territory on the east. Its westerly border stops just short of the Bering Sea. Farther north, in fact as far north as you can get and still be in North America, lies **Far North Alaska.** Finally, **Southwestern Alaska** takes in the westernmost approaches of the Alaska mainland, the Alaska Peninsula, Kodiak Island, the long, long string of Aleutian Islands that extends almost to Japan, plus the Pribilof Islands and others of the Bering Sea.

In this book I include a sixth region, **Canada's Yukon Territory,** because—since it is adjacent both to Southeast and Interior Alaska—you cannot drive from the Alaska panhandle to the main body of Alaska without going through this friendly, fascinating portion of Canada.

Some Notes and Cautions

First, a bit about the Alaska lifestyle and dress. Because we are off the beaten path, things are pretty informal all over the state. Friendly is a way of life up here, and you never have to worry about asking an Alaskan for help, or directions, or for the answer to what you think may be a dumb question. "Comfortably casual" is the dress code of the day, every day, even in big city hotels and restaurants. Ladies can certainly wear a cocktail dress or dressy pantsuit in the evening, and their escorts can likewise wear a coat and tie if they'd like, but it really isn't necessary.

For outdoor wear, comfortable walking shoes (or broken-in boots if you're a hiker) are a must. The weather can vary wildly all over the state, so plan to do what Alaskans do: Dress in layers that start with light shirts and/or undershirts then graduate to heavier shirts, sweaters, and even ski-type parkas. The latter are especially useful if you plan glacier cruises, campouts, or travel in the Arctic. Layering allows you to add protection or to peel off excess clothing as the weather dictates. *Very important:* A lightweight combination windbreaker/raincoat should always be at the top of your pack or suitcase.

Now about money: Truth to tell, the cost of living is higher in Alaska than in most other states, but the differences are narrowing all the time. Depending on where you are (in a large, easily accessible city or a remote bush community), costs for lodging and food could be the same as you're accustomed to paying, or only a few percentage points higher—or they could be a great deal more. I have tried to show prices for most admissions, meals, overnights, and other costs. At the time of this writing all the prices (plus telephone numbers, addresses, e-mails, Web sites, and other such data) were current. But things can change; hotel and meal prices, in particular, may well be higher when you make your trip. When a hotel or B&B price is quoted here, it's usually for a double. Singles may (or may not) be less; extra guests in a room usually cost more. There is no statewide sales tax in Alaska, but most municipalities impose one on goods, services, and overnight accommodations. Sales taxes are not included in the prices quoted in this book. Keep in mind that many businesses are open only in the summer—either May through September or June through August—and prices quoted here reflect summer rates.

Remember that when you travel in the Yukon, distances are measured in metric kilometers, not miles; when speed limits are posted at 90 kilometers per hour, that's the same as 55 miles per hour in the United States. Likewise, our Canadian friends pump gasoline in liters, not gallons.

Cell phones are commonplace in Alaska, but they can be unpredictable in remote areas or even areas that aren't so far from city centers. Cell-phone service is improving, but if you bring a phone, don't rely on it for communications. Also, while cities in Alaska have all the conveniences of Lower Forty-eight places, including 911 service, such emergency response systems are not in place in smaller bush communities.

Friends from Outside often ask "When is the best time to visit Alaska?" The answer is, anytime you want to come. Summer obviously ranks as Alaska's most popular season, but the "shoulder" months of May, September, and early October offer the advantages of fewer crowds, often discounted prices, and an unhurried, more relaxed pace of living.

Winter, perhaps surprisingly, is coming into its own with an active statewide agenda of downhill and cross-country skiing, sled dog mushing and racing, winter carnivals, and viewing the eerie and spectacular aurora borealis, the northern lights. Obviously you have to dress for the season (snug long johns, heavy sweaters, and extrawarm outerwear for tours and activities out of doors), but if you use common sense and take the advice of the locals, you can happily and safely experience Alaska during the time of year many Alaskans enjoy their state the most.

Finally . . . it seems incredible but, more than four decades after becoming the forty-ninth state of the United States, Alaskans still get asked if we use U.S. currency and stamps. The answer, of course, is emphatically yes—though if you arrive here with Canadian dimes, quarters, and other small change in your pocket or purse, merchants will accept them at face value. Canadian dollars, on the other hand, may be accepted according to current value on the international money exchanges.

Now, enough of the technical stuff. Read on. Come. Visit. Enjoy!

—Melissa DeVaughn

Southeast Alaska

Incredible place, Southeast Alaska. It's a place of islands—more than 1,000—and a land of lush forests, snowcapped mountains, cascading waterfalls, steep-walled fjords, and magnificent glaciers. From the glaciers fall tens of thousands of huge and minuscule icebergs that dot the seascape and glitter within great bays and inlets. It is a region of proud and skillful Tlingit, Haida, and Tsimshian Native peoples, whose totems and other works of art are beginning to receive the recognition they deserve. It is a land, too, with a colorful, gutsy gold rush past and a place where today huge salmon, monster halibut, and bountiful trout await the angler's lure in salt water, lakes, and streams.

It's an easy place to get to, despite a lack of road access. Literally scores of elegant cruise ships embark each week in summer from West Coast ports en route to the Southeast Alaska panhandle. Stateroom-equipped ferryliners of the Alaska Marine Highway System likewise ply these waters from Bellingham, Washington, and from Prince Rupert, British Columbia. And of course the jets of Alaska Airlines, plus other carriers in the summer, depart daily from Seattle and other cities in the Lower Forty-eight states en route to the land that nineteenth-century

SOUTHEAST ALASKA

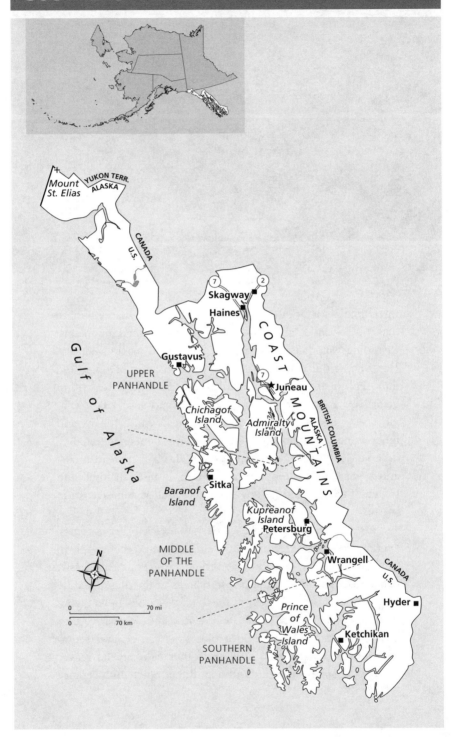

Mount
St. Elias

YUKON TERR.
ALASKA

CANADA
U.S.

Skagway

Haines

Gustavus

UPPER
PANHANDLE

Chichagof
Island

COAST MOUNTAINS

ALASKA
BRITISH COLUMBIA

★Juneau

Admiralty
Island

Gulf of Alaska

Baranof
Island

Sitka

Kupreanof
Island

Petersburg

MIDDLE
OF THE
PANHANDLE

N

0   70 mi
0   70 km

Wrangell

CANADA
U.S.

Hyder

Prince
of
Wales
Island

Ketchikan

SOUTHERN
PANHANDLE

naturalist John Muir called "one of the most wonderful countries in the world." Here's what Southeast Alaska holds in store for visitors these days.

Southern Southeast

Alaskans call **Ketchikan** their First City because it's the first Alaskan port of call for cruise ships, ferries, yachts, and many airlines en route to the forty-ninth state. Spread out along the shores of **Revillagigedo Island** (the name is Spanish and almost unpronounceable; locals just say "Revilla"), the town is just a few blocks wide, but it's miles long. The hustling, bustling city's economy lies in commercial fishing and tourism. Timber, once a thriving business, has all but halted in Southeast, but a few persons still make their living with small logging projects. Sportfishing for salmon, halibut, and freshwater species can be superb. So is the sightseeing at local totem parks and from the decks of small cruisers that explore nearby islands and waters.

For travelers who seek a cruiselike experience, the small ships of half a dozen companies offer comfortable vessels with staterooms, dining rooms, ample decks, observation lounges, and bars—but not the Vegas-like theaters, ballrooms, casinos, boutiques, and crowds of the big liners. It's great the way a number of these boats can nose into small bays and inlets for close-up looks at bears, deer, and other wildlife. Also pleasureable are the whales. When they are in the vicinity, the skipper can cut the engine and drift for a half hour or more to watch the water acrobatics of the great beasts. One option is available from **Classic Alaska Charters** (907–225–0608, www.classicalaskacharters.com), which offers a 40-foot motor yacht for custom trips of five days or more. This is the perfect choice for those who want a personalized or flexible itinerary, or for groups or families who want a vessel all to themselves.

TOP 10 PLACES IN SOUTHEAST ALASKA

Alaska Chilkat Bald Eagle Preserve

Alaska Icefield Expeditions

Alaskan Brewing Company

Alaska's Boardwalk Lodge

Chilkoot Trail

Dyea Campground

Glacier Bay National Park and Preserve

Laughing Raven Lodge

Seawolf Wilderness Adventures

Sitka Wildlife Quest

For a whole slew of cruise packages aboard smaller vessels, check out *Cruise West* (888–851–8133; www.cruisewest.com). They operate eight ships in Alaskan waters, each carrying no more than 130 travelers. Guests enjoy wildlife viewing from the forward lounges and the generous decks as well as overnight accommodations on board. Try the three-night Glacier Bay cruise or the popular eight-night Alaska Inside Passage option, which takes you into smaller ports like Metlakatla and Petersburg in addition to the flagship stops of the larger ships. If you're more interested in wildlife and glaciers, try the Wilderness Inside Passage cruise, an eight-night adventure that showcases the prolific sea life in Icy Strait, Elephant Cove, and Gastineau Channel and includes a stop at a remote Alaskan village. All port stops include optional excursions highlighting local culture. Most of the Cruise West boats set sail from Juneau, with some returning there and others docking in other Southeastern ports.

You'll discover more authentic Native-carved totem poles around Ketchikan than any place else in the world. One of the outstanding collections stands at *Saxman Native Village,* 2½ miles south of Ketchikan on South Tongass Highway. Deeply carved figures represent eagles and ravens, bears and killer whales, and even the figure of a hapless, drowning Indian youth caught in the bite of a giant rock oyster as the tide comes in. Elsewhere in the park you'll find a traditional Beaver Clan community house and on-site carving center. Two 2-hour motor-coach tours by *Cape Fox Tours* (907–225–4846; www.capefoxtours .com) include a visit to Saxman Village and a tour of historic Ketchikan.

The *Totem Heritage Center* (907–225–5900), at 601 Deermount Street, a half mile or so from downtown, houses priceless nineteenth-century totems rescued from decay at abandoned Native villages and sites. They are absolutely majestic, with their deeply carved crests and legends from the cultures of Tlingit and Haida peoples. Admission is $5 and the center is open daily in the summer, 8:00 A.M. to 5:00 P.M. The *Tongass Historical Society Museum,*

Stories in Wood

Totem poles were erected as "story poles" by Tlingit and Haida people who live in Southeastern Alaska, as well as the northwest coast of the United States and Canada, and are unique to these regions. They were usually carved from yellow or red cedar and can stand for fifty or sixty years. Totem poles can be seen today at several locations, including the Totem Bight Park, Saxman Totem Park, and the Totem Heritage Cultural Center near Ketchikan; Klawock Totem Park on Prince of Wales Island; and the Sitka National Historical Park.

downtown at 629 Dock Street, contains exhibits and artifacts from Ketchikan's Native past and its fishing, mining, and timbering heritage. Admission is $2. Call (907) 225–5600 for more information.

Another good totem-viewing location requires a scenic fifteen-minute air flight or one-hour ferry to the Tsimshian Native village of **Metlakatla** on Annette Island.

southeast alaskafacts

The name Ketchikan is derived from the Tlingit word *Kitschk-Hin,* meaning "the creek of the thundering wings of an eagle."

Among sites to see and explore in Metlakatla is the village founder **Father William Duncan's Cottage,** built in 1891 and now a museum that chronicles the history of Annette Island's formerly Canadian Indian peoples and the lay Anglican priest who brought them to Alaska. Admission to the museum is $2; the hours are Monday through Friday 8:30 A.M. to 12:30 P.M., and during scheduled tours, which are offered by **Metlakatla Tours.** The tour takes in the museum, the church, the community fisheries plant, and the **Tribal Longhouse,** which serves as a Tsimshian clan house where dancing and ceremonies take place. The event is followed by a tasty salmon feast. Individual and guided walking tours also are an option. Contact Metlakatla Tours at (907) 886–8687 or www.metlakatlatours.net.

If you're a hiker you'll find Ketchikan a great place to roam from, with lots of ocean, forest, lake, and mountain trails. The 3½-mile **Deer Mountain Trail,** which begins practically downtown and runs to the 3,000-foot summit, provides a particularly grand vista of the city below and nearby islands and ocean waters. Ask for directions to the trailhead at the **Ketchikan Visitor Information Center,** downtown at 131 Front Street. Call the visitor center at (907) 225–6166 or (800) 770–3300 or visit the Web site at www.visit-ketchikan.com.

Earlier we mentioned the opportunity to explore waters around Ketchikan by small sightseeing cruiser. Goldbelt Tourism's **Alaska Cruises** (800–820–2628; www.goldbelttours.com) offers a six-and-a-half-hour excursion from downtown Ketchikan to **Misty Fjords National Monument,** a wondrous 2.2-million-acre national treasure lined by cliffs towering thousands of feet above the sea and waterfalls cascading into the placid waters. View New Eddystone Rock, a volcanic plug rising 237 feet from the waters of Behm Canal, or keep watch for seals, bald eagles, and seabirds. The cost, including a light meal and beverages, is $130 per person. Goldbelt also offers a shorter **Ketchikan Historic Waterfront** day cruise for $50, which takes in areas where many of Ketchikan's historical events took place. Cruise by Ketchikan Creek—the community's former "Creek Street red-light district"—where salmon may be seen jumping as they begin their upstream migration. From the vessel view Saxman

TOP ANNUAL EVENTS IN SOUTHEAST ALASKA

Little Norway Festival,
in Petersburg; held each May to
celebrate Norwegian Independence
Day. For information call
(907) 772–4636.

Juneau Jazz and Classics,
a weeklong celebration in May of
some of the best jazz around.
For further information call the Juneau
Convention and Visitors Bureau at
(888) 581–2201 or go to www.jazzand
classics.org.

Southeast Alaska State Fair,
held each year in Haines. Five fun-filled
days every summer, with parade,
entertainment each night, and more.
For information call (907) 766–2476.

Klondike Road Relay,
held each September; a running road
relay from Skagway, Alaska, to
Whitehorse, Yukon Territory.
For information call the Skagway
Convention and Visitors Bureau at
(907) 983–2854.

Totem Park (with its collection of intriguing totem poles) and Pennock Island, where hardy individuals pursue the pioneering lifestyle. Learn about the island's rain forest from the warmth of the cabin or out on deck.

If you want professionals to organize, equip, and guide you on a Misty Fjord kayaking trip, Betsey Burdett and Geoff Gross offer two-and-a-half-hour to six-day excursions within Misty Fjords National Monument as well as among the Barrier Islands in the South Prince of Wales Island Wilderness area. Their company, **Southeast Exposure** (37 Potter Road; 907–225–8829; www.south eastexposure.com), also offers day trips along the Ketchikan waterfront and into semiwilderness waters nearby. Single fiberglass kayaks rent for $45 per day. Guided two-and-a-half-hour waterfront tours start at $50. A six-day Misty Fjords trip is $950 per person.

Perhaps one of the best ways to see what Ketchikan is really about is to take advantage of one of the best travel bargains around: Rent one of a network of **USDA Forest Service cabins** in the wilderness for as little as $25 per cabin. The forest service maintains more than 150 warm and weather-tight cabins beside remote mountain lakes and isolated ocean shores throughout the **Tongass National Forest,** which makes up most of Southeast Alaska. An additional forty such units exist in Southcentral Alaska's **Chugach National Forest.** Cabins may be reserved for up to a week at a time, and reservations can be made up to 180 days in advance using the toll-free number (877) 444–6777 or accessing www.recreation.gov.

Most units have bunks to accommodate up to six and contain either wood- or oil-burning stoves. Don't, however, expect a "Hilton in the wilderness." You bring your own food, sleeping bags, and other supplies. Privies are "down the path." Mostly these cabins are fly-in units, though you can reach a few by boat or hiking trail. For bear protection Alaskans and visitors often carry 30-06 or larger rifles. No permit is required. It's seldom, however, that someone has to use one. Virtually every town in both regions has charter air services that specialize in serving fly-in campers. Rates vary with the distance you need to fly.

For information about Tongass cabins, call (907) 228–6220 or visit the **Southeast Alaska Discovery Center** at 50 Main Street in Ketchikan (www.fs .fed.us/r10/tongass/districts/discoverycenter). For similar information concerning the Chugach, contact the **Alaska Public Lands Information Center** in Anchorage at (907) 271–2737 or www.nps.gov/aplic/center.

From Ketchikan a popular fly-in-only choice is **Patching Lake Cabin,** a woodstove-equipped mountain lake unit with a skiff on-site. You'll find trout in the water for fishing plus the possibility of deer and black bear in the woods for viewing. (Don't, however, even think of feeding these critters or observing them too closely.) The local USDA Forest Service number for information is (907) 228–6220. Although the cabin rents for only $25 a night, a fly-in charter to Patching Lake would be in the neighborhood of $350 for a party of two.

While in Ketchikan, don't pass up two boating opportunities offered by **Alaska Travel Adventures.** For $85 and three-and-a-half hours of your time, you'll glide across a quiet lake surrounded by forest and mountains. Look closely for bald eagles. A guide will help maneuver the boat while also teaching about the surrounding Tongass rain forest and the plants and animals that flourish there. If you're not keen on paddling, opt for the $89 Wilderness Adventure Cruise and Rain Forest Exploration. You'll start with a guided hike, mostly by boardwalk, through old-growth forest and along a beach, learning about the symbiotic relationship between the indigenous peoples and the lush forest in which they lived. After a hearty snack, take a ride in a motorized raft to look for sea lions, porpoises, harbor seals, and bald eagles. For further information call (800) 478–0052 in Alaska or (800) 791–2673 outside Alaska. The company's Web site is www.alaskatraveladventures.com.

southeast alaskafacts

The Tongass National Forest, in Southeast Alaska, is the largest U.S. forest, with sixteen million acres.

A unique venture among Alaska Travel Adventures's outdoor opportunities is their Backcountry Jeep Safaris. The company offers Jeep-led tours through remote land, most in Southeast Alaska. The Ketchikan-based adventure is one of the company's most popular. It's an all-day adventure that combines off-road riding in your own colorful Jeep Wrangler as well as canoeing in giant canoes. Reach Alaska Travel Adventures at the above numbers and Web site.

Ketchikan-based *Taquan Air* (907–225–8800 or 800–770–8800; www.taquan air.com) has been flying visitors and locals alike on air excursions since 1977, and the company boasts the most experienced pilot staff in Southeast. Taquan offers flight-seeing over Misty Fjords National Monument and three-and-a-half-hour trips to the Anan Wildlife Observatory. The one-and-a-quarter-hour Misty Fjords National Monument trip takes you over some of the most incredible scenery in Alaska, with 3,000-foot-high walls of granite to lush forests to snowcapped mountains. Look for mountain goats, bears, deer, wolves, and moose, and land at a remote location for some real serenity. The rate is $209 per person.

southeast
alaskafacts

More than a thousand islands make up the 500-mile-long Alexander Archipelago, which extends from Icy Bay, north of Yakutat, to the border between the United States and Canada at the south end of Prince of Wales Island.

The longer *Anan Wildlife Observatory* trek is priced at $425 per person and takes you within a stone's throw of some of Alaska's most awesome brown and black bears during the height of the silver-salmon spawning season, July through September. But don't fear: Guides are with you every step of the way, from the plane ride to the observatory to the ½-mile hike along a maintained USDA Forest Service trail that leads to the bears' territory.

One of Taquan's shorter and more affordable flights is the Alps, Eagles, and Totems tour, where for $139 and thirty-five minutes you can view by air the forested fjord while keeping an eye open for bears, goats, and, of course, eagles. The flight takes you over the rustic community of *Herring Cove* before returning along the coast by Saxman Native village to Ketchikan.

It's not located off the beaten path, but the smallish, moderately priced *Gilmore Hotel,* at 326 Front Street (800–275–9423; www.gilmorehotel.com), is often overlooked. The hotel offers a commanding view of Ketchikan's frantic waterfront, taking in fishermen preparing their nets, luxury cruise liners in port, freighters heaped with cargo, and a constant stream of floatplanes landing, taking off, or flying down the channel. Built in 1927 of solid concrete, the hotel's forty rooms are modern, clean, and have full baths and color TVs. Summer rates begin at $99 per night. It's on the National Register of Historic Places. *Annabelle's Famous Keg and Chowder House* off the hotel lobby offers room service or restaurant dining on the premises. The gorgeous 20-foot mahogany bar at Annabelle's is well worth a look-see, as are the murals that depict Ketchikan's notorious old Creek Street red-light district, where Annabelle entertained as a favorite lady of the night in the 1920s.

Speaking of **Creek Street** and its entrepreneurs, do give the lane a stroll, off Stedman Street opposite the big harbor downtown called Thomas Basin. A former brothel called **Dolly's House** (open daily in the summer) has been restored as a museum there, as have numerous other "houses," which now contain boutiques, gift shops, and galleries.

She will never serve the masses, but for a select few visitors who want really personalized tour attention, former schoolmarm Lois Munch will introduce you to Ketchikan's Native history, take you to totem parks, tell you about the critters in a saltwater tide pool, explain the flora and fauna of the area, and even show you an occupied eagle's nest. She calls her operation **Classic Tours.** You can't miss her restored, blazing-red '55 Chevy, which she'll use to take you touring. Two-hour tours are $84 per person, and three-hour tours run $99 per person, with a two-person minimum. But call Lois if you're looking for something even more personalized. For $125 per hour for one to two people, she'll create a tour to match your interests to a T. She can be reached by phone at (907) 225-3091, or visit her Web site at www.classictours.com.

For personalized attention that includes accommodations, check out Victorian-style **Madame's Manor** (877-531-8159 or 907-247-2774; www.madamesmanor .com) in the town's historic Nob Hill district. You'll enjoy great views of the Inside Passage, and on rainy days a fireplace warms the formal parlor. Your host will be happy to fill you in on all sorts of insider information, from historical tidbits to advice on sightseeing, dining, and entertainment. Rates start at $95 per night.

For simple and affordable housing, try **Eagle View Hostel** at 2303 Fifth Avenue. The hostel has clean rooms and a friendly staff. Call (907) 225-5461 or visit www.eagleviewhostel.com.

It's not quite the biggest island under the American flag (the Big Island of Hawaii and Kodiak Island in Southwest Alaska rank first and second in that category), but **Prince of Wales Island** (POW) is huge nonetheless: 2,231 square miles of forested mountains, deep U-shaped valleys, lakes, streams, and 900 miles of coastal shores, bays, and inlets. You get to Prince of Wales by state ferry from Ketchikan or Wrangell or by plane. POW is not without controversy: Environmentalists say the island has been overlogged; the timber industry says reforestation is coming along very nicely. Regardless of the difference of opinion, there are still plenty of scenic spots to explore, from secluded coves to seaside villages to lush expanses of old-growth forest. One thing logging has done is create lots of roads (some gravel, others asphalt) that you can use for exploring and camping. Kayaking or canoeing is superb at lots of freshwater and saltwater access points.

If your budget allows, at *Alaska's Boardwalk Lodge* you'll enjoy first-class lodging, amenities, and service along with astounding outdoor adventures on Prince of Wales Island. Tucked beside the ocean next to a pristine tidewater pond, this hand-hewn log lodge is the perfect launching point for your favorite activities, from prime saltwater fishing for halibut, salmon, lingcod, and snapper to fly fishing in the area's abundant streams and lakes to adventure treks to the totems of *Kasaan* and the huge *El Capitan Cave.* Between the made-to-order breakfasts, the gourmet meals featuring surf-and-turf selections, the beautifully landscaped grounds, the inviting outdoor hot tub, and a guest-to-staff ratio that's nearly one to one, you'll likely never have felt so pampered. The guides are first class, and all of the staff is eager to please. High-season rates start at $3,995 for a three-night package including floatplane transport from Ketchikan, lodging, meals, fishing, fishing gear, guide services, and land tours. All visits are customized to the individual needs and desires of the guests. For more information call (800) 764–3918 or visit www.boardwalklodge.com.

For do-it-yourselfers the USDA Forest Service has two campgrounds and more than twenty $25 to $40 rental cabins on lakes and inlets throughout the island. Call (907) 826–3271 in Craig; (907) 828–3304 at Thorne Bay. For reservations call (877) 444–6777 or access www.recreation.gov. The forest service also offers daily tours of the huge El Capitan Cave at the north end of the island. The *Log Cabin RV Park and Resort* (800–544–2205 or 907–755–2205; www.logcabinresortandrvpark.com) offers cabins at $80 per night plus camper facilities and fishing out of Klawock. Beachfront condo units or a log house are $150 a night for two, or $925 for the week. They also rent canoes, skiffs, and outboards and offer charter fishing.

The *Fireweed Lodge* (907–755–2930; www.fireweedlodge.com), also in Klawock, offers eighteen rooms at $129 for doubles plus fishing charters and access to excellent hiking and canoeing.

McFarland's Floatel (888–828–3335; www.mcfarlandsfloatel.com) provides beachfront log cabins at Thorne Bay. The $295-per-night units are suited for up to four guests, but six can fit comfortably for an extra $65 per additional person. Owners Jim and Jeannie McFarland also offer guided and nonguided trips around Thorne Bay. You can rent a 15-foot aluminum skiff for $95 if you want to hit the water on your own.

It would be easy to miss *Hyder,* in southernmost Southeastern. In fact, sadly, most travelers do. If you're Alaska bound, however, and traveling along British Columbia's Yellowhead Highway between Prince George and Prince Rupert, take the 140-mile paved Cassiar Highway north from its junction with the Yellowhead Highway (about 150 miles before Prince Rupert). Then take the access road off the Cassiar to Hyder. This road also leads to Hyder's very close neighbor, **Stewart.** Stewart (population 400 or so) sits in British Columbia, Canada, and Hyder (population 100) lies in Alaska. They're separated by 2⁄₁₀ miles and the **U.S.–Canada border.** Learn more about these communities by visiting their joint Web site, www.stewart-hyder.com.

What's to see in and around Hyder? For one thing, you'll find spectacular glaciers to view, including **Salmon Glacier,** the world's fifth largest, only 20 miles north of town. You'll also find abandoned mine sites, late nineteenth-century buildings to photograph, superb fishing, hiking trails, and—3 miles north of town—a salmon stream and bear observatory where you can see black bears or brownies. Your first stop in this part of Alaska should be at the **Hyder Community Association** building in town. There you can get information on the area as well as check out a small collection of museum items that tell the story of Hyder. In Stewart the **Stewart Historical Society Museum** (250–636–2568; www.stewartmuseum.homestead.com), at 603 Columbia Street, displays wildlife as well as bits and pieces of local history.

The **Grand View Inn,** located ¾ mile from the border on Hyder's main road, has ten clean, private rooms, four with kitchenettes, in quiet, woodsy surroundings. Owners George and Dee Hancock, a brother-and-sister team, recommend the area bear viewing at Fish Creek, which attracts up to 40,000 summertime visitors each year. For current rates contact them at (250) 636–9174 or www.grandviewinn.net.

The Middle of the Panhandle

Wrangell is a natural for the visitor who wants an out-of-the-way travel experience in a locale that's still a little rough around the edges. It's clean, neat, and easy to get around, but everything isn't laid out for you. You get there either by a daily Alaska Airlines jet from Juneau, Ketchikan, or Seattle or by the ferries of the Alaska Marine Highway System. The tour company movers of masses have seemingly passed Wrangell by, at least for now. The mega–cruise ships rarely call, and even medium or small vessels stop much less frequently than in Ketchikan, Sitka, and Juneau. The result is that it's a made-to-order destination for travelers who enjoy ferreting out backcountry or backyard jewels in the rough (literally and figuratively)—from semiprecious garnets you can physically collect yourself on a nearby ledge to some of the best and most photogenic totem poles in Alaska. Now for a little background.

Wrangell history goes back possibly 8,000 years, when someone (no one knows who) carved mysterious stick-figure petroglyph etchings in stone along the seashore. More recently, according to Tlingit oral history, the present Native peoples settled the area more than 2,000 years ago, arriving via the

Stikine River. Sometime in the 1700s a Tlingit chief named Shakes (the first of several to claim that name) selected the present site of Wrangell as home for his people.

In the early 1800s English, American, and Russian ships came exploring. The Russians established Redoubt St. Dionysius in 1834. The English obtained a lease and occupied the same site, calling it Fort Stikine, in 1840. With the sale of Alaska to the United States in 1867, the community came under American jurisdiction and was called Fort Wrangell. Gold mining, fur trading, fisheries, and commerce have been Wrangell's economic staples since.

Recent years have seen the modest beginnings of tourism, and it's true, there's a lot in and around the community for visitors to experience. A good place to visit early, in order to get oriented, is the **Chamber of Commerce Visitor Information Center** at 107 Stikine Avenue, near the city dock (907–874–2381; www.wrangell.com). Another is the **Wrangell Museum,** in the basement of the city community center between the Presbyterian church and the high school at 318 Church Street. The museum is well worth a visit. It includes masterfully carved totemic house posts, dating from 1770 to 1790, from the Bear Tribal House on Chief Shakes Island. Also on display: artifacts from the Russian and British occupations and from the gold rush era, petroglyphs, bird and natural history exhibits, minerals, and various other items.

southeast
alaskafacts

The city of Wrangell on Wrangell Island in Southeast Alaska has been ruled by three nations since its founding by fur traders in 1811: Russia, Great Britain, and the United States.

Hours are 10:00 A.M. to 5:00 P.M. Monday through Friday and variable hours on weekends.

The most notable cultural site in the community is **Chief Shakes Island,** connected to Wrangell by a walking bridge and located in the middle of Wrangell Harbor. The tribal house and totems there are among the best carved and most colorful in Alaska.

You can see some petroglyphs on display at the city museum and library, but most must be sought out at low tide on Wrangell Island's mysterious **Petroglyph Beach State Historic Park** north of town. The etched figures on the rocks, three dozen or more, seem to depict spirit faces, fish, owls, spirals, and other designs, although no one knows what the figures really mean or who created them. To reach them turn left on Evergreen Avenue from the ferry terminal. Walk north on Evergreen about ¾ mile to a boardwalk leading to the beach. Walk down the boardwalk and head right toward the big rock outcropping on the northern high-tide limit of the beach. Don't, under any circumstances, attempt to move these rocks. You may, of course, photograph them.

A moderately difficult hike (due to a rapid ascent) over the **Rainbow Falls Trail** can be short or long, depending on whether you extend the distance by also hiking the high country ridges along the 2⁷⁄₁₀-mile **Institute Creek Trail** that junctions along the way with the Rainbow Falls Trail. The basic route takes you about ¾ mile from its start at mile 4.6 on the Zimovia Highway to an observation platform and a great view of picturesque Rainbow Falls, then later to a sweeping view of Chichagof Pass. Another popular hiking choice in town is **Mount Dewey,** also called Muir Mountain since John Muir climbed it in 1879 and caused a considerable stir among the locals when he lit a huge bonfire at the top. The trail is primitive in places, but the view from the top is considered well worth the effort.

Totem pole on
Chief Shakes Island

If that's not enough outdoor recreation for you, try **Rainwalker Expeditions** for bike and walking tours. Rainwalker Expeditions, operated by Marie Oboczky (907–874–2549; www.rainwalkerexpeditions.com), features two-hour, half-day, full-day, and custom outings suited to your interests. If you want a more remote location, she also offers a floating lodge, the Rain Haven, that sleeps up to five people. Rates start at $650 for two people for two nights, which includes transportation by boat from Wrangell to places like the Anan Wildlife Observatory, a popular option in July and August. Dockside lodging is $85 per person per night. Rainwalker offers kayak rentals for $40 (singles) and $60 (doubles) a day. Guided trips start at $150.

There are two ways to get one or more of Wrangell's well-known garnets. The easiest is simply to buy one from youngsters you'll find selling them at the docks to cruise ship and ferry passengers. Local kids sell the garnets for $1 to $50, depending on size. Or you can purchase a $10 daily permit at the Wrangell Museum and chip your own garnets from **Wrangell Garnet Ledge,** located on the mainland near the mouth of the Stikine River, about 7 miles northeast of Wrangell Island. Waterborne sightseeing tours often stop at the site.

Though you probably didn't travel all the way to Southeast Alaska to play a round of golf, it's worth noting that one of the attractions in Wrangell is the **Muskeg Meadows Golf Course.** This regulation nine-hole course features some of the most spectacular scenery a golfer could hope for, from ocean views to snow-studded mountains to lush rain forest. And what other course has a raven rule? If your ball is stolen by a raven, you may replace it without penalty as long as you have a witness. If you happen to be in Wrangell in April, you can take in the annual opening tournament, held in conjunction with the Wrangell Garnet Festival celebrating the arrival of bald eagles at the Stikine River. For more information on Muskeg Meadows, call (907) 874–4654 or visit www.wrangellalaskagolf.com.

For close-to-town overnight accommodations, call Gordon and Becky Rooney to reserve a room with a private or shared bath at **Rooney's Roost Bed and Breakfast** (907–874–2026; www.rooneysroost.com), located at 206 McKinnon Street just a block from downtown. The Rooneys have completely renovated the century-old home, and breakfasts are a full gourmet affair. Prices start at $100, and all rooms have private baths. Also in town is Wrangell's largest hotel (yet with thirty-four rooms, minute in comparison to large city hotels), the **Stikine Inn,** complete with restaurant and meeting rooms. Prices vary from $115 to $162, depending upon the room, and reservations can be made by calling (888) 874–3388 or visiting www.stikineinnak.com. Another option, this one close to Chief Shakes Island, is the **Hungry Beaver** (907–874–3005) just behind the restaurant and lounge of the same name at 274 Shakes Street. Four comfortable rooms with kitchenettes run $101 for singles. For at least one meal partake of the restaurant's locally famous pizza fare. For the economy minded the **Wrangell Hostel,** operated by the First Presbyterian Church at 220 Church Street, opens mid-May through Labor Day and charges $18 per person per night. Phone (907) 874–3534.

Bruce Harding's **Old Sourdough Lodge,** 1104 Peninsula Avenue, started life some years back as a small bunkhouse for loggers. Today the rustic log lodge offers comfortable accommodations, including the Jacuzzi-equipped Harding River suite that sleeps six, as well as standard rooms with bath. Also on-site: a sauna and steam bath, plus the Sourdough Room cocktail lounge. Standard room rates start at $94 in season for singles; bed-and-breakfast accommodations start at $104 for singles. Meals cost $10 for breakfast or lunch; dinners start at $24. Call (800) 874–3613 for information, or visit the lodge's Web site at www.akgetaway.com.

John Verhey operates **Stickeen Wilderness Adventures,** offering day trips through forested wilderness up the Stikine River aboard the eighteen-passenger *Triton* and *Kraken*. The latter vessel carries six passengers and can be chartered for small groups. Both vessels were specifically designed and built to navigate the Stikine. The company also offers trips south of Wrangell to **Anan Wildlife Observatory,** the only black bear observatory in Southeast Alaska. The Stikine River and Anan trips cost $170. If you'd like to travel past the coastal mountains to experience a different climate (translate: less rain), Verhey will arrange excursions to Telegraph Creek in conjunction with Sunrise Aviation. For information call (800) 874–2085 or visit www.akgetaway.com.

Verhey also is owner of **Alaska Vistas,** which he established in 1995 as the first paddle-sports outfitter in Wrangell. He offers fully guided kayak trips, Stikine River raft trips, Anan bear tours, and jet boat tours. Single kayak rentals are $47 per day, and doubles rent for $57 per day. Fully guided rates include everything you'll need for a safe and comfortable experience. Guided trips vary from $190 to $2,400 per trip, depending upon what you want to do. Serious river runners might try the Stikine River raft trip.

southeast alaskafacts

The Stikine River is the fastest-flowing navigable river in North America.

The $2,400-per-person rate includes lodging and meals before and after the trip in Wrangell, nine days on the river, plus gear, food, and charter flight to Telegraph Creek from Wrangell. Call (866) 874–3006 or visit www.alaskavistas.com.

For another option try Eric Yancey's **Breakaway Adventures,** a jet boat tour operation that's been on the Stikine River for more than ten years. Yancey's tours, priced at $135 to $170 per person with discounts for groups, seniors, and children, take passengers up the Stikine River and to **LeConte Glacier,** whose claim to fame is that it is the southernmost saltwater glacier in North America. The 22- and 28-foot inboard jet boats also travel to the Anan Wildlife Observatory. Passengers will receive an area map and historical tour along the way. For more information call Yancey at (907) 874–2488 or (888) 385–2488 or visit www .breakawayadventures.com on the Internet.

Remember those bargain-priced ($25 to $40 per night) fly-in USDA Forest Service cabins in the wilderness? Twenty-two of them are located in the Wrangell Ranger District, including one near the Anan Wildlife Observatory. Call (907) 874–2323 for information. For reservations call the park reservation system at (877) 444–6777 or visit www.recreation.gov. If you're a hot-tub buff, ask for information about the **Chief Shakes Hot Springs** tubs (one sheltered, one not) that the forest service has placed along the Stikine River about 22 miles from Wrangell.

High above the surface, **Sunrise Aviation** (907–874–2319 or 800–874–2311; www.sunriseflights.com) will take you flight-seeing over the Stikine River and several glaciers, ice-clogged LeConte Bay, and various high-country lakes, for $452 on a plane that holds five passengers. Custom flight-sees and drop-offs for wilderness adventures also are available. On the ground, Mark Galla's ***Alaska Peak and Seas*** (907–874–2454; www.wedoalaska.com) will take you into the backcountry for just about any trip you can imagine.

If you're tired of running with the crowd or dealing with big tour companies that run the show from outside the state, take in all that this part of the state has to offer with ***Alaska Charters and Adventures*** (888–993–2750; www.alaskaupclose.com). With a limit of six guests per boat, Alaska Charters promises the kind of intimate experiences with the wilderness that you just can't get when you're part of a big group. Whether it's the Stikine River by jet boat, a trek to Anan Wildlife Observatory or LeConte Glacier, kayaking, canoeing, fishing, or whale watching, you'll be able to arrange it with this locally owned company specializing in custom tours.

Back in 1897, when the rest of the world went crazy over gold in the Klondike, Norwegian-born Peter Buschmann came north, too, but only as far as Mitkof Island in Southeast Alaska. He settled there to fish and eventually build a salmon cannery and sawmill. Other Norwegians, noting the great fisheries of the region, the abundant ice from nearby LeConte Glacier, and the majestic surroundings, joined Buschmann and his family and named their community ***Petersburg.***

Today, Peter's burg thrives as one of the most active fishing ports in the United States. Fishermen seine, troll, and gillnet for salmon in the summer; seek halibut into the fall; fish for herring in the spring; go after crab in the winter; and harvest shrimp year-round. Sport fishing for salmon and halibut is especially rewarding.

About 3,000 Alaskans call Petersburg home. Most of them fish or work in the fisheries industry or in businesses that service the fishermen. In the summer one of the most pleasant no-cost "tours" you can take is simply to wander in Petersburg's three public harbors along 2½ miles of floats, taking in the 1,200 or so commercial fishing vessels that may be in port at any one time. Tourism is a rapidly growing but not yet dominant industry in Petersburg, and therein—as in Wrangell—lies much of the community's charm. The town is "real." And it's clean, neat, well laid out, and noticeably Norwegian, with its Scandinavian rosemaling floral designs on buildings and homes and its huge, white 1912 ***Sons of Norway Hall*** downtown (complete with a ***Viking sailing vessel*** ready to put to sea). If you're lucky you'll find Norwegian seafood specialties on menus at local restaurants. (Beer-batter halibut is a particular pleaser. So is the tiny, succulent, popcorn-sized shrimp for which the community is known.) The town, no surprise, is nicknamed Little Norway, and its biggest celebration is the *Little Norway Festival,* timed each May to celebrate Norwegian Independence Day.

A good place to start your visit is the *Petersburg Visitor Information Center* at First and Fram Streets. Office hours are 9:00 A.M. to 5:00 P.M. Monday through Saturday and noon to 4:00 P.M. Sunday in the summer. Phone (907) 772–4636 or (866) 484–4700 for information or visit www.petersburg.org.

The community's biggest visitor attraction is nearby LeConte Glacier, one of the most active in North America, with a constant succession of icebergs calving and crashing explosively from its wide face into the frigid waters of LeConte Bay. Many days the big and little bergs literally carpet bay waters from shore to shore, and sightseeing boats must gently push the ice aside as they cruise in front of the glacier.

The waters of North Frederick Sound, also near Petersburg, provide superb viewing of another major visitor attraction: great humpback whales. Large numbers of these gentle giants feed here in the summer months, to the considerable delight of visitors as well as locals. Several charter operators offer LeConte Glacier and whale-watching excursions. One of your best options is the *Kaleidoscope Cruises* tour (800–868–4373; www.petersburglodgingandtours.com), with marine biologist and naturalist Barry Bracken as your captain. With more than thirty years' experience, Bracken is well versed in glacier ecology as well as marine wildlife. He'll take you aboard his 28-foot *Island Dream* in search of whales, other marine wildlife, and calving glaciers. Tours are five to ten hours. Rates start at $175 per person for the five-hour tour, and a ten-hour customized trip for groups of up to four people is $140 per boat per hour.

Another fine way to experience Petersburg is by taking part in one of *Tongass Kayak Adventures*' (907–772–4600; www.tongasskayak.com) guided sea-kayaking trips. A $70, four-hour tour of Petersburg Creek takes place almost daily through the summer. Or opt for a more challenging three-night, $930 LeConte Glacier Bay trek or an eight-night glaciers and whales package for $2,350.

For a bird's-eye view of LeConte Glacier, you can book a flight-seeing excursion with *Pacific Wing* (907–772–4258; www.pacificwing.com). A forty-five-minute flight costs $160 per person for two passengers and $130 per person for three passengers.

For the visitor who enjoys walking tours, the tabloid-sized *Viking Visitor Guide,* available at the visitor center, provides an easy-to-follow walking-tour map covering more than thirty points of interest, from major fish-processing plants along the waterfront to *Eagle's Roost Park* off Nordic Drive just a few minutes' walk from downtown. One or two eagles are almost always in residence to pose for pictures on their craggy perches.

You'll know you've arrived at the ***Clausen Memorial Museum,*** located at Second and Fram Streets, when you see the large bronze sculpture called *Fisk* (Norwegian for "fish"), which displays the many species of fish to be found in these waters. Inside, exhibits vary from an old-time fish-gutting machine (called an iron chink) to the re-created office of a pioneer cannery owner. There are also fur farming exhibits; Native artifacts, including an old Indian canoe; and early-day community photographs. Don't miss the two huge wall-mounted salmon, one of them the largest king ever caught (126½ pounds) and the other, the world's largest chum (a 36-pounder). The museum's phone number is (907) 772–3598.

Those who are in the area to fish—and want to do it on their own—should check out ***Doyles Boat Rentals*** (907–772–4439; www.doylesboatrentals.com), which rents fast 18-foot skiffs to reach the best fishing spots. The boats are also nice for obtaining a scenic view of the town from the water or for touring around to see the sites.

The USDA Forest Service rents numerous cabins in the national forest around Petersburg, including ***Ravens Roost,*** one of the relatively few forest service shelters you can hike to. It's located on the mountain behind Petersburg Airport, nearly 4 miles by trail or 3 by helicopter. The Raven Trail begins near the orange-and-white tank south of the airport with 1 mile of boardwalk through muskeg (spongy bog) before the trail's ascent begins. The middle section is relatively steep, then flattens along the ridgetop. The easy way to enjoy the experience is to fly in by helicopter, then hike out downhill. The cabin rents for $35 per night per party. For details call (877) 444–6777 or visit www.recreation.gov. ***Temsco Helicopters*** will drop you off at the cabin for $376, which is its minimum charge for a half-hour flight. Call (907) 772–4780 for more information.

When Petersburg folk talk of driving "out the road," they're referring to the 34-mile ***Mitkof Highway,*** along which you can visit the ***Falls Creek Fish Ladder*** near mile 11, and the ***Crystal Lake Fish Hatchery*** and ***Blind Slough Recreation Area*** at mile 17.5. Birders visiting in the wintertime will especially enjoy the ***Trumpeter Swan Observatory*** at mile 16.

Whether it's fishing, sightseeing, or just plain relaxing you're looking for, ***Alaska Sport Haven*** (800–772–4741; www.alaskasporthaven.com) is a nice option. The lodge is 14 miles south of Petersburg on the island of Kupreanof. Amenities include hot showers and kitchen, boat rentals, charters, and self-guided or guided hunting and fishing trips. Lodging facilities can accommodate up to six people, and meals are included. Full-service package prices that include the use of a chartered boat or skiff as well as meals, gear, and bait are $250 to $400 per night.

For the fisherman, *Secret Cove Charters* offers quality fishing and whale-watching trips through the island-studded waters of the area. Prices start at $245 a day. For more information call (907) 772–3081 or visit www .secretcovecharters.com.

If you're looking for a downtown lodging location, call the *Tides Inn* at First and Dolphin Streets (907–772–4288 or 800–665–8433; www.TidesInn Alaska.com). Ask for a room overlooking the harbor. Owner Gloria Ohmer was born and raised in Petersburg, and she's an absolute fount of knowledge about things to see and do. Rates start at $75 in the winter and $90 in the summer, including complimentary continental breakfast. Nonsmoking rooms are available.

Nordic House Bed and Breakfast, 3 blocks north of the ferry terminal (806 South Nordic Drive; 907–772–3620; www.petersburgbnb.com), offers a view of Wrangell Narrows, boats, planes, and sometimes even wildlife. Rates are $78 to $99, depending upon the room and whether it has a shared or private bath. A private room with bath and kitchenette is $125 for a double. The *Rocky Point Resort,* 11 miles south of town on Wrangell Narrows, offers saltwater fishing for salmon, halibut, trout, crab, and shrimp in protected waters. Package getaways include a cabin, a motorized skiff, meals, fishing gear, and freezing facilities so that you can take your catch home. Call (907) 772–4405 or visit www.rockyptresort.com for reservations and information.

For one of life's memorable seafood dining experiences, plan at least one dinner at *Rooney's Northern Lights Restaurant* (907–772–2900), located at 203 Sing Lee Alley. At this favorite local spot, you'll enjoy waterfront dining and a menu that offers burgers, espresso, ice cream, and desserts in addition to fresh seafood. Rooney's serves breakfast, lunch, and dinner, with beer and wine available.

Many Alaskans and most visitors rank *Sitka* the most visually beautiful community in the state. Perched at the base of majestic mountains on Baranof Island, the community looks westerly toward Pacific Ocean waters upon hundreds of big and little, near and distant isles, mountains, and a massive volcano. Native Alaskan and Russian history abounds in this community. It

Second to One

When you visit Sitka you visit the largest city, in area, in the Western Hemisphere. It's the second largest in the world. There are 4,710 square miles within the unified city and borough municipal borders. Juneau, at 3,108 square miles, comes in third; Kiruna, Sweden, with 5,458 square miles, ranks as the world's largest city.

was the hub and headquarters of Russian America and the czars' vast sea otter–pelt gathering and trading empire until the United States purchased Alaska in 1867. Sitka served as Alaska's territorial capital until the early years of the twentieth century. It is, today, a forestry, fishing, travel, and education center.

Be sure to visit the **Sheldon Jackson Museum,** at 104 College Drive in Sitka. Actually, the octagonal-shaped building itself ranks as something of an artifact, having been constructed in 1895 as the first concrete structure in Alaska. It's named for the nineteenth-century Presbyterian missionary and educator who supplied a large portion of the collection. Jackson suppressed some aspects of Native culture, but he did import 1,300 reindeer from Norway in an attempt to aid the Eskimos. The museum is small and sometimes overlooked, but most visitors find it well worthwhile. The well-presented collection emphasizes the Native peoples of Alaska—Tlingit and Haida Indians of the Southeast, Athabascan Indians of the Interior, Aleuts from the Southwest, and Inupiats of the far north. You'll never get a better, closer look at a Tlingit dugout canoe, an Athabascan birch-bark canoe, an ancient two-passenger Aleut baidarka (kayak), and two Inupiat kayaks. You'll see Indian battle armor as well as exquisite Inupiat fur parkas. The museum operates 9:00 A.M. to 5:00 P.M. daily in summer; 10:00 A.M. to 4:00 P.M. Tuesday through Saturday in winter. Admission is $4. For information visit the Web site at www.museums .state.ak.us or call (907) 747–8981.

For visitors with RVs or tents, the campgrounds of choice in Sitka are clearly the two **USDA Forest Service campgrounds at Starrigavan Bay,** nearly 8 miles north of town on Halibut Point Road. Both feature separated, private campsites surrounded by thick, towering trees. Near the entrance to the upper campground you'll also find one of Alaska's easiest walking trails. The **Starrigavan Estuary** wheelchair-accessible trail, a ½-mile elevated boardwalk, takes you beside open wetlands and into deep and dark woods of spruce, hemlock, and alder trees.

Another short and gentle hike, this one at the south end of Lincoln Street on the shores of Sitka Sound, lies within **Sitka National Historical Park.** Actually you can enjoy two trails there—one a 1½-mile stroll back into Alaska history on the site of the bloodiest battle fought between Tlingit Indians and nineteenth-century Russians, the other (less frequented by visitors) a ¾-mile jogging course.

If your tastes run far off the beaten path, you may consider chartering a boat for a drop-off at the sea-level trailhead of the **Mount Edgecumbe National Recreation Trail** on Kruzof Island, about 10 miles west of Sitka. The 6⁷⁄₁₀-mile trail up the side of this volcanic crater (a look-alike for Japan's

Mount Fuji) is steep and usually takes about eight hours. From the summit the view of ocean waters and myriad islands is a mind boggler.

If you've never experienced the fun of a kayak ride, here's a good place to start. Alaska Travel Adventures offers a three-hour **Sitka Sea Kayaking Adventure,** led by experienced guides through protected island waterways. The $99, three-hour tour often includes views of deer, brown bears, seals, and (always) eagles. For advance reservations or more information, call (800) 478–0052 in Alaska or (800) 791–2673 outside Alaska (Web site: www.alaska adventures.com). **Sitka Sound Ocean Adventures** (907–747–6375; www.ss oceanadventures.com) will likewise outfit you with single- or double-seat kayaks for half-day ($35 and $45, respectively), full-day ($52 and $62), or longer trips in Sitka Sound and environs.

A Place of Honor

If you happen to wander through Sitka National Historical Park's visitor center, and you marvel at the beautiful Tlingit totem poles there with their twin wolf design and intricate carvings, you can thank the Indians of the Tlingit Eagle clan for making them, and you can thank my father-in-law, whose Tlingit name is Shuk Shah Ni Ish, for putting them there.

The year was 1962 and my father-in-law, park historian George Hall, had learned that several totem poles and a house front—made up of nine wooden planks incised with an elaborate Tlingit bear design—were in the dilapidated, roofless remains of an old house. As soon as he saw the ornate poles, he knew they had to be protected.

Tlingit Alex Andrews, a friend of my father-in-law and "a man of admirable character," helped form a group that went to the old house, removed the poles and planks, and moved them to another house to protect them from the elements. Tlingit Patrick Paul was the clan custodian, and he also helped.

At this new location, a party was about to get under way to celebrate saving the poles. The Tlingit women were cooking, the men were preparing for song. And my father-in-law, little did he know, was about to be given the honor of a lifetime.

Midway through the celebration, Alex called George forward. His actions—helping save the precious Eagle-clan poles from a sure demise—reminded the Tlingits of something one of their own people would do. In fact, it reminded them of someone they admired, a Tlingit long dead but now thought to be reborn—in my father-in-law. For that, they gave him the name, Shuk Shah Ni Ish, "mountain," "bird," "person." And they later "gave" Shuk Shah Ni Ish the poles and the house front to place them where he thought was best. His choice: the visitor center, where they will be preserved for everyone.

—Melissa DeVaughn

Sitkan Jane Eidler arranges fascinating ninety-minute historic *walking tours* of downtown Sitka, taking in a lofty view of ocean and islands from *Castle Hill* (where "Russian America" officially became "Alaska, U.S.A." in 1867); a re-created *Russian Blockhouse;* the old Russian cemetery; the *Lutheran cemetery* where, interestingly, Russian Princess Maksoutoff lies buried; historic houses; the *Saint Michael's Russian Orthodox Cathedral;* the *Russian Bishop's House* (part of Sitka National Historical Park); and more. Primarily these are group tours, but you can call (907) 747–5354 to see if there's a group scheduled with which you can tag along.

On days when cruise ships are in port—which is almost every day in the summer—the *Sitka Tribe of Alaska's Tribal Tours/Historical and Cultural Sightseeing Tours* offers a tour from the perspective of the Tlingit people who lived here before, during, and after the Russians. The narrated two-and-a-half-hour excursion, priced at $44, takes in Sitka National Historical Park, Sheldon Jackson Museum, a narrative drive through Sitka's Native village, and a Native dance performance. A one-hour historic sightseeing drive is $15. For do-it-yourselfers, Sitka Tribal Tours offers a great way to see the town on your own and at your own pace. Their $10 pass is good for a full day, and it gives you access to points of interest throughout town. For details call (907) 747–7290.

The USDA Forest Service lists twenty-four fly-in or boat-in cabins accessible from Sitka. Probably the most exotic in all of Alaska is the *White Sulphur Springs Cabin,* on nearby Chichagof Island. It features a weather-tight log cabin with large windows facing out from a picturesque rocky beach onto the broad Pacific—plus an adjacent structure containing an oversize hot springs bath (almost a pool) with the same awesome ocean view. (*Note:* Rental of cabin does not include exclusive use of the hot springs. Locals, fishermen, and visitors can and do frequent this spot.) Getting to this cabin is costlier than most because you have to helicopter in, but if you can afford the tariff, the trip itself will rank as one of your vacation highlights of a lifetime. The local forest service number in Sitka is (907) 747–6671. For reservations call (877) 444–6777 or access www.recreation.gov on the Web.

For a wildlife-viewing excursion geared toward the independent traveler, check out the *Sitka Wildlife Quest,* a two-hour cruise scheduled for Tuesday and Thursday evenings, or you can opt for a three-hour tour on weekends. Both take in some of the great bays and narrow passages in and around Sitka. While on the water, look for sea otters, three species of whales (humpback, killer, and minke), brown bears, sea lions, black-tailed deer, seals, and eagles. The tour is $59 for the evening trip and $79 for the weekend one. For more information call (888) 747–8101 or (907) 747–8100 or visit www.allenmarinetours.com.

Castle Hill: A Palace Fit for a King— or at Least a Governor

Once a rocky fortress, surrounded on three sides by water, Castle Hill still is the high point between downtown Sitka and the bridge to Japonski Island. Here the Russian governors, beginning with Alexander Baranov, presided over Russian America. Two buildings occupied the site before the "castle" was built. The first was destroyed by fire, the second by earthquake. The castle, or "Baranov's Castle," was built in 1830 and was renowned for its opulence in what was then a remote and wild country.

A light placed at the top of the castle to guide mariners made the building the first lighthouse in Alaska.

After the U.S. purchase of Russian America in 1867, Baranov's Castle fell into disrepair; in 1894 it burned to the ground.

Today Castle Hill is a historic monument where Russian cannons bristle from the hill's crest and a commanding view of Sitka and the surrounding islands can still be had. Ramps have been constructed to make the one-time fortress wheelchair accessible.

Here's another quality wildlife viewing excursion by water: **Sitka's Secrets** (907–747–5089; www.sitkasecret.com) offers three-hour trips for $120 on the 27-foot vessel *Sitka Secret* to **St. Lazaria National Wildlife Refuge** for a view that sets birders cackling. **St. Lazaria,** a sixty-five-acre island some 15 miles west of Sitka, contains the nests of an estimated 2,000 rhinoceros auklets, 5,000 common and thick-billed murres, 2,000 tufted puffins (comical little creatures sometimes called sea parrots or flying footballs), 450,000 fork-tailed and Leache's storm petrels, plus eagles and other winged species. En route there's a good possibility you'll view whales, seals, sea lions, and sea otters.

Duane and Tracie Lambeth's **Sitka Sportfishing and Dove Island Lodge** (888–318–3474; www.aksitkasportfishing.com) is the place to go if you want to experience both saltwater and freshwater fishing in a relaxed setting. From the picturesque Dove Island, you can spend your days fishing and your evenings paddling around in a kayak or relaxing in a spacious hot tub. The Lambeths have boats ranging from 16 to 38 feet and can get you just about anywhere in Sitka Sound and the surrounding area. A new lodge has been added to the already breathtaking resort area, so guests can enjoy new amenities—and a fire pit right at water's edge.

The primary goal of the **Alaska Raptor Rehabilitation Center,** at 1000 Raptor Way (800–643–9425; www.alaskaraptor.org), is healing injured birds of prey, especially eagles, but the center has a worthy program for two-legged human types as well. With the $12 admission fee, visitors can walk through the center's seventeen-acre campus, which is home to more than 200 recovering birds each year, including peregrine falcons, bald eagles, golden eagles, and countless owls. A ¼-mile nature trail offers visitors a chance to see bald eagles close-up in an uncaged natural habitat, as does the Bald Eagle Flight Training Center. And if you've got extra time, try something really different and volunteer at the center. A training program offers volunteers a minilesson in raptor rehabilitation.

If you're into two-wheel tripping, **Island Fever Diving and Adventures** (907–738–1535; www.islandfeverdiving.com) offers mountain biking as well as "Bike and Hike" tours. They also offer diving and snorkeling charters, with all gear supplied.

Sitka contains a bevy of B&Bs, virtually every one of them more than adequate; several are outstanding. Among the latter: **Alaska Ocean View Bed and Breakfast,** run by Carole Denkinger, provides gourmet breakfasts at times convenient to her guests plus snacks around the clock. These latter munchies are best enjoyed while basking in an outdoor spa on her red cedar executive-home patio. As the name implies, the view takes in ocean, islands, and mountains, yet the B&B is near harbors, shopping, and restaurants. Rates range from $89 for a single to $199 for a suite. For information call (907) 747–8310 or (888) 811–6870 or visit Denkinger's Web site at www.sitka-alaska-lodging.com.

Burgess Bauder's Lighthouse is, well, different. It's not exactly a B&B, since the host doesn't reside in or near the premises. But it certainly isn't your usual lodge or inn, either. It's a real lighthouse that Bauder constructed and located on an island a few minutes by boat from downtown Sitka. Bauder provides you with a skiff for coming and going if you stay three days or more, though you may not wish to stray far from the tranquil surroundings. Small wooden hot tubs offer relaxing moments in the evening. The lighthouse will sleep eight. The two bedrooms located in the tower offer particularly commanding views. You do your own cooking. Rates start at $150. Call (907) 747–3056.

Another great home-away-from-home option is **Sitka Rock Suites,** offering eleven waterfront and water view studios and one-bedroom and two-bedroom suites. You enjoy gorgeous views and can do some wildlife watching right from your deck. Rates run from $60 to $195 per night, and if you're inclined to stay awhile, they also rent by the month in the off-season. For more information call (907) 747–3740 or visit www.sitkarocksuites.com.

Port Alexander is one of those small, isolated communities that infrequent visitors end up raving about. Located at the southern tip of Baranof Island, the town once boasted 2,000 residents. Today there are about 50, among them Peter Mooney, who with his wife, Susan Taylor, operates **Laughing Raven**

Lodge, a secluded getaway offering wildlife viewing, hiking, kayaking, ing. Rooms are located right by the water, so don't be surprised if you're awakened during the night by whales spouting. Four rooms are available, each with its own bath, and skiffs and kayaks are available for exploring the water. Packages include room, board, guided fishing, fish processing, and packaging. Call (907) 568–2266 or (800) 768–7752 or visit www.portalexander.com on the Internet. Call Alaska Airlines at (800) 426–0333 for travel information to Sitka. Package prices average out to about $700 per day and include airfare from Sitka.

The Upper Panhandle

Juneau, Alaska's state capital, is arguably the most scenic capital city in the nation. The most populated portion of town sits on the shores of Gastineau Channel, backed up by awesomely steep Mount Juneau, Mount Roberts, and various other peaks in the 3,000-foot-and-higher class. Within Juneau's 3,108 square miles you'll find big bays, tiny inlets, thickly vegetated islands, and numerous glaciers (including *Mendenhall Glacier,* the second most-visited river of ice in Alaska). The town also contains large portions of the Juneau Icefield—a 1,500-square-mile, high-altitude desert of hardpack ice and snow that extends from behind the city to beyond the Canadian border. It's from the overflow of this ice field that Mendenhall, Taku, and other great glaciers descend. Juneau had its start in 1880 as a miners' camp after a local Indian chief, Kowee, led prospectors Joe Juneau and Dick Harris over Snowslide Gulch into Silver Bow Basin. They found, according to Harris's account, gold "in streaks running through the rock and little lumps as large as peas or beans."

You can see exhibits of the community's gold-mining history in the small, often overlooked *Juneau–Douglas City Museum* at Fourth and Main Streets, open 9:00 A.M. until 5:00 P.M. weekdays; 10:00 A.M. to 5:00 P.M. weekends. Admission is $4. For more information check out www.juneau.org/parksrec/museum on the Web, or call (907) 586–3572.

You can view more history (including Eskimo, Indian, and Aleut displays) and wild animal dioramas (including a spectacular multistoried eagle's nest tree) in the *Alaska State Museum,* 395 Whittier Street, a couple of blocks from downtown. If traveling with young children, don't miss the Discovery Room on the second floor where kids can climb aboard a child-size copy of Captain

southeast alaskafacts

The Juneau Icefield, in the Coast Mountains north of Juneau, covers more than 1,200 square miles and is the source of more than thirty glaciers, including the Mendenhall, Taku, Eagle, and Herbert.

James Cook's eighteenth-century vessel *Discovery,* stroke wild-animal pelts, and dress in period costumes. Museum admission is $5. Hours are 8:30 A.M. to 5:30 P.M. seven days a week. For information call (907) 465–2901 or visit www.museums .state.ak.us.

Also often passed by—but for history buffs well worth the effort of a few blocks' climb to Chicken Ridge from downtown—is **Wickersham House,** the restored Victorian home of Judge James Wickersham, a pioneer jurist and Alaska territorial (nonvoting) delegate to Congress. You can see the judge's arti- fact collection and period furniture as well as interpretive displays and a grand hilltop view of the city's business district. Daily informal tours of the century-old house (213 Seventh Street) range from a half hour to several hours, depending upon how much time and interest you have. Sip tea from bone china teacups and learn about Wickersham's fascinating and adventurous life. The house is listed as a state historic site, and tours are held daily in the summer, except Wednesday. A suggested donation of $2 helps keep the place up. Call (907) 586– 9001 or visit www.dnr.state.ak.us/parks/units/wickrshm for more information.

Juneau is blessed with an incredible number of hiking trails, many of them remnants of old mining roads dating from the 1920s or earlier. If you lack wheels, you can easily reach several from downtown Juneau, including the **Mount Roberts Trail** (2⁷⁄₁₀ miles one way), which begins at the end of Sixth Street; **Perseverance Trail** (3½ miles one way), which you access by walking up Gold Street to Basin Road; and the **Mount Juneau Trail** (2 steep miles one way), which begins as a side trail about ½ mile along the Perseverance Trail. The Mount Roberts and Mount Juneau treks meander through thick forests until they break out, finally, above timberline for awesome aerial views of green forests, Gastineau Channel, and Douglas Island, across the water.

Near Mendenhall Glacier, 13 miles north of downtown, the **West Glacier Trail** (3½ miles one way) takes you from the parking lot on the west side of Mendenhall Lake through alder and willow forests for a mostly gradual climb up the side of Mount McGinnis. Your destination is a 1,300-foot vantage point from which you can look down on the rolling white expanse of the glacier. If you want knowledgeable local expertise while you're trekking in the area, **Gastineau Guiding** (907–586–2666; www.stepintoalaska.com) offers daily escorted hikes along forest trails to saltwater shores and alongside historic remains and relics of the community's gold-producing heyday. Prices range from $28 to $66 per person depending upon the location and duration of the hike. The **City and Borough of Juneau** offers free guided hikes on Wednes- day and Saturday during the summer. Call (907) 586–5226 for details.

Beer aficionados take note: **Alaskan Brewing Company**'s (www.alaskan beer.com) amber beer and pale ale brews have taken gold medals and blue ribbons in tasting competitions across the country. You can tour Alaska's pioneer microbrewery on Shaune Drive off Old Glacier Highway, about 4 miles from downtown. The company offers free tours and tastings 11:00 A.M. to 5:00 P.M. daily, but it's the most fun on bottling days. Call (907) 780–5866 for bottling days and times. Speaking of tasting brews, Alaska's best-known saloon, the *Red Dog,* is located downtown at 278 South Franklin Street, but don't overlook the saloon in the *Alaskan Hotel and Bar,* at 167 South Franklin. The big, ornate back bar there is worth a look-see whether or not you imbibe. The hotel, incidentally, was built in 1913 and offers refurbished rooms with private and shared baths. The summer rates are about $60 for a room with a shared bath and $80 for a private bath. Phone (800) 327–9347 or (907) 586–1000 or visit www.thealaskanhotel.com.

About dining in Juneau: The opportunities are mouthwateringly wide, from Mexican cuisine downtown at *El Sombrero* (157 South Franklin; 907–586–6770) to arguably Alaska's best Friday clam chowder at the old-fashioned *Douglas Cafe* (907–364–3307) across the bridge at 916 Third Street, in the community of Douglas. The cafe is perhaps the only restaurant in Juneau that features the tasty amber clams and amber mussels. Virtually unknown to the tourist trade is the small *Hot Bite* (907–790–2483), open summers only on the dock at Auke Bay, 13 miles north of downtown. There the proprietors have raised the creation of hamburgers to an art form.

Dockside in downtown Juneau you'll find a couple of great eateries with terrific waterfront views. For fine dining and fresh seafood, you can't beat the *Twisted Fish Company* (907–463–5033). While you're waiting for your table, you can shop for goodies to take home at the adjoining *Taku Store, Smokeries, and Fishery* (800–582–5122; www.takustore.com). This family-owned business provides fresh seafood to many Alaskan restaurants, and they're happy to offer samples of their smoked salmon to visitors. Their seasoned rubs, especially the Sugar Maple Dry Rub, are great with salmon, halibut, and even plain old chicken. *Doc Waters Pub* (907–586–3627) is another favorite

Silver Bow and Gold

An Auk Tlingit Indian named Chief Kowee is the true discoverer of gold in the Juneau area, not Joe Juneau and Dick Harris, the two prospectors often credited. It was Kowee who brought ore samples to entrepreneur Richard Pilz, hoping to bring prosperity to his people. Pilz then outfitted Harris and Juneau and sent them to find the source. When they returned empty-handed, Kowee led them to the source at Gold Creek in Silver Bow Basin in 1880.

hangout, with a casual menu, great views of the water, and indoor as well as outdoor seating.

The long-standing **Silverbow Inn** (120 Second Street; 907–586–4146 or 800–586–4146) is worth a stop for those who enjoy a history lesson. The inn offers a few rooms for the night, but although thoroughly modern, shows its late-nineteenth century age. The bagel shop below is a nice place to enjoy breakfast away from the bustle of the main tourist drag on South Franklin.

If you're a Friday visitor, plan to pick up a sack lunch at any of several downtown sidewalk vendors and head for the **State Office Building**—the S.O.B., in local parlance. There in the structure's great atrium, local and visiting organists perform each week on a grand and lusty old Kimball theater pipe organ, to the considerable delight of scores of brown-bag lunch consumers perched on benches and ledges.

One of the best ways to really appreciate Juneau is by staying in one of those nifty USDA Forest Service cabins scattered throughout the area. There are five cabins you can hike to straight from Juneau and dozens that are accessible by air or boat. Two of the closer (and therefore less costly to reach by plane) lakeside cabins are the **East Turner Lake** and **West Turner Lake** units up Taku Inlet, south of the city. Trout and char fishing can be productive from either end of the lake, and wildlife watching can include brown bears (from a distance, please!), deer, mountain goats, and waterfowl. The cabins rent for $25 to $45 a night. Reservations may be made by calling (877) 444–6777 or signing up on the Web at www.recreation.gov.

Don't overlook the **Alaska State Parks cabins.** They are equally nice, and several are accessible by trail. The **Juneau Convention and Visitors Bureau** on Egan Drive can give you more information at (888) 581–2201 or www.traveljuneau.com.

Alaska Discovery (800–586–1911; www.akdiscovery.com) is one of the state's longtime and very special practitioners of the outdoor guiding art. The company has an office in Juneau and offers everything from a five-day Glacier Bay Kayaking Escape, starting at $1,990, to nine-day float trips into the Arctic wilderness, starting at $3,050.

Their Bears of Pack Creek trip takes you by air to the nearby island that Tlingit Indians called *Kootz-na-hoo,* or "Fortress of the Bears." This trip offers an almost unparalleled opportunity to view brown (grizzly) bears in their natural forest habitat at and near **Pack Creek,** where the USDA Forest Service has constructed an elevated observation platform. The three-day trip is fully guided. It includes floatplane transportation from Juneau, kayak paddling in protected waters, ample time ashore for hiking and bear viewing, rubber boots and gear, plus meals and beverages. Participants must be fourteen years or older. The cost is $1,090 per person with a three-person minimum. To best capture the Pack Creek experience, budding photographers may be interested in **Dolphin Charters** (510–527–9622 or 800–472–9942; www.dolphincharters.com) guided trips to the sanctuary. Travel aboard the company's midsize boats for eight to ten days and learn from professional photographers how to best capture these bruins on film. Trips depart from several Southeast communities, including Juneau, and rates start at $3,995. Traveling by water provides access to remote locations accessible only by boat. Besides the masterful bears, look for humpback and orca whales, sea lions, seals, and bald eagles. A warm bed, hot showers, and professionally prepared meals are all part of this more-pampered version of visiting Pack Creek.

Here's another Pack Creek option: Among a variety of fishing and wildlife viewing excursions packaged by **Alaska Fly 'n' Fish Charters** (907–790–2120; www.alaskabyair.com) is a one-day guided floatplane visit to the bear sanctuary. Like Alaska Discovery, the company is one of several allowed to guide a limited number of visitors at this truly world-class viewing site. An Alaska Fly 'n' Fish guided trip to Pack Creek runs $395 per person. Fly-in freshwater fishing packages are available for $495 per person, as are $110-per-person-and-up trips for glacier flight-seeing, with a five-person minimum. For more information from the Juneau Ranger District, including a list of approved guiding companies and procedures for getting an unguided visit permit, call (907) 586–8800 or visit www.fs.fed.us/r10/tongass. You can get this information in person at 8510 Mendenhall Loop Road in Juneau, but travelers who wait until they get here usually find the limited number of permits are long gone. The Web site also lists air charter companies that transport permit holders to Pack Creek.

In Juneau, **Alaska Travel Adventures** offers a splashy Mendenhall Glacier Float Trip down almost all white water on the Mendenhall River for $99; a Historic Gold Mining and Panning Adventure in the shadow of the old AJ mine for $49; Glacier View Sea Kayaking through protected waters north of town, priced at $85; and the outdoor **Gold Creek Salmon Bake,** now located on Salmon Creek near the hospital, for $35. This, incidentally, is Alaska's longest-running salmon bake and many, including my Juneau friend Pete, say it's the best in the state. The menu includes not only fresh king-salmon steaks (grilled on an open pit over alder coals and glazed with a brown sugar and butter sauce) but barbecued ribs, baked beans, lots of other trimmings, plus your choice of complimentary wine, beer, coffee, or soft drink. All this in sheltered surroundings alongside a sparkling stream and waterfall at the site of old mine diggings. And don't forget the live folk music to enhance the entire scene. To avoid a cast of thousands, call ahead (800–478–0052 in Alaska, 800–791–2673 outside Alaska, or 907–789–0052 locally), ask when the busloads of cruise ship passengers are expected, then plan your own arrival earlier or later. To visit Alaska Travel Adventures online, go to www.alaskaadventures.com. Also on-site: the *Juneau Raptor Center,* where you'll find live eagles and other birds of prey plus exhibits you can enjoy and learn from. There's no charge for viewing the birds. Call (907) 586–8393.

Still another kayak rental firm, *Juneau Outdoor Center* (907–586–8220; www.juneaukayak.com), offers kayak and outboard rentals, guided tours, and free advice. The knowledgeable and experienced staff can help plan a boating adventure in Southeast and teach first-time paddlers about safety, self-rescue, and basic paddling skills. The company will deliver you and your rental boat anywhere on the Juneau road system. Delivery charges range between $50 and $125, depending on location and circumstance. Single kayaks rent for $50 a day; double kayaks rent for $70 per day. Discounts are applied to trips longer than six days. The outdoor center is located at the Douglas Boat Harbor at 101 Dock Street.

If skiing's your thing and you're in Juneau during the winter months, *Eaglecrest Ski Area,* about twenty minutes from downtown off North Douglas Highway, offers slopes (and two double chairlifts) for everyone from beginner to expert. For information in season call (907) 790–2000 or visit www .skijuneau.com.

You'll find numerous ways to see glaciers around Juneau—on motor-coach tours, from boats, during hikes, and looking down from airplanes. Perhaps the most exciting way to see glaciers (short of actually hiking there on your own) is by helicopter. Several companies have filled that niche, including *Era Helicopters* (800–866–8394; www.flyera.com), *Coastal Helicopters Inc.* (800–789–5610; www.coastalhelicopters.com), and *Temsco Helicopters* (877–789–9501; www.temscoair.com). During these flights you not only fly over one or more rivers of ice, you also touch down and disembark from your chopper for twenty minutes or so of frolicking on the hardpack ice. Fares are in the $200 to $400 range. All three companies offer tours that include exciting sled dog rides on the glaciers. Be sure to ask for specials.

One of Southeast's most dramatic sights is *Tracy Arm Fjord,* a long, deep, meandering waterway whose steep walls rise for thousands of feet. Whales, seals, mountain goats, deer, and bears are among the wildlife viewing possibilities. *Auk Nu Tours* (800–478–3610; www.auknutours.com) offers a trip into the fjord, which culminates in an extended stay at the faces of the twin tidewater Sawyer glaciers. The all-day cruise includes lunch and beverages and costs $147 per person, plus tax.

Francis and Linda Kadrlik's *Adventures Afloat* (800–3AFLOAT or 907–586–3312; http://home.gci.net/~valkyrie) will likewise introduce you to the

A small cruise vessel in Tracy Arm Fjord

wilderness of Southeast Alaska with a flight-seeing arrival at their base of operations. In this case the base is the elegant 106-foot classic yacht MV *Valkyrie,* your floating home for day and multiday ecotours that include wildlife watching, exploring, and fishing from the smaller (32-foot) *High Roller.* Prices start at $559 per person a day, with discounts for groups.

If you're planning to keep both feet on terra firma, there are a couple of land-based options in Juneau. One is a visit to the ***Shrine of St. Therese,*** overlooking Lynn Canal at mile 23 of the Glacier Highway. After St. Therese was pronounced patroness of Alaska in 1925, local priest Father William LeVasseur envisioned a retreat center in her honor. Hundreds of volunteers moved thousands of rocks to build the quaint chapel and surrounding buildings. Today the shrine is part of a retreat center that includes gardens, a labyrinth, and cabin rentals. The shrine and grounds are open daily from 8:30 A.M. to 10:00 P.M. Cabin rentals are modest, with prices starting at $35 per night for the Hermitage Cabin, which has no running water or electricity. The cabins are intended for visitors seeking solitude in an atmosphere of retreat. For more information visit www.shrineofsainttherese.org.

The ***Chez Alaska Cooking School*** provides another unusual option—this one for visitors who'd like to learn how to prepare some of the incredible fresh foods, particularly seafood, that grace Alaskan tables. For $15 you can join one of the daily three-hour demonstration classes, each of which culminates with a feast of the delicious dishes you helped prepare. Call (907) 790–4329 or visit www.chezalaska.com to find out how you can join in the fun.

You'll find a number of good-value B&B accommodations in and around Juneau. Here's one B&B about 11 miles from downtown and close to Juneau's

Bold and Beautiful Lituya Bay

In 1958 an earthquake rattled the land in Southeast Alaska along the Fairweather fault, and a huge chunk of earth—40 million cubic feet of dirt and rocks—broke off from a piece of mountainside and landed in a picturesque T-shaped body of water known as Lituya Bay. It's hard to say there is a "prettiest" place in Alaska. Snow-tipped mountains, aquamarine glaciers, forested hillsides, and broad sweeping rivers all have a way of capturing the eye. But Lituya Bay, on the passage north from Cross Sound to the community of Yakutat, might just qualify.

On this day though, July tenth to be exact, you would not have wanted to be in Lituya Bay. As the landslide thundered into the water, it caused a giant wave—called a splash or seiche wave—that surged to the opposite side of the bay at the alarming height of 1,740 feet, taller than the 1,250-foot Empire State Building.

The wave plucked the trees along the bay like a gardener pulling weeds. It scoured the soil down to bedrock. Surely any animals in the wave's path were swept out to sea and gone forever. Later, the unearthed trees floated in the bay like matchsticks, stripped of their bark and branches, and twisted into splinters. Even loggers couldn't salvage the useless debris.

The Lituya Bay seiche wave set a record that has never come close to being broken. The second-highest recorded seiche wave was a mere 230 feet, caused by a landslide in a lake in Norway.

number-one visitor attraction, Mendenhall Glacier: Guests at **Pearson's Pond Luxury Inn** enjoy private baths, queen beds, private entries and decks, robes, slippers, kitchenettes, fireplaces, and self-serve continental breakfasts plus the use of the spa, barbecue, rowboat, kayaks, and bikes. Rates begin at $329 for double rooms. For details call (907) 789–3772 or (888) 658–6328 or visit www.pearsonspond.com.

Heading up to mile 21 of the Glacier Highway, you'll find **Alaskan Williwaws,** a former cannery transformed into beyond-the-ordinary accommodations. Privacy is the watchword here: five acres of remote beachfront property at the end of a private road, with private docks and private beaches where you might catch a glimpse of whales and sea lions cavorting in the water. Hosts Daniel and Kristine Malick offer a one-bedroom cabin and a two-bedroom lodge. Rates start at $100 per night, and prices include fishing gear. For more information call (907) 789–2803 or (888) 337–9617, or visit www.williwaws.com.

Exceptional accommodations can also be had at **Alaska's Capital Inn Bed and Breakfast** (907–588–6507 or 888–588–6507; www.alaskacapitalinn.com). This exquisitely restored 1906 home perched on a downtown hillside overlooking the harbor and the mountains features several rooms, from the former maid's quarters at $149 per night to the sumptuous Governor's Suite with double whirlpool and private fireplace for $279 per night. Period antiques grace all the rooms, and gourmet breakfasts include specialties like lemon soufflé hotcakes and Dungeness crab eggs Benedict.

The *Juneau International Hostel,* located at 614 Harris Street, is a particular pleasure for fans of hosteling. It's located in a large, historic, rambling house on the side of a hill called Chicken Ridge. Clean, spacious, and wheelchair accessible, it's just a few blocks above downtown Juneau. In spite of its relatively large capacity (forty-eight beds, sitting room with fireplace and library, laundry), it's filled almost all the time in the summer. Reservations are a must. The cost is $10 for adults. Call (907) 586–9559 or visit www.juneauhostel.org.

If your plans call for a trip between Juneau and Sitka, one of the most pleasant ways to travel between the two ports is via ferries of the *Alaska Marine Highway System.* Try to catch whichever ferry happens to be stopping at Hoonah, Tenakee Springs (most trips), and Angoon. Of course, you don't have to be heading to Sitka to visit these small communities; you can, if you like, simply take a round-trip from Juneau to one or all three, then return by ferry or small plane to Juneau. Call (800) 642–0066 for information or reservations. Online reservations can be made at www.ferryalaska.com; you can also request a free DVD about the ferry system.

Located on the northeast shore of Chichagof Island, about 40 miles and three ferry hours north of Juneau, lies *Hoonah,* a thriving village of mostly Tlingit Indian people. If you're not laying over, check with your ship's purser and see if you have time to mosey into the village (about a fifteen-minute walk). If you don't, at least take the time to visit the graveyard right across the highway from the ferry dock. You'll find some graves there that are quite old, others new, some traditional with angel figures, others marked with the distinctive Russian Orthodox Church's cross—its distinctive cross bar pattern—and still others with cast figures from the Tlingit Indian totemic tradition.

In town you'll find two restaurants plus lodging, grocery, gift, and general merchandise establishments. Overnighters will find *Sportsman's Bed & Breakfast* at 257 Second Street clean and pleasant. Rates are $75 for a single, and $95 for a double; call (907) 945–3218 for reservations. Want to see a genuine brown (grizzly) bear while you're in the area? Check out the village garbage dump (honest), about 2 miles from town. But do not walk to the site. Get someone to drive you, or hire a cab. These critters are big and wild.

Between Hoonah and Sitka, the ferry stops occasionally at *Tenakee Springs,* long enough sometimes for passengers to run with towel in hand to the community's hot springs for a quick, relaxing soak. The springs, incidentally,

southeast alaskafacts

In June 1986 Hubbard Glacier advanced so quickly that it sealed off Russell Fjord, turning the saltwater inlet into a freshwater lake. Concern for the fate of seals and porpoises trapped by the ice led to several unsuccessful rescue attempts. In October of that year, the ice dam broke and the animals escaped. The 80-mile-long glacier, which terminates in Yakutat Bay, has advanced at least ten times since the last ice age.

provided one of the principal reasons for the community's founding back in 1899. Miners would journey to the site every winter when cold weather shut down their "diggin's" and they'd stay for weeks or months. The tradition continues, sort of. Lots of Juneauites, Sitkans, and other Southeast Alaska residents still come to take in the waters, both winter and summer. Interestingly, there are posted hours for men's bathing and other hours for women. But never the twain meet, at least not in the 5-by-9-foot bathing pool. You'll find several overnight options in Tenakee Springs, including furnished cabins for rent from longtime Alaskans Elsie and Don Pegues's **Snyder Mercantile Company** (907–736–2205). Rates are $85 per night for a three-room cottage; be advised that the toilet is across the road and the water isn't potable. Another option is to book a sportfishing package from **Tenakee Hot Springs Lodge** (907–736–2400; www.tenakeehot springslodge.com). Rates start at $75 per person and include access to the kitchen; meals and fishing charters can be arranged. Fishing in the area is first rate; beachcombing and hiking are likewise, and chances are you'll see sea life in the water—humpback whales, seals, sea lions, and otters. The one-way ferry trip from Juneau to Tenakee Springs costs $34.

The Tlingit village of **Angoon** offers yet another offbeat destination from Juneau. Located on the northwest coast of Admiralty Island, the community is accessible by ferry and by air from Juneau, which is 60 air miles away. Two very comfortable lodging possibilities at Angoon—the **Favorite Bay Inn** and the **Whalers' Cove Sportfishing Lodge**—provide all the comforts with easy access to sportfishing, kayaking, canoeing, and simple sightseeing. Worth a visit: nearby Tlingit Indian village. The islands and waters of Kootznahoo Inlet and Mitchell Bay are prime kayaking locales. To contact the inn or lodge, call (800) 423–3123. Rates at the inn start at $209. For information on the lodge visit www.whalerscovelodge.com. Call for sportfishing package rates. A one-way ferry trip from Juneau to Angoon costs $36; airfare through **Alaska Seaplane Service** (907–789–3331) is $99.

Here's one of the most economical day cruises you can experience in Alaska. Twice a month on Sunday mornings, the smaller ferry, *LeConte,* departs from Auke Bay terminal (about 14 miles north of Juneau) for the picturesque fishing village of **Pelican,** on the northwest corner of Chichagof Island. The route takes you through Icy Straits, past prime whale-watching waters off Point Adolphus. Along the way you may view sea lions, seals, bears, deer, eagles, and other wildlife. Arrival at Pelican is at midday, and you have an hour and a half to walk along the town boardwalks, stroll around the commercial fishing docks, and watch as commercial fishers unload halibut, salmon, crab, and black cod at the cold storage plant. You can have lunch at the popular **Rose's Bar and Grill** (907–735–2288). The return ferry departs midafternoon and arrives seven hours later in Juneau. If that's too much time afloat, you can fly back on Alaska Seaplane Service (907–789–3331) for $135. The ferry trip from Juneau is $48. Call (800) 642–0066 or visit www.ferryalaska.com. For fully equipped lodging, plan to stay at the **Highliner Lodge.** The rooms and suites are comfortable, and if you decide to stay longer, you can rent one of their boats and toodle around in the water. Hostel-style rooms start at $175, while suites range from $200 to $500 per night, depending on the number of occupants and whether there's a harbor view. For more information call (907) 735–2476.

The people of **Haines** will tell you, perhaps with some justification, that their community has the best summer weather in Southeast Alaska. The warmer, drier air of the Yukon interior regions, they say, flows over Chilkat Pass into the Chilkat Valley and brings with it more sunshine and less rainfall than other panhandle communities experience. Whatever the reason, Haines and vicinity do offer the visitor a pleasurable place to perch for a day or a few days.

Sadly, many visitors pass Haines by. They're in such a toot to get off the ferry and rush north to the main body of Alaska, they miss many of Haines's considerable pleasures—pleasures like the Tlingit Indian dancing and cultural exhibits at old Fort William Henry Seward; like the old fort itself (now a National Historic Landmark), with its rows of elegant officers' homes and its traditional military parade ground; like a fascinating museum of Southeastern Alaska, a new museum of natural history, and a state park that many rank among America's most pleasurable.

You get to Haines aboard the ferries of the Alaska Marine Highway System, either from Skagway, an hour's sailing from the north, or from Juneau, about four and a half hours from the south.

Passengers-only water taxis make several round-trips daily between Haines and Skagway. Or you can drive to Haines over the 151-mile Haines Highway, which joins with the Alaska Highway at Haines Junction, Yukon Territory, Canada. You can also fly to Haines. Several excellent small-plane carriers provide frequent scheduled flights from Juneau and Skagway. Rugged coastlines, thickly forested islands, high-rising mountains, and Davidson and Rainbow Glaciers are only a few of the sights you encounter along the way.

Once you're in Haines, a good place to stop for advice, a map, and literature is the ***visitor information center*** (907–766–2234 or 800–458–3579; www .haines.ak.us) on Second Avenue South, about a block from the Haines downtown business district. Only a few minutes' walk from the visitor center is the ***Sheldon Museum and Cultural Center*** (907–766–2366; sheldonmuseum.org), on the harbor end of Main Street. This museum literally had its start in 1893, when Steve Sheldon, at the ripe old age of eight, purchased a piece of the original transatlantic cable and began a lifetime of collecting. He arrived in Haines from his native Ohio in 1911 and met and married a woman from Pennsylvania, also an avid collector. Their family hobby has resulted in what is now the Sheldon Museum, a collection that encompasses Tlingit basketry and totemic art (including a rare, unfinished Chilkat ceremonial blanket), mementos of Fort Seward (later called Chilkoot Barracks when it housed the only U.S. troops in Alaska), photos of colorful Jack Dalton, plus pack saddles and other gear Dalton used to clear the Dalton Trail toll road to the Klondike. You can also see the shotgun he kept loaded behind the bar of his saloon. The museum is generally open 10:00 A.M. to 5:00 P.M. Monday through Friday and 1:00 to 4:00 P.M. weekends. Admission is $3.

trivia: topthis

What is believed to be the tallest Sitka spruce in Alaska stands near the Naha River, 35 miles north of Ketchikan. The behemoth is 250 feet tall and measures 71 inches around at its base. If confirmed by state forestry officials, it will top the old record holder, a 185-foot tree at Exchange Cove on Prince of Wales Island.

Another museum, the ***American Bald Eagle Foundation***'s (907–766–3094; baldeagles.org), features a collection of Southeast Alaska natural history. Displayed in a beautiful diorama of taxidermy are the animals, birds, and fish of the region. The foundation is a block from the visitor information center, at the intersection of Second Avenue South and the Haines Highway.

Haines's premier attraction is unquestionably ***Fort William Henry Seward,*** established in 1904, renamed Chilkoot Barracks in 1922, and deactivated in 1946. The government sold the entire fort to a group of World War II veterans in 1947, and although their plans to create a business cooperative did not fully work out, the fort's picturesque buildings have been largely preserved. You can, in fact, sleep and dine in any of several grand old officers' quarters, which now serve as hotels, motels, or B&Bs. Other old structures still at the fort include warehouses, the cable office, and barracks. One large building now houses the ***Chilkat Center for the Arts.*** In still other fort buildings you can see contemporary Tlingit craftsmen of ***Alaska Indian Arts*** (AIA) fashion large and small works of traditional totemic art from wood, silver, fabric, and soapstone. Totem poles carved and created by AIA on the fort grounds can be seen all over Alaska and, indeed, the world. You'll see totemic art, too, at the **Totem Village Tribal House,** also on the fort parade grounds. The **Chilkat Indian Dancers** perform here on weeknights throughout the summer; admission is $10 per person. Adjacent to the structure is a traditional trapper's log cabin of the kind you might find in Alaska's bush country. For more information call (907) 766–2540 or visit www.tresham.com.

Adjacent to the fairgrounds at the northern edge of the city (Haines is home to the **Southeast Alaska State Fair** each August), you'll come to some gold rush–era buildings that may seem vaguely familiar. These buildings, now called **Dalton City,** served as the set for the Walt Disney movie *White Fang,* based on Jack London's novel. When the moviemaking ended, the Disney company donated the set to the community. The buildings may be of recent origin, but they present an authentic picture of a gold rush community during the tumultuous time of the Klondike gold stampede. Picture-taking opportunities abound.

A site often overlooked by visitors is **Chilkat State Park,** about 8 miles south of town on Mud Bay Road. You don't have to be a camper to enjoy this forested 6,000-acre wonderland on the Chilkat Peninsula. For visitors seeking just an afternoon outing, there are ample trails, saltwater beach walks, and gorgeous views of Davidson and Rainbow Glaciers. The state charges $10 for camping here.

In the late fall and early winter, throngs of eager birders arrive to visit the **Alaska Chilkat Bald Eagle Preserve,** just a few minutes' drive from the city. There 2,500 to 4,000 American bald eagles gather each year to feast on a late run of Chilkat River salmon. This is the world's largest concentration of bald eagles, and the spectacle is easily seen from turnoffs alongside the highway. A number of eagles and many other bird species can be viewed there year-round, and other wildlife is frequently spotted, especially during summer float trips down the stream.

Chilkat Guides, Ltd., offers daily Bald Eagle Preserve Raft Trips through some of the most spectacular portions of the Chilkat River and the preserve. This is a gentle float in spacious 18-foot rubber rafts. Eagles, bears, moose, even wolves, if you're lucky, may be seen during the four-hour trip. The tour begins with a van pickup near the old army dock, and includes a 30-mile drive to the preserve. Then comes the float downriver to a haul-out spot near the Indian village of Klukwan. The price is $79 for adults. For more details call (888) 292–7789 or visit www.chilkatguides.com.

Both Chilkat Guides and Juneau-based Alaska Discovery package float trips down the magnificent **Alsek and Tatshenshini Rivers,** which flow out of the Canadian interior. These twelve- and nine-day trips, respectively, open up some of the world's most awesome mountain/glacier/wild river country. Exciting white water, relaxing floats, abundant wildlife, and wild-country treks are only a few of the features of these premier experiences, which begin in Haines and end at Yakutat, for a jet flight back to Juneau. Prices for the Tatshenshini trip are $2,895 for Chilkat Guides and $3,350 for Alaska Discovery. For the Alsek, Chilkat Guides charges $3,395 and Alaska Discovery costs $3,850. Contact Chilkat Guides at the number above; Alaska Discovery can be reached at (888) 678–6235; www.akdiscovery.com.

Another option for shorter sightseeing of the area is with *Alaska Nature Tours,* one of Haines's longest-running tour operators. The company offers guided hikes that range from relatively easy to strenuous all-day affairs. Try the Chilkat Rainforest Nature Hike, which travels through rain forest, coastal meadow, and beach over its 3-mile course. The hike comes with a picnic lunch and is perfect for those who want to take it easy and enjoy the scenery. The four-hour, mostly flat trek is $75. Hikers who want a challenge could climb *Mount Ripinsky,* a local favorite that will take all day to climb. The reward for this strenuous hike is stunning views of ice-capped mountains and vistas from some 3,600 feet above town. The cost is $110. For more information contact Alaska Nature Tours at (907) 766–2876 or www.kcd.com/aknature.

Here's something different to try while in Haines: Visit an operating cannery to learn about the history of salmon canning in Alaska. *Tsirku Canning Co.,* at Fifth Avenue and Main Street, has re-created an authentic salmon canning line with antique equipment it has collected from canneries around the state. Every piece has been reconditioned so they all work perfectly. "The cannery has the only three-piece can reform line left in existence, which demonstrates how the old cans were shaped from flat metal pieces into a usable can," the company boasts.

Tours of the cannery are held daily except Sunday and take about an hour. The cost is $10 for adults and free for children younger than twelve. Call (907) 766–3474 or visit www.cannerytour.com.

Bicyclists can join other pedalers on day rides or longer tours through *Sockeye Cycle* of both Haines and Skagway. In Haines they're located on Portage Street uphill from the dock in Fort Seward. Their excursions include the one-day or overnight *Chilkat Pass* bicycle adventure into the *Tatshenshini/Alsek Provincial Park,* a part of the largest protected United Nations International Wilderness Area in the world. The price per person is $185 for the day trip and $412 for the overnighter, which includes four meals. Even more challenging is a 350-mile nine-day Golden Circle Tour north from Haines up the Haines Highway to Canada's Yukon, east to Whitehorse in the Yukon Territory on the Alaska Highway, then south on the Klondike Highway to Skagway. The trip costs

$2,341. Rentals are $14 for two hours, $25 for four hours, and $35 for eight hours. For details about these and other trips, call (907) 766–2869 in Haines, (907) 983–2851 in Skagway. The Web address is www.cyclealaska.com.

Shane and Janis Horton are the owners of *Chilkoot Lake Tours,* and they offer an easygoing float or fishing trip on the lake of the same name. The trip is $85 per person for two hours of unforgettable sightseeing. The Hortons also operate *Eagle's Nest Motel,* near the center of town, and *Eagle's Nest Car Rental.* Cars rent for $49 per day, $294 per week, or $20 per hour with 100 free miles per day. Motel rooms are not five-star but comfortable and well equipped, and the Hortons claim they are the nicest in town. Call (800) 354–6009 or (907) 766–3779 or visit www.alaskaeagletours.com.

For some of the best local seafood, stop by the *Hotel Halsingland* (907–766–2000 or 800–542–6363; www.hotelhalsingland.com) for full dinners starting at about $19. The hotel offers rooms starting at $119 for a double. A limited number of economy rooms with shared baths are available, starting at $69.

For a relaxed atmosphere and healthful food, check out *Bear-Ritto's Eatery* (907–766–2117) in the Bear Den Mall on Main Street across from the Sheldon Museum. One of the cafe's specialties is Haines's own birch-syrup ice cream.

The historic building that houses the *Fort Seward Lodge, Restaurant, and Saloon* was constructed in the early 1900s as the fort's post exchange. In those days it included a gym, movie house, library, and two-lane bowling alley as well as a soda fountain. The latter was a popular place with tourists, who enjoyed watching the soldiers' pet bear (named Three Per, for 3 percent beer), who would beg for ice-cream cones when she couldn't entice the soldiers to give her beer. Three Per has long since gone to bear heaven, but the building is still popular with visitors, who can enjoy all-you-can-eat crab dinners in season, rent rooms with private or shared baths, and savor a favorite libation in the bar. Rooms start at $50 for an economy single; meals and saloon charges are in the moderate range. For more information phone (907) 766–2009 or (877) 617–3418 or visit www.ftsewardlodge.com.

Also on fort grounds: Norman and Suzanne Smith's *Fort Seward Bed and Breakfast,* house number 1 on Officers' Row, features stately Jeffersonian rooms with fireplaces, cable TV, and awesome views of Lynn Canal. Full sourdough-pancake breakfasts are included in the $89 to $135 rate for two. For information phone (907) 766–2856 or (800) 615–NORM or visit www.fortsewardalaska.com. Also on the parade grounds in Officers' Row are *Fort Seward Condos,* owned and operated by Ted and Mimi Gregg. These completely furnished bedroom apartments come with fully equipped kitchens. The Greggs were among the original purchasers of the fort back in the '40s and have a wealth of memories and history to share. Rates start at $125 per night. Call (907) 766–2708 or visit www.fortsewardcondos.com. Dave Nanney's *Chilkat Eagle Bed and Breakfast* sits next to the Chilkat Center for the Arts. It's small, intimate, and was built in 1904 as NCO quarters. Hospitality is practiced here in six languages: English, Spanish, French, Japanese, Dutch, and Italian. The rate is $80 for a double. Call (907) 766–2763 or visit www.eagle-bb .com.

If you want to stay on the waterfront, check out *A Sheltered Harbor Bed and Breakfast.* There are five rooms with private baths, and breakfasts are a tasty, filling affair. Prices range from $70 for a single to $120 for the suite. For more information call (616) 780–1128 or visit www.geocities.com/asheltered.

southeast alaskafacts

Early on October 24, 1918, the SS *Princess Sophia,* a passenger vessel carrying 350 people, went aground on Vanderbilt Reef in Lynn Canal. Forced off the reef the following evening by storm and high tides, the *Princess Sophia* sank and all aboard perished.

If you're looking for charming historical accommodations right in town, you won't do better than *A Summer Inn Bed and Breakfast* at 117 Second Avenue (907–766–2970; www.summer innbnb.com). Originally owned by one of Soapy Smith's illustrious con men, this well-kept five-bedroom house features full breakfasts and an on-site innkeeper. Rates are $75 for a single and $90 for a double.

Bear Creek Camp and International Hostel (907–766–2259; http://bear creekcabinsalaska.com) offers a lot of options—regular cabins, cabins with bunk beds, campsites, plus a separate shower house and bathrooms. There's also a kitchen for guests' use in another cabin. The camp and hostel are situated among trees and mountains about a mile from downtown. Call ahead for ferry pickup. The nightly fee is $18 for a bunk in the hostel, $48 for a cabin, or $12 for a campsite. To get there head out Mud Bay Road. When you come to Small Tract Road, turn left and drive for about ¾ mile. It's around a corner and on the left.

For a unique experience, check out *Valley of the Eagles Golf Links* (907–766–2401; www.hainesgolf.com). Located right next to the ocean on glacial rebound lands that are rising almost an inch a year, the course features spectacular scenery, including trout and salmon streams. It's not uncommon to see tracks where moose or bear have ambled across the artificial turf, which has been installed to protect the area from the effects of harsh chemical fertilizers. Don't expect perfect, manicured greens, but that's all part of the charm.

For off-road adventures of just about every variety, *Alaska Cross Country Guiding and Rafting* offers transportation by helicopter, fixed-wing aircraft, river raft, and airboat. (A note about airboats for the uninitiated: They're very loud.) Alaska Cross Country also offers white-water rafting, glacier hiking, cross-country skiing, snowshoeing, and guided photography trips through the Chilkat Bald Eagle Preserve. Call (907) 767–5322 for details.

Dolly Varden Alaska runs a nice three-hour kayaking and mountain biking tour out of Haines for $157 per person. It starts with a bike ride along the ocean to Chilkoot Lake State Recreation Site, where you'll get a quick lesson in kayaking and paddle off in hopes of seeing bears, eagles, and even an occasional seal that has followed salmon into the lake. For more information call (866) 298–6287 or visit www.DollyVarden.com. If you like more independent water excursions, **Alaska River Outfitters** (907–766–3307) will rent you a raft, pack your food, and drop you at a put-in location on either the Tatshenshini or the Alsek River.

When you're ready to leave town, if you're Skagway bound and don't have a car, consider **Chilkat Cruises & Tours** (907–766–2100 or 888–766–2103; www.chilkatcruises.com), which can ferry you in thirty-five minutes across the water what would take six hours to drive. The large, comfortable *Fairweather Express* and *Fairweather Express II* make up to twenty-six crossings per day and have plenty of observation-deck space for sightseeing. The cost is $54 round-trip or $30 one way.

In the annals of the nineteenth-century American frontier, no town had a more frantic, frenzied, fascinating history than **Skagway.** This city at the northern end of Lynn Canal, some 90 miles north of Juneau, was packed to overflowing during the "Days of '98," when thousands of would-be gold seekers poured into the community to outfit themselves for treks to the Klondike gold fields. It was one of the most lawless towns under the American flag. Jefferson "Soapy" Smith and his gang of toughs and con men controlled the city, prompting the superintendent of the Canadian North West Mounted Police across the border to call it "little better than hell on earth." Amazingly well preserved, with many structures from the late nineteenth and early twentieth centuries still standing and in use, much of the town today makes up the **Klondike Gold Rush National Historical Park.** And there's still a lot of violence in this town . . . but it's all make-believe, a nightly reenactment of the July 8, 1898, shoot-out between "good guy" citizen Frank Reid and "bad guy" desperado Soapy Smith. (Both men died in the encounter.)

There's more to Skagway than gold rush structures and shoot-outs, though. There is, for instance, the **White Pass & Yukon Route.** Declared an International Historic Civil Engineering Landmark by the American Society of Civil Engineers—a designation achieved by only fourteen other projects, including the Eiffel Tower in Paris and the Statue of Liberty in New York—the narrow-gauge railway provides one of North America's premier rail experiences. Construction of the line between Skagway and Whitehorse, Yukon, began, against horrendous grades and incredible natural obstacles, in 1898. The builders clawed and blasted their way to the 2,885-foot White Pass in 1899 and to Whitehorse the following year. The WP&YR today carries visitors from Skagway, at sea level, to the pass in the incredibly short distance of only 20 miles. Called the Summit Excursion, the fully narrated three-hour tour is $98 and takes in the most spectacular of the cliff-hanging mountain and lush valley sights. Another option is the six-hour, $150 excursion to *Lake Bennett* and on to Carcross, Yukon Territory, where some 20,000 stampeders camped during the winter of 1898 after climbing and crossing the Chilkoot Pass. (They then proceeded by boat and raft through additional lakes, rapids, and riverways to the Klondike.) For reservations or information call (800) 343–7373 or visit www.whitepassrailroad .com.

And speaking of the railroad, the headquarters and information center of the Klondike Gold Rush National Historical Park is located in the restored old *WP&YR Depot,* at Second Avenue and Broadway. You'll find historical photos, artifacts, and film showings there plus visitor information about the town and current conditions on the *Chilkoot Trail.* Walks through the downtown historic district guided by park service rangers leave from the center several times daily. The National Park Service, at substantial effort, has restored a number of Skagway's most historic buildings, including the *Mascot Saloon,* Third Avenue and Broadway, built in 1898, and the *Trail Inn and Pack Train Saloon,* Fourth Avenue and Broadway, constructed in 1908. *Captain Benjamin Moore's cabin,* a half block west of Broadway between Fifth and Sixth Avenues, dates from 1887; the good captain was there, waiting for the gold rush to start, when the first stampeders clambered ashore a decade later. Call (907) 983–2921 for walking tour schedules. The tours are free of charge.

The city also has a free self-guided walking tour that takes in downtown businesses as well as some of the Victorian-style homes in the community. Maps are available at the visitor center. For further information call (907) 983–2854.

Other worthwhile stops in Skagway include the *Corrington Museum of Alaska History* (907–983–2579), at Fifth Avenue and Broadway, with exhibits from prehistory to modern-day Alaska, and *Gold Rush Cemetery,* about 1½ miles north from downtown, where Frank Reid and Soapy Smith lie buried.

The *Arctic Brotherhood Hall,* at Second Avenue and Broadway, is worth a look-see if for no other reason than an interesting photo opportunity. It's old, having been built in 1899 to house "Camp Skagway Number 1" of a once-thriving Alaska-Yukon fraternal organization of gold seekers. And its curious, false-fronted facade is covered with more than 20,000 (count 'em, 20,000) individual pieces of big and little rounded pieces of driftwood.

During the Klondike gold rush, Skagway was the jumping-off place for the White Pass Trail of '98 horse and wagon route to the Yukon. For stampeders who couldn't afford either pack horses or wagons, the nearby community of **Dyea** (pronounced Dy-EE) was the starting point for the famous Chilkoot Trail to the gold fields. The trail today is part of the Klondike Gold Rush National Historical Park and, like trekkers of old, you, too, can hike from Dyea (accessible by gravel road, 9 miles north of Skagway) to Lake Bennett. It's a three- to six-day walk, with some shelters along the way. For details from the park superintendent's office, call (907) 983–2921.

Although the Chilkoot Trail is the best-known trail in the area, the hiker with limited time can enjoy several other hiking options, including the easy, woodsy **Lower Dewey Trail**, less than a mile long. You'll find the **Skyline**

The Chilkoot Trail of the Great Gold Rush Days

My husband and I are planning a trip on the famed Chilkoot Trail, which during the 1898 Klondike gold rush was the route gold seekers toiled up to Lake Bennett in Canada. It is a famous trail; old sepia-toned prints captured hordes of laden prospectors making their way up "the Scales," which seemed to climb straight to heaven. So it is with anticipation that I look forward to this trip—as long as my husband doesn't repeat his antics of the last time he was on this trail, more than twenty years ago when he was but a young lad of sixteen.

He was a Boy Scout—the Scout law is to be "trustworthy, loyal, helpful, friendly, courteous, kind, obedient, cheerful, thrifty, brave, clean, and reverent"—and he traveled with Troop 211. It was a three-day trip in which the Scouts would do like the gold miners, hauling their packs and themselves clear to the top. All seemed to be going well, until a Scout of large proportions, we'll call him Norm, began to complain about all the weight he had to carry (including the double-burner Coleman stove he had insisted earlier that he must have in order to cook his canned food). Scoutmaster Mr. Weston, tired of hearing Norm's complaints, made the rest of the Scouts take Norm's belongings and redistribute the weight evenly among themselves. Obviously, moans and groans ensued, but like good Scouts they followed their orders.

It wasn't until Norm had reached the top of the great pass that he realized the joke was on him. Bent on revenge, the "trustworthy, loyal, helpful, friendly, courteous, kind" Scouts had discreetly filled Norm's pack with rocks so that the poor child never got relief after all.

Remind me not to complain during *our* trip.

—Melissa DeVaughn

Trail and A.B. Mountain longer (more than 3 miles to the summit), more strenuous, but greatly rewarding. ("A.B.," incidentally, stands for Arctic Brotherhood, a gold rush fraternal organization.)

A Chilkoot Trail map and maps of area hiking destinations are available at the city and park service visitor centers.

For the truly adventurous, try Alaska's all-time favorite winter sport in the middle of the summer. *Alaska Icefield Expeditions* (907–983–2299; www.ak dogtour.com) has teamed up with *Temsco Helicopters* (907–983–2900 or 866–683–2900; www.temscoair.com) to offer spectacular glacier flight-seeing by helicopter combined with a glacier landing and sled dog rides. Meet professional mushers and their four-legged teammates and go for a sled dog ride on the Denver Glacier. The entire tour, including cruise-ship transfer, helicopter ride, sled dog expedition and return trip, costs $449 per person.

Another dry-land option is to go for a wheeled dogsled ride with *Alaska Sled Dog Adventures.* The two-and-three-quarter-hour tour is $109 and encompasses a short history of sled dogs and the sport of mushing, the ride on the sled, and lots of adorable photo opportunities. Or if dogs are not your animal of choice, there is the option of horseback riding. The three-and-a-half-hour slow ride and sightseeing trek is $165 per person. Call (907) 983–4444 or visit www.alaskasleddog.com.

While in Skagway, don't pass up the chance to see a true piece of history on Seventh Avenue and Spring Street. Built in 1900, the McCabe Building is the first granite building in the state of Alaska, and it was originally intended to be a women's college. The building now houses the *Skagway City Hall* and *Skagway Museum and Archives* (907–983–2420; www.skagwaymuseum.org). The collection includes "good guy" Frank Reid's will, the tie "bad guy" Soapy Smith was wearing during the shootout, an Eskimo kayak, and an Indian canoe. Admission is $2.

Also in Skagway is *At the White House Bed and Breakfast,* a beautifully renovated Victorian-style home that was almost destroyed by fire in the late '70s. Owners Jan and John Tronrud have done an excellent job decorating the home. Rates start at $125. For further information call (907) 983–9000 or visit www.atthewhitehouse.com.

Historic *Skagway Inn Bed and Breakfast,* at Seventh and Broadway, traces its origins to 1897 and its days as a brothel providing "services" for lonely gold stampeders. Today the inn contains ten rooms restored to Victorian charm. Some rooms share a bath. Innkeepers Karl and Rosemary Klupar offer full breakfasts, home-baked muffins, fresh-ground coffee, piping-hot tea, courtesy van service (including transportation for hikers to the start of the Chilkoot Trail), and Alaskan expertise. Rates start at $99 for a double. Call (907) 983–

2289 or visit www.skagwayinn.com. In the evening, incidentally, you can purchase dinner at the restaurant there called *Olivia's at the Skagway Inn.* This is probably Skagway's most expensive restaurant, but expect it to be worth the tariff. It is a fine dining experience.

Skagway Home Hostel has served more than 50,000 guests in a historic home that dates from 1901. Dorm rooms begin at $15 per night, with couples' rooms going for $50 per night. Even at those prices you'll enjoy a host of amenities, including use of the fully equipped kitchen and backyard barbecue, hot showers, free bicycle and Internet use, access to a library of books, and a help-yourself policy to the fresh goodies in the garden out back. It's conveniently located a block and a half from shops and restaurants, and the friendly hosts will help you book local tours and activities. For more information call (907) 983–2131 or visit www.skagwayhostel.com.

Perhaps the strangest "cabin" in the USDA Forest Service wilderness cabin network is the retired White Pass & Yukon Route *Denver Caboose,* located 5½ miles north of Skagway. The view, a stunner, takes in the Skagway River and the Sawtooth Mountains. Visitors may rent this unit for $35 a night, just like most others in the system, but instead of flying, hiking, or boating in you reach the caboose by—you guessed it—taking the train! For information call (877) 444–6777 or go to www.recreation.gov.

For a truly off-the-beaten-path camping experience, travel 9 miles down the road to the *Dyea Campground.* There are many things about this hidden treasure that make it so special. First, it only costs $6 per night to camp. Second, it is located among lush green trees, which make the air feel particularly clean and clear. And third, if you're like me and enjoy a closer-to-nature experience, there are only the basics—pit toilets, water from a simple pump, and lots of space to spread a tent and enjoy the surroundings. No humming generators here! For further information on the campground, call the park service at (907) 983–2921.

For bicyclists, *Sockeye Cycle,* of Skagway and Haines, offers a five- or ten-day Canol Road Tour, which explores the sparsely populated Northeast Yukon Territory via an old World War II dirt road. The cost is $2,105 for ten days and includes special mountain bikes and gear as well as lodging and three meals a day. For information call (907) 983–2851 in Skagway or (907) 766–2869 in Haines, or visit the Web site at www.cyclealaska.com.

Skagway is the southern terminus of the *Klondike Highway,* which extends into British Columbia and Canada's Yukon Territory. Each fall, on a designated weekend in September, the highway becomes less a highway and more a race course as hundreds of running teams from all over the United States and Canada arrive to race in stages all the way to Whitehorse, 110 miles away. For dates and information about the ***Klondike International Road Relay,*** contact the ***Skagway Convention and Visitors Bureau*** at (907) 983–2854 or www.skagway.com.

Glacier Bay National Park and the Community of Gustavus

No question about it. ***Glacier Bay National Park and Preserve*** is one of the extraordinary parks of the nation. Home to sixteen massive, glistening saltwater glaciers and the site of hundreds of huge and little valley and mountaintop ice masses, Glacier Bay National Park is all about the power of ice in shaping a land. It's a place where the relentless grinding force of glaciers has carved deep, steep-walled saltwater fjords and U-shaped mountain valleys, and it's a place of stark, barren, rocky expanses where glaciers have only recently receded. It's also a land of mature, lush spruce and hemlock forests, where the ice receded decades ago. It's a place where the word *awesome* comes frequently to mind.

Glacier Bay National Park lies some 60 miles west of Juneau, accessible by cruise ship, yacht, jet, or light aircraft. Visits can be as short as a day trip out of Juneau or as long as a week or more. The community of ***Gustavus,*** easily reached by air, abuts the park and provides a rich variety of guiding, fishing, lodging, and supply services.

If you want lodging within the park boundaries, your only choice (though highly pleasurable) is ***Glacier Bay Lodge*** on the shores of ***Bartlett Cove.*** The lodge is a fifty-six-room resort located 10 miles from the community of Gustavus. It contains fully modern guest rooms, dining room, cocktail lounge, small gift shop, and the ***National Park Service Glacier Bay Visitor Center.*** Rooms begin at $150 per person per night. Ask about rooms with a view of the cove and about packages that include meals, the Glacier Bay Tour, and transfers from Gustavus. For a brochure or reservations, call (907) 264–4600 or visit www.visitglacierbay.com.

The sightseeing yacht *Baranof Wind* departs Bartlett Cove daily for a full day, which includes close-up looks at glaciers, thousands of birds, and good prospects of viewing brown bears and mountain goats on land plus whales, porpoises, and seals in the water. Park service naturalists accompany each sailing. The fare, including lunch onboard, is $156.50. Package tours that include whale watching, kayaking, flight-seeing, and fishing can be arranged. For information call (907) 264–4600 or visit www.visitglacierbay.com.

Now about Gustavus, next door to the park. Funny place this town. Except it's not a town, because the 300 strong-willed, individualistic citizens who live

True and Unexpected

Justice Creek in Glacier Bay National Park and Preserve was named by the National Park Service after a story by Jack London titled "The Unexpected," in which justice was provided by two prospectors who, in the absence of a court, tried and executed a third person for murder. The story was based on actual events that happened in the vicinity of the creek. On October 6, 1899, one M. S. Severts calmly shared dinner with hosts Hannah and Hans Nelson and two other guests, Sam Christianson and Fragnallia Stefano. When he'd finished eating, Severts got up, went outside, and returned with a Colt .45 revolver. He fired two shots, killing Stefano and wounding Christianson, before turning the gun on Hannah. Hans leaped to her rescue. The couple hired Indians to guard the killer for several weeks while they tried to flag down passing ships. Having no success, they tried Stefano themselves, procured a signed confession, and hung him.

there have voted repeatedly not to become any sort of official city with trappings like mayors or government. But Gustavus is a definable community because these same people—as friendly and sharing and helpful as they are fiercely independent—manage to provide everything that they need in order to happily reside there. They're equally prepared to provide travelers with everything they need to visit for a few days or a season. The setting is awesome, bounded on three sides by the snowcapped peaks of the Chilkat Range and the Fairweather Mountains and on the fourth by smooth, sandy, saltwater beaches. The community spreads itself sparsely over miles of flat countryside and includes boundless opportunities for berry picking, hiking, bicycle riding, kayaking, golfing, whale watching, freshwater and saltwater angling, beachcombing, birding, and just gawking.

For such a small community, Gustavus has no shortage of fine lodging. The first place that comes to mind is the *Gustavus Inn,* once a rural homestead and now a comfortable, inviting inn for weary travelers. The home was built in 1928 and served a pioneer family with nine children. In 1965 the new owners—Jack and Sally Lesh—did some renovations and opened their doors to guests. Today, one Lesh generation later, David and JoAnn Lesh carry on the tradition. The food continues to be the inn's strong point, with fresh seafood in great quantity. And there are ample opportunities to borrow a bicycle and go for a ride, fish from the banks of the nearby Salmon River, hike on the many trails and backroads, or just wander your way into relaxation. Rates start at $185.00 per adult, $92.50 per child, including all meals. Call (800) 649–5220 or visit www.gustavusinn.com.

Gustavus's second inn, the *Glacier Bay Country Inn,* likewise offers an Alaskan, high-quality experience in a setting of verdant forests and majestic mountains. Here, too—in a distinctive structure with multiangled roofs, dormers, decks, and log-beamed ceilings—informally gracious living and fine dining are trademarks. The charge is $198 per person, based on double occupancy, including three full meals. Cabins are also available, starting at $230 per person per night. For further information or reservations, visit www.glacierbayalaska.com or call (800) 628–0912.

Another all-inclusive option is the ***Bear Track Inn*** (907–697–3017 or 888–697–2284; www.beartrackinn.com), a handcrafted log lodge with 30-foot ceilings and fourteen spacious rooms. The rate of $495 per person, double occupancy, for two days and one night, includes transportation from Juneau, lodging, and meals. Also included are fishing, wildlife viewing, and kayaking.

If you'd prefer to stay right in Gustavus, check out the ***Growley Bear Inn.*** This log cabin with a carved bear out front is just a five-minute walk from downtown, such as it is. Rates are $145 per day, including a full breakfast plus in-room television, compact fridge, and private bath. For more information call (907) 697–2712 or visit www.gustavus.com/growleybear.

Glacier Bay, with its protected arms and inlets, provides ideal kayaking waters for sightseeing at sea level. ***Glacier Bay Sea Kayaks,*** operated by longtime Alaskans Bonnie Kaden and Kara Berg, has been renting these crafts to visitors for many years, by the half day or full day; they also offer guided kayaking in the park, including all gear and equipment. Prices start as low as $30 a day. Call (907) 697–2257 for information or visit www.glacierbayseakayaks.com. Berg's husband, former Glacier Bay ranger Mike Nigro, spends his time on the water as owner/operator of ***Gustavus Marine Charters*** (907–697–2233; www.gustavusmarine charters.com). Captain Nigro is an Alaska veteran whose company is one of a limited number of charter concessions authorized by the National Park Service to operate within the park. His vessel, the MV *Kahsteen*, has comfortable sleeping quarters and a spacious main cabin and open fly bridge for effortless viewing and photography. Meals include salmon, halibut, and Dungeness crab, but special diets can be accommodated with adequate notice. Sport anglers can choose from king- and silver-salmon fishing as well as halibut fishing. Trips range from a two-day sightseeing trip through the East Arm of Glacier Bay for $900 per person to a five-day Glacier Bay expedition for $2,250 per person.

Newer to the kayak-renting scene yet equally as qualified is ***Sea Otter Kayak Glacier Bay,*** across from the store on Dock Road. The owners will pick you up at the airport or dock, outfit you with a kayak and all the necessary gear, and deliver kayaks to their appropriate destination. They can even arrange travel and lodging for out-of-town visitors. Rates begin at $51 for a single and $56 for a double for a full day. Rates decrease for multiday rentals. For more information call (907) 697–3007 or visit www.he.net/~seaotter.

Award-winning **Alaska Discovery** operates water and hiking tours in the park, catering to both one-day visitors with or without outdoor experience and to knowledgeable kayakers and rafters who seek a rigorous wilderness adventure. Call (800) 586–1911 for more details or visit www.akdiscovery.com.

Another option is to cruise Glacier Bay aboard the *Seawolf,* a 97-foot ocean yacht with six cabins, a twelve-passenger capacity, and activity areas for all to enjoy. The *Seawolf* crew promises a maximum of five hours of travel each day, leaving plenty of time for exploring by water or land. Try guided kayaking with their sturdy double boats and quiet paddles, or go for a nature hike along the shore. Watch the whales, touch a glacier, or pick berries by the handful in season. It's all part of the **Seawolf Wilderness Adventures** philosophy of making nature more than just a spectator sport. The six-day Glacier Bay Adventure runs $3,180 per person. The folks at Seawolf can also help you create a customized adventure. Try to contact them during the off-season, as communications are spotty once they're aboard the vessel. For more information call (907) 957–1438 or visit www.seawolfadventures.net.

Spirit Walker Expeditions offers tours from a one- or two-day trip by kayak to nearby (and aptly named) Pleasant Island to their five- to ten-day expedition among the (also aptly named) **Myriad Islands,** where hundreds of tiny isles make up a miniature Inside Passage. Prices for these trips range from a $230 day trip to a $3,825 weeklong Myriad Island adventure, which includes bush plane airlift from Gustavus. Call (800) KAYAKER for more details or visit www.seakayakalaska.com.

The 70-foot *Steller,* formerly a state research vessel, provides a floating base for kayakers and motor skiff sightseers on **Glacier Bay Adventures** four-day trips. The main search is for humpback whales, but the vessel frequently encounters Steller sea lions, sea otters, porpoises, seals, and minke whales. Visitors usually spend one day in Dundas Bay, where a shore visit allows anglers to sample freshwater fishing in the Dundas River. For more details call Dan Foley at (907) 697–2442.

Jim Kearns's **Fairweather Adventures** offers lodging and marine wildlife tours at the mouth of Glacier Bay, on the banks of the Salmon River. Kayak trips, sportfishing, beach excursions, and exploring are all available. Lodging and meals are provided at the breathtaking **Meadow's Glacier Bay Guest House.** Phone (907) 697–2334 for details or visit www.fishglacierbay.com.

When you're ready to leave Gustavus, call **Air Excursions,** which is the primary airplane carrier for the community. Fares are about $80 one way to Juneau. For more information call (907) 697–2375 or visit www.airexcursions.com.

For more information in general on the community of Gustavus, call (907) 697–2245.

Places to Stay in Southeast Alaska

GUSTAVUS

Glacier Bay Country Inn;
(800) 628–0912,
www.glacierbayalaska.com
A distinctive inn.

Glacier Bay Lodge;
(800) 451–5952,
www.glacierbaytours.com
A fifty-six-room resort on the shores of Bartlett Cove; dorm rooms also available for thrifty travelers.

Gustavus Inn;
(800) 649–5220,
www.gustavusinn.com
Comfortable, inviting inn.

HAINES

Bear Creek Camp and International Hostel;
(907) 766–2259,
www.kcd.com/hostel

Chilkat Eagle Bed and Breakfast,
67 Soap Suds Alley;
(907) 766–2763,
www.eagle-bb.com
Near Lynn Canal.

Eagle's Nest Motel,
mile 1 on Haines Highway;
(800) 354–6009,
www.alaskaeagletours.com

Fort Seward Bed and Breakfast,
house number 1
on Officers' Row;
(907) 766–2856,
(800) 615–NORM, or
www.fortsewardbnb.com
Awesome views of Lynn Canal.

Fort Seward Lodge, Restaurant, and Saloon;
(907) 766–2009 or
(800) 478–7772,
www.ftsewardlodge.com

Hotel Halsingland;
(907) 766–2000,
www.hotelhalsingland.com

On the Beach Inn B&B,
on scenic Tanani Bay;
(907) 766–3992,
www.onthebeachinn.com

A Sheltered Harbor Bed and Breakfast;
(616) 780–1128,
www.geocities.com/asheltered
On the waterfront.

A Summer Inn Bed and Breakfast,
117 Second Avenue;
(907) 766–2970,
www.summerinnbnb.com

HOONAH

Sportsman's Bed and Breakfast,
257 Second Street;
(907) 945–3218

HYDER

Grand View Inn;
(250) 636–9174,
www.grandviewinn.net
On Highway 37A,
Hyder's main road.

JUNEAU

Driftwood Lodge,
435 Willoughby Avenue;
(907) 586–2280 or
(800) 544–2239,
www.driftwoodalaska.com
A popular lodging for lawmakers in the state capital for the legislative session.

Juneau International Hostel,
614 Harris Street;
(907) 586–9559,
www.juneauhostel.org

Silverbow Inn,
120 Second Street;
(907) 586–4146 or
(800) 586–4146,
www.silverbowinn.com
Historic hotel with modern accommodations.

Westmark Baranof Hotel,
127 North Franklin Street;
(907) 586–2660 or
(800) 544–0970,
www.westmarkhotels.com
In historic downtown Juneau.

JUNEAU AREA

Alaskan Williwaws,
mile 21 Glacier Highway;
(907) 789–2803 or
(888) 337–9617,
www.williwaws.com

Pearson's Pond Luxury Inn;
(907) 789–3772 or
(800) 658–6328,
www.pearsonspond.com
A B&B inn.

KETCHIKAN

Gilmore Hotel,
326 Front Street;
(907) 225–9423 or
(800) 275–9423,
www.gilmorehotel.com
Has a commanding view of Ketchikan's frantic waterfront.

Madame's Manor,
324 Cedar Street;
(907) 247–2774 or
(877) 531–8159,
www.madamesmanor.com
In Ketchikan's historic Nob Hill District.

KETCHIKAN AREA

Eagle View Hostel;
(907) 225–5461,
www.eagleviewhostel.com

PELICAN

Highliner Lodge;
(907) 735–2476

PETERSBURG

Nordic House Bed and Breakfast,
806 South Nordic Drive;
(907) 772–3620,
www.petersburgbnb.com

Rocky Point Resort,
11 miles south of town on Wrangell Narrows;
(907) 772–4420,
www.rockyptresort.com

Tides Inn,
First and Dolphin Streets;
(907) 772–4288,
www.TidesInnAlaska.com

PORT ALEXANDER

Laughing Raven Lodge;
(907) 568–2266 or
(800) 768–7752,
www.portalexander.com
A secluded getwaway for wildlife viewing, hiking, kayaking, and fishing.

SITKA

Alaska Ocean View Bed and Breakfast,
1101 Edgecumbe Drive;
(907) 747–8310,
www.sitka-alaska lodging.com
The name says it all.

Burgess Bauder's Lighthouse;
(907) 747–3056.
Located on an island a few minutes by boat from downtown Sitka; use of skiff included.

SKAGWAY

At the White House Bed and Breakfast;
(907) 983–9000,
www.atthewhitehouse.com
Beautifully renovated Victorian-style home. Two blocks from downtown.

Skagway Home Hostel;
(907) 983–2131,
www.skagwayhostel.com
Dorm and couples' rooms; bicycle and Internet use.

Skagway Inn Bed and Breakfast,
Seventh and Broadway;
(907) 983–2289,
www.skagwayinn.com
Twelve rooms restored to Victorian charm.

WRANGELL

Hungry Beaver,
274 Shakes Street;
(907) 874–3005.
Rooms with kitchenettes.

Old Sourdough Lodge,
1104 Peninsula Avenue;
(800) 874–3613,
www.akgetaway.com
Rustic lodge with comfortable accommodations.

Rooney's Roost Bed and Breakfast,
206 McKinnon Street;
(907) 874–2026,
www.rooneysroost.com
Just a block from downtown.

Stikine Inn;
(888) 874–3388,
www.stikineinnak.com
Wrangell's largest hotel, with thirty-three rooms, restaurant, and meeting rooms. One block from ferry terminal.

Wrangell Hostel,
220 Church Street;
(907) 874–3534.
Operated by the First Presbyterian Church mid-May through Labor Day.

Places to Eat in Southeast Alaska

GUSTAVUS

A Bear's Nest Café;
(907) 697–2440,
www.gustavus.com/bearsnest
Features organic breads, soup, seafood, and salad.

HAINES

Bamboo Room Restaurant and Pioneer Bar,
near corner of Second and Main;
(907) 766–2800,
www.kcd.com/bamboo
Breakfast, lunch, dinner, and full bar.

Bear-Ritto's Eatery;
(907) 766–2117.
Healthful food in the Bear Den Mall.

Fort Seward Lodge, Restaurant, and Saloon;
(907) 766–2009.
All-you-can-eat crab dinners in season.

JUNEAU

Douglas Cafe,
918 Third Street;
(907) 363–3307.
Perhaps the only restaurant
in Juneau that features
amber clams and amber
mussels; all that and
(arguably) Alaska's best clam
chowder, too.

Dragon Inn,
213 Front Street;
(907) 586–4888.
Tasty Chinese in downtown.

Mike's Fine Food & Spirits;
(907) 364–3271.
Fine dining at affordable
prices.

Twisted Fish Company,
550 South Franklin Street;
(907) 463–5033.
Fresh seafood on the
waterfront.

Westmark Baranof Hotel,
127 North Franklin Street;
(907) 586–2660,
www.westmarkhotels.com
Fine dining in historic
downtown Juneau.

KETCHIKAN

**Annabelle's Famous Keg
and Chowder House,**
326 Front Street;
(907) 225–9423.

PETERSBURG

**Rooney's Northern Lights
Restaurant,**
203 Sing Alley;
(907) 772–2900.

SKAGWAY

Olivia's at the Skagway Inn,
Seventh and Broadway;
(907) 983–2289,
www.skagwayinn.com
A fine dining experience.
Pricey, but worth it.

WRANGELL

Hungry Beaver,
274 Shakes Street;
(907) 874–3005.
Locally famous pizza;
restaurant and lounge.

Canada's Yukon

So, you may be asking, what is a chapter about part of Canada doing in an Alaska guidebook? Actually, there are a couple of reasons.

First of all, if you're driving from Southeast Alaska to Alaska's interior, you have to go through a small sliver of Canada's British Columbia and a big hunk of Canada's Yukon. From Haines or Skagway at the northern end of the Southeast Alaska ferry system, you can drive the 152-mile Haines Highway or 98 miles of the Klondike Highway to junctions with the Alaska Highway. From there your route lies northwesterly through Canada's Yukon Territory to the rest of Alaska.

Second, from the traveler's point of view, visiting Canada's Yukon is really part of the North Country experience. Aside from a few artificial differences, like Canada's metric road signs, or gasoline pumped in liters instead of gallons, you'll notice few distinctions between the Yukon and Alaska's interior region. Both are lands of rolling hills, majestic mountains, fish-filled lakes, and vast, untrammeled wilderness areas teeming with moose, caribou, bears, and wolves.

In both Interior Alaska and the Yukon, you'll marvel at a sun that nearly doesn't set during the summertime, and in both

CANADA'S YUKON

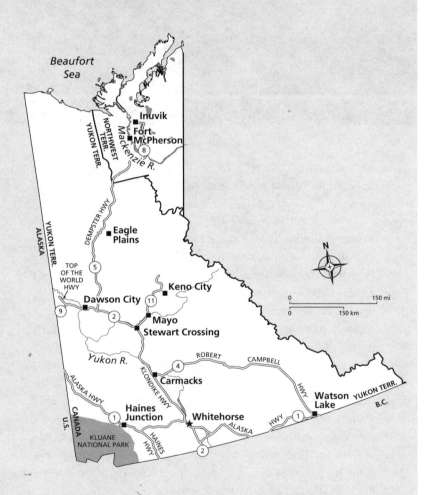

Beaufort
Sea

Inuvik

Fort
McPherson

⑧

NORTHWEST
TERR.

YUKON TERR.

Mackenzie R.

DEMPSTER HWY

■ Eagle
Plains

YUKON TERR.

ALASKA

TOP
OF THE
WORLD
HWY

⑤

Keno City ■

Dawson City ■

⑪

⑨

②

■ Mayo
■ Stewart Crossing

Yukon R.

ROBERT

CAMPBELL

KLONDIKE HWY

④

■ Carmacks

HWY

ALASKA HWY

Watson
Lake ■

YUKON TERR.

CANADA

U.S.

Haines
Junction

①

★ Whitehorse

ALASKA

①

B.C.

KLUANE
NATIONAL PARK

HAINES
HWY

②

N

0   150 mi
0   150 km

you'll find friendly, helpful, outgoing folk who revel in their Native heritage, their gold rush past, and their present-day frontier lifestyle.

The main arterial road of the Yukon Territory is the Alaska Highway, referred to by many tourists—but few Alaskans or Yukoners—as the Alcan. (It's rather like calling San Francisco "Frisco." Everyone will know what you're talking about, but knowledgeable visitors will observe the local preference.) The fabled road begins at Dawson Creek in British Columbia, meanders through the Yukon Territory to the Alaska border, and ends at Delta Junction, Alaska— a total journey of 1,422 miles.

The two largest cities of the Yukon are Whitehorse, present-day capital of the territory, and Dawson City (not to be confused with Dawson Creek, B.C.). It was near the present site of Dawson City, in 1896, that the discovery of gold on a tributary of the Klondike River set off one of the world's wildest stampedes.

In both Alaska and the Yukon, you'll see numbers on frequent mileposts or kilometer posts beside the highways. These numbers represent miles or kilometers from a highway's beginning. Home and business addresses and even cities are often referenced in miles or kilometers. Whitehorse, for instance, is shown in a Yukon government guidebook as being located at kilometer 1,455.3 on the Alaska Highway. In this Canadian section of this book, we'll identify most sites by their kilometer-post markings, although in discussing short drives and distances, we'll frequently refer to miles, since most U.S. residents have a better feel for mileage measurements. When, in the next chapter, we're back in Alaska, U.S.A., highway references will be in miles.

Here's a word of explanation about the layout of this chapter. It assumes you'll be traveling northerly through the Yukon to Interior Alaska either from Skagway (over the southern half of the Klondike Highway), Haines (over the Haines Highway), or Dawson Creek (at the start of the Alaska Highway). So, to start with, the chapter discusses sights and options along each of these three

TOP 10 PLACES IN CANADA'S YUKON

Carcross	Kluane Lake
Discovery Claim	Midnight Dome
Herschel Island	Sign Post Forest
Inn on the Lake Bed and Breakfast	SS *Klondike*
Jack London's cabin	Takhini Hot Springs

northbound approaches to Whitehorse. After a discussion of things to see and do in Whitehorse, the chapter describes the northern portion of the Klondike Highway from near Whitehorse to Dawson City. After suggesting a round-trip on the Dempster Highway from Dawson City to Inuvik in Canada's Northwest Territories, it deals—still Alaska-bound—with the Top of the World Highway north and west from Dawson City to the point where it crosses the border and meets Alaska's Taylor Highway. The Taylor, in turn, is described from northernmost Eagle to Tetlin Junction on the Alaska Highway, 80 miles northwest of the Alaska border.

Finally, the chapter backtracks to Whitehorse and lists your Alaska Highway options between that city and the point where you cross into Interior Alaska and the United States again. Of course, if you're departing Interior Alaska and heading southerly to southeast Alaska or Dawson Creek, British Columbia, follow the listings in reverse.

Remember that as of 2008, passports are required for reentry to the United States even when traveling by road. Remember to check restrictions on bringing firearms, alcohol, and certain fresh foods across the U.S. and Canadian borders. For up-to-date information visit www.travel.state.gov.

Customs stations may be a few miles on either side of the actual border, with several miles separating the U.S. and Canadian customs stops in some locations. Obviously, you only need to stop at the border-crossing station for whichever country you're *entering;* you're not required to stop when you're exiting. And be sure to check customs operating hours when planning your trip. Some stations are open twenty-four hours, but others, such as the U.S. border crossing on the Top of the World Highway, are open only twelve hours per day. If the customs checkpoint is closed, the road will be gated and you'll have to wait at the border until it reopens.

The Klondike Highway: Skagway to Whitehorse

Don't let the start of the ***Klondike Highway*** out of Skagway scare you. The first 10 or 11 miles climb at a pretty steep grade, from sea level to 3,000 feet plus, but after that the going's relatively level and certainly no worse than other mountain roads in the Lower Forty-eight and elsewhere. The road is two lanes wide and asphalt paved for its 98-mile (159-kilometer) length, and it roughly parallels the historic Trail of '98 from Skagway to the Klondike gold fields. It rises from lush, thickly vegetated low country to high rocky mountain and lake terrain with picture-postcard views and cascading waterfalls.

At kilometer 43, take the turnout to the east for a spectacular view of *Tormented Valley,* with its little lakes, stunted trees, and rocky landscape of big and little boulders. The historic remains of an ore-crushing mill for the *Venus Mine* can be seen and photographed at kilometer 84. Twelve kilometers farther there's a spectacular view of *Bove Island* and a portion of the Yukon's southern lakes system.

The community of *Carcross,* on the shores of Lake Bennett, lies at kilometer 106. Stop by the visitor reception center in the old *White Pass & Yukon Train Depot* (867–821–4431), where you can get tourist information. Among the off-the-beaten-path stops in this historic gold rush community are the *Matthew Watson General Store* and the *Barracks,* where you can soak up the atmosphere while you shop. If you've got postcards to mail, stop by the *Carcross Post Office,* where they'll stamp your passport with your choice of several commemorative postmark stamps. Several prominent figures from the Klondike gold rush are buried in Carcross, including Kate Carmacks and Skookum Jim, but due to vandalism, the cemetery has been closed to the public.

If time permits, turn right at kilometer 107 and head northeast on the paved 34-mile Tagish Road to *Tagish,* Yukon Territory, then head south on the good but mostly gravel 60-mile Atlin Road to *Atlin,* British Columbia. The

ANNUAL EVENTS IN CANADA'S YUKON

Yukon Quest Sled Dog Race:
Held each February, this 1,000-mile race goes from Whitehorse to Fairbanks and reverses directions each year.
(867) 668–4711;
www.yukonquest.com

Yukon Sourdough Rendezvous Festival:
Held in late February in Whitehorse, this weird and wacky festival is designed to "combat cabin fever."
(867) 667–2148;
www.yukonrendezvous.com

Gertie's International Dart Tournament:
Held every May in Dawson City. Draws some of the world's best darters. Call the Klondike Visitors Association at (867) 993–5575.

Yukon International Storytelling Festival:
Whitehorse, August. Storytellers from around the circumpolar world.
(867) 633–7550;
www.storytelling.yk.net

Yukon Gold Panning Championship:
Held in July in Dawson City as part of Canada Day festivities. Call the Klondike Visitors Association at (867) 993–5575.

Fireweed Festival:
In Faro each August. A horticulture show, plus triathlon, squash tournament, dance, and Yukon folk songs.
(867) 994–2375.

drive takes a little more than two hours. Atlin is a favorite getaway for Southeast Alaskans, many of whom have summer cottages there. *Atlin Lake* is a huge, meandering, spectacular body of water with lots of recreational opportunities. In the community itself you can visit the *Atlin Historical Museum* in the town's original one-room schoolhouse. Admission is $2.50. September through June the museum is open on request; it's open daily in the summer. Phone (250) 651–7522 or e-mail heritage@atlin.net. While there, for a small donation you can tour the *MV* **Tarahne,** which once carried freight and passengers across Atlin Lake to Scotia Bay. Tours of the drydocked vessel are available during summer. Also worth noting in town is the cold, bubbly water at the mineral springs under the gazebo at the north end of town. You can rent motorbikes or houseboats, take flight-seeing excursions around the area, or engage a guide for excellent lake and stream fishing. The community has a hotel plus several B&Bs and inns, including *Quilts and Comforts Bed and Breakfast* (on Pillman Road, off the Atlin Highway; 250–651–0007 or 800–836–1818), which has a spectacular view of Atlin, the mountains, and its extensive award-winning flower garden. Afternoon Tea in the Garden is served to parties of eight or more during summer and, as the B&B's name implies, there are quilts to be had, for sale or just for admiring. Room rates start at $75 for a single, $85 for a double.

yukontrivia

Work on the White Pass and Yukon Route railway began in 1898. By July 6, 1899, the rails topped the summit and reached Lake Bennett. The narrow-gauge railway connected Carcross and Whitehorse in June 1900, and on July 29, 1900, the golden spike was driven at Carcross, marking completion of the entire line.

If fishing is part of your goal, give *Atlin Wilderness Adventures* a call (250–651–7621). Owners Aaron and Glen McKenzie specialize in fishing and sightseeing on Atlin Lake. Or try *Brewery Bay Charters,* another local operator, at (250) 651–7674 or www.atlin.net/tourcomp.htm#bbcharters.

When you leave you can avoid duplicating about a third of your route back to Carcross by joining the Alaska Highway at *Jake's Corner* (about 60 miles north of Atlin).

Back on the Klondike Highway, a few minutes' drive beyond Carcross lies *Caribou Crossing,* a six-acre theme park with live Dall sheep, Stone sheep, bighorn sheep, lynx, an old-time trapper's cabin, the only mounted saber-toothed tiger in existence, plus a cafe and gift shop. On the same property, but in a separate building, is the *Museum of Yukon Natural History,* a privately owned collection of mounted Yukon wildlife in authentic dioramas, including the world's largest mounted polar bear at 11 feet 8 inches from nose to tail. Admission is $7.25 to visit both attractions. Call (867) 821–4055 or visit www.cariboucrossing.ca. Hours for both are 8:30 A.M. to 5:00 P.M. daily.

Here's a Yukon superlative for you—a "smallest," not a "biggest." At kilometer 111 you pass the **Carcross Desert,** at 260 hectares (640 acres), the smallest desert in the world. Glaciers and a large glacial lake originally covered the area, and when the glaciers retreated they left sand deposits on the former lake bottoms. The well-named **Emerald Lake,** nestled in the hills farther along at kilometer 120, is the subject of thousands of photo exposures each year.

At kilometer 157, 98 miles beyond its starting point at Skagway, this portion of the Klondike Highway junctions with the Alaska Highway. You're just a few minutes' drive south of Whitehorse. The northern portion of the Klondike Highway, which extends all the way to Dawson City, recommences just north of Whitehorse.

The Haines Highway: Haines to Haines Junction

The Haines Highway (which several Canadian publications call the Haines Road) runs 152 miles (246 kilometers) from the water's edge in Haines, Alaska, to **Haines Junction** on the Alaska Highway, west of Whitehorse. They're spectacular miles, sometimes paralleling the path of the old Dalton Trail to the Klondike. In the process they traverse thick green forests in the Chilkat Valley at lower elevations and high, barren, mystical plains once you've climbed over Chilkat Pass. Your travel log will record frequent views of piercing sawtooth mountains plus lakes that contain monster-size trout. The road is two lanes, asphalt, and open year-round.

About 9 miles from Haines, you enter the Alaska Chilkat Bald Eagle Preserve

yukonfacts

The Yukon Territory comprises 193,380 square miles.

The population of the Yukon Territory is approximately 33,500.

Herschel is the Yukon Territory's only island.

where, in winter, thousands of American bald eagles gather to feast on the still-abundant salmon of the Chilkat River. If you want to stop, use pullouts and viewing areas about 10 miles farther down the road.

At mile 40 you'll arrive at U.S. Customs, but if you're Canada-bound you don't have to stop until you cross the U.S.–Canada border and come to **Canada Customs and Immigration Station** a couple of minutes farther on. (Remember, kilometer posts now replace mileposts in metric-minded Canada.)

You'll cross Chilkat Pass (elevation 1,065 meters; 3,493 feet) at kilometer 102 and come to **Million Dollar Falls Campground** at kilometer 167. There's pleasant camping and fishing here, and it's an excellent picnicking choice, even if you don't want to spend the night.

Approaching kilometer 188, you come to the **St. Elias Lake Trail,** a novice- and intermediate-friendly hiking trail through subalpine meadows. It's a 6⁶⁄₁₀-kilometer (4-mile-plus) trek that offers a good chance to spot mountain goats beyond the lake.

You have another camping and fishing opportunity at big, long **Dezadeash Lake** (pronounced DEZ-dee-ash), home to lake trout, northern pike, and grayling at kilometer 195.

At kilometer 202 you can hike **Rock Glacier Trail** in **Kluane National Park,** a half-hour walk to the rocky residue of a former glacier and a panoramic view. Rock glaciers are a unique landform created when glacial ice and frost-shattered rock mix and flow downhill.

Haines Junction, Yukon Territory, lies at Haines Highway kilometer 246, nearly 153 miles from the road's start in Haines, Alaska. Whitehorse lies about 100 Alaska Highway miles east.

The Alaska Highway: Watson Lake to Whitehorse

Amazingly, the 2,288-kilometer (1,422-mile) Alaska Highway was constructed and connected in eight months and twelve days as a military road during World War II. Construction started March 8, 1942, and ended October 24; it was one of the most remarkable road-building feats in modern history. The road, then and now, commences in **Dawson Creek, British Columbia,** originating at the huge, picture-worthy **Milepost 0 Monument** on Tenth Street in downtown Dawson Creek. It ends at Delta Junction, Alaska. It's an asphalt road all the way, though the quality of the pavement varies, and you'll likely encounter gravel detours from time to time as road crews strive to improve the highway and your vacation experience.

The first major Yukon Territory (Y.T.) community you'll come to (and, therefore, our starting point in this section) is **Watson Lake,** at kilometer 1,021. The **Alaska Highway Interpretive Centre,** at the junction of the Alaska and Campbell Highways, is a good place to pick up the latest data on road conditions as well as visitor attractions in the area. One of them, the mind-blowing **Sign Post Forest,** started in this way: Back in 1942, the American soldier Carl K. Lindley of Danville, Illinois, one of thousands of U.S. servicemen constructing the Alaska Highway, got homesick and erected a sign indicating the mileage back to his hometown. Others did the same, and a tradition took hold. Later, after the war, civilian motorists started driving along the road from the Lower Forty-eight states to Alaska, and they erected signs, too, more than 27,000 signs to date. Among them you'll find one license plate from Virginia that reads AAW–7191. How do I know? I put it there.

Just beyond kilometer 1,162 you cross the Continental Divide, separating lands that drain into the Pacific Ocean from those that drain into the Arctic Ocean. Just off the highway at kilometer 1,294, you arrive in the mostly Native community of *Teslin,* originally a summer home for Tlingit Indians from Southeast Alaska and British Columbia. The *George Johnston Museum,* open from 9:00 A.M. to 7:00 P.M. in summer, houses the largest Tlingit Indian artifact collection in the Yukon. You'll see dioramas, rare historical photographs, George Johnston's 1928

yukontrivia

Whitehorse, the capital of the Yukon Territory, was named for the nearby rapids of the Yukon River, where the frothing water looked like the manes of white horses. The name has been used since 1887.

Chevrolet, and many post-European and early Yukon exhibits. The museum honors Johnston, a Tlingit Indian who was born in 1884 and died in 1972. An expert photographer, Johnston brought the car, a first in these parts, to Teslin. Admission is $5 for adults. Phone (867) 390–2550 or visit www.gjmuseum.yk.net.

Nine miles north of Teslin, at kilometer 1,306, *Mukluk Annie's Salmon Bake* (867–390–2600) serves up salmon and barbecued ribs, steaks, and pork from 11:00 A.M. until 9:00 P.M. There are also houseboat rides on Teslin Lake every evening at 8:00 P.M., free to salmon-bake customers and guests at Mukluk Annie's motel there. Jake's Corner and access to the Atlin Road lie beyond kilometer 1,392; you come to Whitehorse city limits at kilometer 1,455, about 40 miles later.

Whitehorse is the Yukon Territory's "big city," a modern community of 23,400. It's home to about two-thirds of all the Y.T.'s residents and serves as its hub and transportation center. The town's origins lie in the construction of the White Pass & Yukon Route railway from the ocean port of Skagway early in the century. Its economy today relies on government, trade, and tourism plus minerals and mining activity.

If you're driving, make the *Yukon Visitor Reception Centre,* at kilometer 1,455 at Second Avenue and Hanson Street, your first stop in the Whitehorse area. It's operated by Tourism Yukon and contains lots of good information and laser-disk visuals, especially about Yukon national parks and historic sites. It's also one of your best sources for up-to-date highway data.

Call (867) 667–3084. Located beside the center is the **Yukon Transportation Museum** (867–668–4792; www.yukontransportmuseum.ca), which features North Country transport, from dogsleds and stagecoaches to a WP&YR railcar replica and vintage aircraft. Admission is $6. Another source of visitor information, particularly for sites in and around Whitehorse, is the **Whitehorse Chamber of Commerce Information Centre** in town, at 302 Steele Street (867–667–7545). If you enjoy historical sites, the information center is a great place to pick up walking-tour brochures for many Yukon communities.

Perhaps your best source of information, though, is Jeanette Bringsli at the **City of Whitehorse** at 2121 Second Avenue. She can tell you, practically off the top of her head, just about anything you want to know about Whitehorse, and she'll do it with a smile to boot. Phone (867) 667–6401 or visit www.city .whitehorse.yk.ca or www.visitwhitehorse.com.

Not to be missed is the **MacBride Museum** (First Avenue and Wood Street; 867–667–2709; www.macbridemuseum.com), 5,000 rambling but fascinating square feet of artifacts, historic photographs, maps, and exhibits that cover the Yukon from ancient prehistory to the present. The real Sam McGee's cabin (of Robert Service fame) can be seen here, as well as horse wagons and steam engines. Admission is $7. The museum is open weekdays, in the summer, from 9:00 A.M. until 6:00 P.M., and weekends 10:00 A.M. to 7:00 P.M.

Everybody does a tour of the **SS Klondike,** the largest stern-wheeler to ply the Yukon River, and you should, too. It's located literally on the shores of the Yukon River, near the Robert Campbell bridge. The 210-foot ship was built in 1929, sank seven years later, but was refloated and rebuilt in 1937. It continued in service until the fifties. Now designated a Parks Canada National Historic Site, it's been restored to reflect one of the North Country's prime methods of travel during the late 1930s. Admission is $6.15. Call (867) 667–3910 or (800) 661–0486.

You'll probably never have a better chance to see Yukon wildlife than during a drive-through tour of the **Yukon Wildlife Preserve.** (Contact

The Bishop Who Ate His Boots

The well-known gold rush story "The Bishop Who Ate His Boots" was the inspiration for the famous scene in Charlie Chaplin's movie *The Gold Rush*. Lost at 40 below and out of provisions, Bishop Stringer decided to boil his and his companion's sealskin-and-walrus-sole boots for seven hours, then drink the broth. According to the bishop, it was "tough and stringy, but palatable and fairly satisfying." Bishop Stringer lost fifty pounds during the ordeal, but eventually found his way to a Native village, where he was nursed back to health.

Stern-wheeler SS *Klondike,* Whitehorse

867–633–2922 or visit www.yukonwildlife.ca.) In 750 acres of forests, mead-ows, and marshlands you can view caribou, elk, bison, moose, mountain goats, sheep, musk ox, mule deer, snowy owls, and rare peregrine falcons. The ***Yukon Conservation Society*** sponsors free guided hikes around the Whitehorse area during the summer, providing an opportunity to learn about the unique northern flora and fauna as well as the natural history and geology of the land. Call (867) 633–2922 or visit www.yukonconservation.org. The conservation society can be reached at (867) 668–5678.

An interesting dining experience can be had at a local favorite: ***Klondike Rib and Salmon BBQ*** at Second Avenue and Steele Street downtown (867–667–7554). Here you can sample Alaska salmon and halibut, Texas-style barbecue ribs, English-style fish-and-chips, plus their specialty—arctic char, caribou, and musk ox.

For the traveler in search of art, the ***Yukon Arts Centre,*** at Yukon Place on College Drive (867–667–8575; www.yukonartscentre.com), offers a spectacular view plus the territory's largest art gallery, a theater, and an outdoor amphithe-ater. There is no charge, but donations are accepted. Summer hours are Tues-day through Sunday, 10:00 A.M. to 6:00 P.M. Hours during the rest of the year vary slightly. A ***Yukon Permanent Art Collection***—showing northern land-scapes and lifestyles as portrayed by prominent Canadian artists—is displayed in the foyer of the Yukon Government Administration Building on Second Street. Open weekdays only, 8:30 A.M. to 5:00 P.M.

June through August, escorted ***Whitehorse Heritage Buildings Walk-ing Tours*** originate every hour on the hour, 9:00 A.M. to 4:00 P.M., Monday through Saturday at the Donnenworth House, 3126 Third Avenue. Phone

(867) 667–4704 or e-mail yhma@yknet.yk.ca. There is a $4 fee. There's also a local cemetery tour. If you can't join an escorted tour, pick up the self-guided *Walking Tour of Yukon's Capital* from local merchants.

You don't have to be Anglican (Episcopal) to visit the **Old Log Church** (867–668–2555) located a block off Main Street on Elliott Street and Third Avenue. The sanctuary building, constructed in 1900 for the Church of England, and the log rectory next door are rich in Yukon's history. Exhibits, artifacts, and relics tell the story of the Yukon's history from precontact life among aboriginal peoples to early exploration and beyond. Admission is $3. Tours are conducted daily 10:00 A.M. to 6:00 P.M.

Takhini Hot Springs lies twenty to thirty minutes from downtown Whitehorse; don't miss it. You get there by driving roughly 9 miles north of the Yukon Visitors Reception Centre on the Alaska Highway, then nearly 4 miles north on the Klondike Highway to the Takhini Hot Springs Road. You then travel about 6 miles west to the well-marked springs area. This place offers some of the most pleasant soaking and swimming waters you'll find in the North Country as well as the opportunity to chat in really relaxing surroundings with Yukoners, Alaskans, and fellow travelers. Facilities here are fully modern, with changing rooms, showers, and a coffee shop on-site. If you're RV camping or tenting, plan to stay in the campground there. Activities, besides bathing and swimming, include hiking and horseback riding. The charge for the hot springs is $7.00; for camping, $14.50 to $25.00. For information call (867) 633–2706 or visit www.takhinihotsprings.yk.ca.

Another option just outside town is **Inn on the Lake Bed and Breakfast** (867–660–5253; www.exceptionalplaces.com), which is a special place. If you don't want to just sit around during your visit, take advantage of the inn's complimentary golf passes, or go mountain biking, kayaking, canoeing, or windsurfing. There is a Jacuzzi suite and personal steam rooms, and, to top it all off, the food is great. Prices range from $179 for a room with a bath to $229 for the deluxe, two-bedroom Presidential Suite.

In town there are many other accommodations, among them **Historical House Bed and Breakfast** (5128 Fifth Avenue), originally built for none other than Sam McGee. The place features priceless antique furniture, which is perfect for the setting. While there, be sure to converse with the proprietor, Bernie Phillips, who also happens to be the city councillor. Bernie will be glad to entertain you on his caribou horns—just ask. Rooms are $95, Canadian, for a double in the summer. Phone (867) 668–3907 or visit www.yukongold.com.

Longtime Yukoners Mary Anne and Jacques Boily operate **Red Door Bed and Breakfast** at 61 Teslin Road, a five-minute drive from downtown Whitehorse. Featuring a landscaped yard with fountain, rock garden, and deck, this

B&B offers a private entrance and laundry facilities for guests. Walking trails are nearby. Furnished with brass beds and antiques, the Red Door is a comfortable option with rates starting at $70 per night. Call (867) 633–4615 or visit www.bbcanada.com/reddooryukon.

If getting on the Yukon is your goal, stroll down to the waterfront, across from MacBride Museum, and take your pick of **Yukon Riverboat Tours.** Prices and times vary, but several operators make the decision easy.

From Whitehorse, if you're driving, you have two choices for travel north and west to the main body of Alaska. You can continue on up the Alaska Highway, driving west and then northwest to Haines Junction, Kluane National Park, Beaver Creek, and the U.S. border, or you can drive northerly on the Klondike Highway to Carmacks, Minto, Stewart Crossing, and Dawson City, where you can connect with the Top of the World Highway to the Alaska border.

The Klondike Highway: Whitehorse to Dawson City

The northern portion of the Skagway to Dawson City Klondike Highway starts at kilometer 1,487 on the Alaska Highway, about 9 miles beyond Whitehorse. The first major stop along the way is **Carmacks,** at kilometer 357. (Remember, kilometer posts show the distance from Skagway.) The community is historically important as a stern-wheeler steamboat stop on the Yukon River route between Whitehorse and Dawson City. **Up North Adventures** offers some fine canoeing that passes through the Carmacks area if you want to start a trip from Whitehorse. Enjoy a half-day, full-day, or overnight self-guided trip along the Yukon River, with prices starting at $40, Canadian. Longer, guided trips range from five to fifteen days and start at $1,350, Canadian. If you like what you see at Up North, check out their other adventures, including guided and self-guided kayak trips, motorboat tours, bicycle tours, and guided ATV tours. They'll shuttle you to and from destinations through the Yukon and into Alaska as part of your self-guided adventure. Call (867) 667–7035 or visit www.upnorth.yk.ca.

At kilometer 380.5 you can see the **Five Finger Rapids** from an observation deck built as part of the Five Finger Rapids Day Use Area of trails and picnic sites. If you have an hour and don't mind the 219 stairs, you can hike down for a closer look at these treacherous rapids.

For campers or picnickers, the Yukon government's **Tatchun Creek Campground** is at kilometer 382.4 of the Klondike Highway, with twelve sites and fishing for grayling and salmon in season. And if you don't mind driving 8 kilometers off the road, there's also great camping at nearby **Tatchun Lake,**

yukontrivia

Dawson City's world-famous gambling hall is named for Diamond Tooth Gertie, a bona fide Yukon dance hall queen. Gertie Lovejoy's nickname came from the sparkling diamond she had wedged between her two front teeth. Just as the miners made their fortunes mining gold from the earth, she made hers mining nuggets from the pokes of lonely miners.

with twenty sites. Overnight camping costs $12. Phone (867) 667–5340.

At kilometer 537 you come to **Stewart Crossing,** where you have the opportunity to take a side excursion (about 150 miles round-trip) over the **Silver Trail** through scenic woods and water country to the mining communities of **Mayo, Elsa,** and **Keno City.** If you plan to overnight here, the Yukon government **Five Mile Lake Campground,** just east of Mayo, offers generous campsites, kitchen shelters, launch sites, a swimming beach, and an obstacle course where kids can work off energy. The charge is $8 per night.

More pampered lodging can be had at **Keno Cabins B&B,** a quaint outpost with two cabins ($75, Canadian, for the smaller, and $95, Canadian, for the larger one) that sleep up to four people each. They come complete with coffeemaker, TV, and sauna; full breakfasts are available on request. Contact Keno Cabins at (867) 995–2829.

The **Mining Museum** (867–995–2792) at Keno City is a particular delight, with displays that vary from old-time mining equipment to baseball uniforms the local teams wore. There's no admission charge, and the museum is open daily from June to September. If the museum piques your prospecting interests, drive down Duncan Creek Road south of Keno City for a guided tour of Duncan Creek Golddusters. There, you'll also be able to try a little gold-panning of your own. You can also grab a walking-tour brochure and check out some of the buildings that date from Keno's heyday as a gold and silver mining center. Or hike through the historic mining areas dotting the alpine meadows and valleys. At the **Keno City Café,** chat with longtime Keno resident and cafe owner Geordie Dobson, or challenge him to a game of cribbage. The cafe is open from 5:00 to 10:00 P.M.

Back on the highway toward Dawson, the high point (literally) of a Dawson City visit comes when you drive the Dome Road from its junction at Klondike Highway's kilometer 717 to the top of **Midnight Dome** for a panoramic view of the city, the Yukon and Klondike Rivers, the Bonanza gold fields, and the Ogilvie Mountains. Awesome.

Dawson City, of course, is where it all began—the frenzied, frantic, fabled stampede for North Country gold. It started in 1896 when George Carmack, Skookum Jim, and Tagish Charlie found "color"—lots of it—in a Klondike River tributary called Rabbit Creek, later renamed Bonanza Creek. The rush cata-pulted into international prominence when the vessel *Portland* steamed into Seattle on July 17, 1897, and the *Seattle Post-Intelligencer* screamed "Gold! Gold! Gold!" in its banner headline. A "ton of gold" was proclaimed in the story that followed. The rush was on.

Tens of thousands of gold seekers (most of them ill prepared and with-out the slightest concept of the rigors they would face) crowded aboard almost any boat that would float out of West Coast ports and headed for Skagway and the White Pass, Dyea and the Chilkoot Pass, or St. Michael on the Yukon River. Their common goal was Dawson City and the rich gold country around it. It's said that 100,000 gold seekers set out for the Klondike. Some 30,000 made it.

Today the rush to the Klondike continues, but it's a vastly more comfort-able odyssey. Travelers come not to extract riches but to see the place where all the excitement happened. Thanks to eleventh-hour rescue restorations by the national and territorial governments, Dawson City looks remarkably as it did more than a century ago, when it sprang up on the Yukon River shores. Old buildings and landmarks were saved from certain rot and destruction, including the magnificently refurbished 1899 **Palace Grand Theatre,** where the park service holds daily presentations such as "Mounties in the Klondike" and "Who Really Discovered Gold?" (admission $6.40). At **Diamond Tooth Gertie's** (867–993–5575), you can legally gamble away your "poke" at real gaming tables (as many a prospector did in '98) for an admission charge of $6. At the historic old **1901 post office,** at Third Avenue and King Street (open noon to 6:00 P.M.; 867–993–7200), your first-class letters and postcards will be canceled the old fashioned way—by hand. Collectors can purchase commemorative stamps.

The Rush Is On

George Washington Carmack is credited with discovering gold at Bonanza Creek, setting off the great rush north for Klondike gold.

It was in 1896 that Carmack and two brothers, Tagish Charlie and Skookum Jim, went looking for gold in the Klondike region. Another prospector, Robert Henderson, reported good color on Gold Bottom Creek but said he didn't want any "Siwashes" (Jim and Charlie were Indians) on Gold Bottom.

So the three partners went looking for their own creek and staked Rabbit Creek, soon to be known as Bonanza Creek. Their strike was the richest in North America and made them wealthy men. They shared their bounty without dispute. They didn't tell Henderson of their discovery, and he did not share in the riches.

Before beginning a foray to any of these sites, it's probably wise to get oriented at Tourism Yukon's ***Dawson Visitor Reception Centre,*** at Front and King Streets (867–993–5566; www.dawsoncity.org). While you're there, take time to view some Yukon attractions on laser videodisc players and maybe even take part in one of the ***Dawson City walking tours*** ($6.40) that originate at the site several times daily. If you plan to extend your trip to Inuvik and Canada's Northwest Territories via the Dempster Highway, cross the street from the Dawson reception center and get highway and other information from the ***Northwest Territories Information Centre*** (867–993–6167).

yukontrivia

The Yukon Territory's Mount Logan, at 19,550 feet, or 5,959 meters, is Canada's highest mountain.

The Yukon Territory's official flower is fireweed.

There are about 250 active mines in the Dawson gold fields.

At ***Jack London's cabin*** (867–993–5575) near Grant Street and Eighth Avenue, you can take part in interpretive tours, daily in the summer, that showcase London's cabin that was discovered in the Yukon wilderness. The structure was carefully disassembled, and half the logs were used to re-create the writer's cabin at its present site in Dawson City. The other half went into the construction of an identical cabin at Jack London Square in Oakland, California. Curator Dick North is one of the premier experts on Jack London as well as author of several books, including one on the famous "Mad Trapper." Admission is $2. At Eighth Avenue and Hanson you'll find the ***Robert Service cabin,*** where poetry is recited daily in the summer. Call (867) 993–7200 for recital times. Admission is $6.40.

For a really in-depth look at Dawson's history, visit the old ***1901 Territorial Administration Building,*** where the ***Dawson City Museum and Historical Society*** houses its collection of gold rush–era artifacts, paleontological remains, cultural exhibits of the Han Native people, even a collection of narrow-gauge steam locomotives. There are also vintage film showings and lectures. Admission is $7. Call (867) 993–5291 or e-mail dcmuseum@yknet.yk.ca.

Another interesting stop in Dawson is the ***Danoja Zho*** (meaning "long time ago house") ***Cultural Center,*** where you'll learn about the traditional peoples of the Klondike region. In addition to viewing the exhibits, you can join guided tours and watch live performances. The admission charge of $5 is valid for two days. For more information call (867) 993–6768 or visit www.trondek.com.

If you want to get out into the surrounding wilderness, check with ***Ruby Range Adventures*** (867–667–2209; www.rubyrange.com). They offer guided canoe and river expeditions as well as fishing safaris. Tours run from eight to twenty-two days.

Take a gander at what homes used to look like by visiting the **Berton House,** which is used by Dawson's writer-in-residence program. The original house was built in 1901 and was owned for many years by the Berton family, whose son, Pierre, a writer, eventually donated it to the Yukon Arts Council. The home has been renovated and now hosts Canadian writers year-round. For more information call (867) 993–5575 or visit www.dawsoncity.org.

It's not far off the beaten path (in fact, it sits on Front Street and First Avenue, on the banks of the Yukon between King and Queen Streets), but it's a must-see if you value restored historical artifacts. We're referring to the **Steamer Keno,** built in 1922 in Whitehorse for service between Stewart City and Mayo Landing. It's typical of the breed of shallow-draft riverboats that served the North Country from early gold rush times until well into the twentieth century.

The largest wooden-hull, bucket-line gold dredge in North America—old **Gold Dredge Number 4,** two-thirds the size of a football field long and eight whopping stories high—can be seen south of town near the spot where it ceased operations in 1960. The site is beside Bonanza Creek off Bonanza Creek Road, 7%₀ miles south of the Klondike Highway. About 2½ miles farther south you'll find **Discovery Claim** (and a monument to mark the spot) on Bonanza Creek, where George Carmack, Skookum Jim, and Tagish Charlie made their history-making discovery. You can still pan for gold in this very spot. To rent gold-panning equipment, try **Claim 33 Gold Panning and Antiques** (867–993–6447).

Dredge Number 4

Huge, earth-devouring machines once chewed their way up and down the creek beds of the Yukon River valley, gobbling up everything in their paths, right down to bedrock, processing it all in their complex innards, and spitting out mounds of rubble behind them. Their trails can be traced across the valley floors like giant worm tracks 50 feet high.

The dredges are all gone save one. Dredge Number 4 is now a Parks Canada Historic Site. This 3,000-ton monster made three passes up and down the valley, averaging 22,000 grams a day. In 1960 it sank and was neglected for thirty-two years.

In 1992 it was resurrected, and today you can tour its rusting interior. There were seventy-two buckets, each weighing two-and-a-half tons, in a continuous chain that pulled material up from the creek bed and dumped it into the dredge's internal gold-sluicing works. Those who remember when it was in operation say that the vibration of the dredge in action was so great that it could be heard 11 miles away and felt 9 miles in any direction.

At the ***Dawson City Bed and Breakfast,*** at 451 Craig Street, you're situated in a quiet, beautiful setting overlooking both the Klondike and Yukon Rivers. Breakfasts are full service. The owners will pick you up at the airport, bus, or waterfront if you don't have your own wheels. Rates are $98 for a double with a shared bath, $115 for a private bath. Call (867) 993–5649 or visit www.dawsonbb.com.

White Ram Manor Bed and Breakfast is within walking distance of most Dawson City attractions. Look for the pink house at Seventh Avenue and Harper Street. Accommodations include full breakfasts, use of kitchen facilities for other meals, hot tub, barbecue, and picnic area. Rates are $59 to $109. Call (867) 993–5772 or (866) 993–5772 or visit www.bbcanada.com/whiterammanor.

Another longtime lodging favorite is the ***Downtown Hotel*** (867–993–5346), located 1 block from Diamond Tooth Gertie's and 1 block from the Grand Palace Theatre. And if you want to prove that you're a real sourdough, have a Sour Toe Cocktail in the hotel's ***Sourdough Saloon.*** Yes, that's a real (preserved) human toe at the bottom of your glass. Or spend the night in a restored brothel, ***Bombay Peggy's*** (867–993–6969; www.bombaypeggys.com). For meals and another great lodging option in the center of town, try ***Klondike Kate's*** at 1102 Third Avenue (867–993–6527; www.klondikekates.com), with patio dining and a nice selection of entrees.

A pleasant day trip from Dawson City is ***Fishwheel Charters***' two-hour tour of the Yukon River. The operators are licensed First Nations river pilots, and they will take you approximately 6 miles downriver to the historic site of Fort Reliance. There you can enjoy tea and bannock and learn about the river's history—past, present, and future. Call (867) 993–6237 for an appointment. Incidentally, in the wintertime, the company offers sled dog rides and tours.

When you're ready to leave Dawson City, you have three driving choices. You can retrace the Klondike Highway south to the place just outside of Whitehorse where it meets the Alaska Highway, then continue north on the Alaska Highway to the main body of Alaska. Or you can take the ***Top of the World Highway*** to the place at the Alaska border where it meets the ***Taylor Highway,*** which, in turn, also connects with the Alaska Highway in Alaska. Or you can keep going north and east via the ***Dempster Highway*** to ***Inuvik,*** in the Mackenzie Delta, not many miles from the shores of the Arctic Ocean. (Of course, when you've made it to Inuvik, you have to turn around and drive back the way you came. The Dempster doesn't meet or loop with any other highway.)

The Dempster Highway: Dawson City to Inuvik

The Dempster, the third choice, definitely deserves consideration. It stretches 741 kilometers (460 miles) from its starting place about 41 kilometers (25 miles) south of Dawson City on the Klondike Highway. It ends in Inuvik, Northwest Territories, surely one of the most literally colorful communities in North America, with almost every hue of the rainbow represented on homes and buildings.

Along the highway you pass sometimes through valleys bounded by great granite mountains, at other times over high flat plains, with rolling hills in the distance. Sometimes your route is the legendary trail of the valiant North West Mounted Police who patrolled the region by dogsled in the days before the highway was built.

Accommodations and service stations are rare along most of the route, so top off your tank every chance you get. Halfway to Inuvik, you come at kilometer 371 to **Eagle Plains** and the **Eagle Plains Hotel and Restaurant**, which offers thirty-two comfortable rooms, groceries, vehicle services, gas, and a restaurant that serves the tastiest, most satisfying sourdough pancakes this side of the Canadian border. Take the time to examine the display of historic photos on the walls of the restaurant.

yukontrivia

The lowest temperature ever recorded in North America was in the Yukon Territory. The mercury plummeted to 81.4 degrees below zero in February 1947.

They tell the tragic story of the Mounties' "Lost Patrol" in 1910 and of Inspector W.J.D. Dempster's finding and retrieval of their frozen bodies. Other pictures relate the murderous exploits of the Mad Trapper of Rat River and the manhunt organized against him in 1932. The Mounties, as always, got their man. Rooms cost $126 to $140. Call (867) 993–2453.

At kilometer 402 you cross the **Arctic Circle** (take pictures of the monument), and at kilometer 471 you leave the Yukon Territory and enter the Northwest Territories. From now on, kilometer posts show the distance from this point. At kilometer 86, turn off the highway to visit the nearby community of **Fort McPherson.** You can fill up on gasoline as well as visit the church graveyard where the hapless Lost Patrol members lie buried. Also, if you're in the market for a backpack, duffel bag, or an attaché case, visit the **Fort McPherson Tent and Canvas Factory.** The workmanship is first rate, and almost certainly no one in your hiking club back home will have one with the company's distinctive emblem. Call (867) 952–2179 for information.

At kilometer 269 and the community of Inuvik, don't fail to visit the ***Igloo-shaped Catholic Church.*** Igloo-shaped? It sounds hokey, but the effect when you see it is breathtaking, and the paintings inside, created by Inuvialuit painter Mona Thrasher, are more than inspirational. Take time to see, as well, ***Ingamo Hall,*** a log friendship center with a great hall that has the feel of a baronial mansion.

If you'd enjoy an Arctic country setting for your overnight accommodations, consider the ***Arctic Chalet,*** a B&B lakeside home and cabins. Olav and Judi Falsnes offer simple but nutritious breakfasts and complimentary canoes. (*Note:* Saturday check-ins must be prearranged.) Rates begin at $110 for a double. The Web address is www.arcticchalet.com. Sled dog rides are available in the winter, starting at $100 for an hour of fun. Call (867) 777–3535. If you're camping, go to the ***Chuk Campground,*** about 2 miles from town on the Airport Road. Its hilltop location presents a worthwhile view of the Mackenzie Delta, and its breezes tend to discourage mosquitoes. Rates are $12 for a primitive campsite and $15 with electric hookup. Call (867) 777–7196 for more information.

For the really ultimate in far north travel, fly to ***Herschel Island,*** off the Arctic coast about 150 miles to the northwest (a Yukon territorial park, but accessible from Inuvik) for wildlife viewing as well as a look at the Native Inuvialuit culture from prehistory through the nineteenth-century whaling era. Several air carriers offer the trip. You also can arrange your trip through ***Arctic Nature Tours,*** which offers nature, cultural, adventure, and custom tours by plane and boat. Visit the village of Tuktoyaktuk on the Arctic coast, or go fishing on the Mackenzie River. Prices range from $35 for a two-hour Inuvik town and cultural tour to $800 for a multiday camping trip to Herschel Island. Phone (867) 777–3300 or visit www.arcticnaturetours.com.

Igloo-shaped Catholic Church, Inuvik

The Top of the World Highway: Dawson City to the Alaska Border

Back to Dawson City and the second choice mentioned earlier, driving on the Top of the World Highway to the Taylor Highway. Yes, that's the official name of the road. It begins with a free car-ferry ride over the Yukon River and heads west toward the Alaska border and Alaska's Taylor Highway for 127 kilometers (79 miles). The road, you'll find, really lives up to its name. Much of the time you're on ridgetops looking down on deep valleys. Lots of good scenic photo ops here. It's a good gravel road, but slippery in heavy rains. About 105 kilometers (66 miles) beyond Dawson City, you'll cross the *U.S.–Canada border.*

The Taylor Highway: Jack Wade Junction to Eagle and Tetlin Junction

We're now going to talk about part of Alaska again, even though this chapter deals largely with the Canadian Yukon. Travel on the Taylor Highway is so logically connected with the Top of the World Highway from Dawson City, it just doesn't make sense to have you jump pages into other sections of the book.

At *Jack Wade Junction,* where the Taylor and the Top of the World Highways meet, turn north on the Taylor Highway and drive 65 miles to visit *Eagle,* a small but historically important community in the Alaska scheme of things. Still standing is the *Wickersham Courthouse* where Judge James Wickersham dispensed frontier justice during Eagle's gold rush days early in the twentieth century. Still intact as well are the old Waterfront Customs House, a military mule barn, water wagon shed, NCO (noncommissioned officers) quarters, and other structures that were part of old Fort Egbert. The federal Bureau of Land Management (BLM) has renovated and

yukontrivia

The Yukon River and its tributaries drain almost one-third of Alaska.

restored portions of the old fort where, incidentally, Captain Billy Mitchell once served a tour of duty. BLM also maintains a campground just beyond Fort Egbert. The *Eagle Historical Society* (907–547–2325; www.eagleak.org) conducts daily tours of the community, starting at 9:00 A.M. at the courthouse. The cost is $5. You can visit the National Park Service headquarters for the *Yukon–Charley Rivers National Preserve* (907–547–2233; www.nps.gov) on the banks of the Yukon near Fort Egbert. Staffers will show you a video about the national preserve and answer any questions.

Gray Line of Alaska's luxury river vessel **Yukon Queen** operates between Eagle and Dawson City, Yukon. The company transports passengers between Eagle and Anchorage or Fairbanks by motor coach as part of packaged land tours. Call (907) 456–7741 or (867) 668–3225 for details.

yukontrivia

About 3 percent of the Yukon Territory is covered by wetlands, a much lower percentage than for the rest of the country. The Yukon's inland waters comprise 1,792 square miles, or 4,481 square kilometers.

After your Eagle visit, backtrack south on the Taylor Highway to Jack Wade Junction. The distance from Jack Wade Junction to Tetlin Junction, and the Alaska Highway, is about 96 miles. When you've gone about 30 of those miles, around mile 66, slow down and look for *Chicken.* No, this isn't a joke; it's a town . . . sort of. It's said the community got its name because the miners back in the gold rush days couldn't spell *ptarmigan,* which some called an Alaska chicken anyway. The original mining camp is now abandoned private property and is closed to general traffic. If you turn off the Taylor Highway at the Airport Road, you'll come to the *Chicken Creek Cafe,* known for its pies and baked goods and the gathering place from which tours depart daily at 1:00 P.M. for old Chicken. Nearby you'll find the *Chicken Saloon* and *Chicken Mercantile Emporium,* where you can buy a Chicken hat, a Chicken pin, and, naturally, a Chicken T-shirt. *Chicken Discount Gas and Propane* gives you an opportunity to keep your gas tank full.

The Taylor Highway ends (or begins, depending on which way you're traveling) at Tetlin Junction, mile 1,302 on the Alaska Highway, where there's lodging, food, and gas if you've perilously coasted in without buying fuel on the Taylor Highway.

The Alaska Highway: Whitehorse to the Alaska Border

Back in Canada's Yukon and beyond Whitehorse about 90 miles lies Haines Junction, at the junction of the Haines Highway from Haines, Alaska, and the Alaska Highway at kilometer 809. The community calls itself the Gateway to *Kluane.* Kluane (pronounced clue-AW-nee) is the Yukon's biggest lake. Its namesake, *Kluane National Park and Preserve,* is one of the preeminent wilderness national parks of North America.

Especially for the hiker, mountain climber, canoe enthusiast, kayaker, and river runner, Kluane National Park is a place to spend days, not hours. To get oriented, visit the *Kluane National Park and Preserve Visitor Centre,* about ⅖ mile east of the junction with the Haines Highway and just off the Alaska Highway. There you'll see an international award-winning audiovisual presentation about the park, and you'll be able to pick up information about long and short hiking trails and canoe/kayak routes. Summer hours are 8:00 A.M. to 8:00 P.M. daily; call (867) 634–7250 or visit www.parkscanada.ca.

To see Kluane from the air, arrange a flight-see with *Ranger Air Charters,* which is based in Whitehorse. The company can take you for a quick ride or arrange a drop-off and pick-up in remote areas for hiking, fishing, or just plain exploring. Call (867) 633–4368.

For a double treat, stay at *Dalton Trail Lodge,* at Dezadeash Lake bordering the park. The rooms are luxurious, and the double treat comes at dinnertime with scrumptious Swiss cuisine. Meals and accommodations are $205, Canadian, per person. One-week packages start at $2,300, Canadian, per person, or $2,700, Canadian, per person if you add fishing. Call (867) 634–2099 or visit www.daltontrail.com.

If you just need a quick place to camp, the *Cottonwood RV Park and Campground* is a good choice. It's right on the road, but I'll always have fond memories of the place after spending a beautiful July Fourth camped overlooking Kluane Lake, when a rainbow seemed to shine right in the tent. Cabin rentals also are available. Phone the Mobile Operator at 2M3972, Destruction Bay Channel (dial 0 and ask the operator to assist with your call), or visit www.yukonweb.com/tourism/cottonwood. Winter contact is available at (613) 968–9884.

About 35 miles beyond Haines Junction, 3 kilometers off the highway at kilometer 1,693, the Sias family (six generations of Yukoners) operates *Kluane Bed and Breakfast.* Accommodations are heated A-frame cabins with mountain views, showers, cooking facilities, and a beach. Guests share bath and kitchen facilities. Rates start at $65 per night. For more information call (867) 841–4250. On the road to the bed-and-breakfast, be sure to check out the remains of *Silver City,* a once-thriving mining community abandoned in 1924.

Another lodging option in Haines Junction is the *Raven Hotel and Restaurant* (mile 181 Alaska Highway), which features wonderful European meals in a gorgeous dining room with a view of the St. Elias Mountains. Hosts Christine and Hans Nelles make their pasta from scratch, so come with high expectations. There are twelve well-appointed, nonsmoking rooms with hardwood furniture, private bath, telephone, television, and room service. One of the rooms is designed for travelers with special needs. The dining room is open to hotel guests first, serving others as space permits. Call (867) 634–2500 or visit www.yukonweb.com/tourism/raven.

At the **Sheep Mountain Visitor Centre,** kilometer 1,706.8, you can frequently spot a herd of Dall sheep on the nearby slopes. An interpretive trail leads to Soldier's Summit, which was the site of the opening ceremony for the Alaska Highway on November 20, 1942.

At the village of **Burwash Landing,** kilometer 1,061.5, the **Kluane Museum of Natural History** (867–841–5561) contains natural history exhibits featuring wildlife of the region as well as Indian artifacts, costumes, and dioramas.

Here's another North Country travel superlative: **Beaver Creek,** at kilometer 1,934, is Canada's westernmost community. **Tourism Yukon's visitor reception center** features a special display of wildflowers and dispenses tons of visitor information especially for visitors entering Canada from Alaska. If you can get a table—there are only four—**Buckshot Betty's** (867–862–7111) in Beaver Creek offers great home cooking and fresh baked goods served up by Betty herself. At kilometer 1,967.5 you arrive at the U.S.–Canada border. Set your clocks back an hour (from Pacific to Alaska time), and start thinking again in miles and gallons.

Places to Stay in Canada's Yukon

ATLIN

Quilts and Comforts Bed and Breakfast,
on Pillman Road off
Atlin Highway;
(250) 651–0007 or
(800) 836–1818.

DAWSON CITY

Aurora Inn,
Fifth Avenue and
Harper Street;
(867) 993–6860.

Bombay Peggy's,
Second Avenue
and Princess Street;
(867) 993–6969.
The only restored brothel in
the Yukon.

**Dawson City Bed
and Breakfast,**
451 Craig Street;
(867) 993–5649,
www.dawsonbb.com

Downtown Hotel,
Second Avenue
and Queen Street;
(867) 993–5346.
Home of the famous Sour
Toe Cocktail.

**White Ram Manor
Bed and Breakfast,**
Seventh Avenue
and Harper Street;
(867) 993–5772 or
(866) 993–5772,
www.bbcanada.com/
whiterammanor

EAGLE PLAINS

**Eagle Plains Hotel
and Restaurant,**
kilometer 364
Dempster Highway;
(867) 993–2453.

HAINES JUNCTION

**Cottonwood RV Park
Campground,**
kilometer 1717
Alaska Highway;
contact Mobile Operator
2M3972 on Destruction
Bay channel,
or call (613) 968–9884
in winter.
www.yukonweb.com/
tourism/cottonwood

Dalton Trail Lodge;
(867) 667–1099 or
(867) 634–2099,
www.daltontrail.com
Bordering Kluane National
Park.

Kluane Bed and Breakfast,
Kilometer 1693
Alaska Highway;
(867) 841–4250.

The Raven,
mile 181 Alaska Highway;
(867) 634–2500,
www.yukonweb.com/
tourism/raven

INUVIK

Arctic Chalet;
(867) 777–3535,
www.arcticchalet.com
Lakeside B&B home and
cabins within walking
distance of downtown.

KENO

Keno Cabins B&B;
(867) 995–2829.
Fully equipped cabins.

WHITEHORSE

**Historical House
Bed and Breakfast,**
5128 Fifth Avenue;
(867) 668–3907,
www.yukongold.com

**Inn on the Lake
Bed and Breakfast,**
20 miles outside Whitehorse;
(867) 660–5253,
www.exceptionalplaces.com

**Red Door Bed and
Breakfast,**
61 Teslin Road;
(867) 633–4615,
www.bbcanada.com/
reddooryukon

Westmark Klondike Inn,
2288 Second Avenue;
(867) 668–4747,
www.westmarkhotels.com

Places to Eat in Canada's Yukon

CHICKEN

Chicken Creek Cafe,
Airport Road (around mile 66
Taylor Highway).
Known for pies and baked
goods.

DAWSON CITY

Klondike Kate's,
1102 Third Avenue;
(867) 993–6527,
www.klondikekates.ca
Casual dining and cabin
rentals in the heart of historic
Dawson.

EAGLE PLAINS

**Eagle Plains Hotel
and Restaurant,**
kilometer 364
Dempster Highway;
(867) 993–2453.
Great pancakes; halfway to
Inuvik from Dawson City.

HAINES JUNCTION

The Raven,
mile 181 Alaska Highway;
(867) 634–2500,
www.yukonweb.com/
tourism/raven
Fine European dining with a
view.

TETLIN

**Mukluk Annie's
Salmon Bake,**
9 miles north of Tetlin;
(867) 390–2600.

WHITEHORSE

**Klondike Rib and
Salmon BBQ,**
Second Avenue
and Steele Street;
(867) 390–2600.
Alaska salmon and halibut,
Texas-style barbecue ribs,
English-style fish-and-chips,
arctic char, caribou, and
musk ox.

Southcentral Alaska

More than half the population of Alaska lives, works, and plays in Southcentral Alaska, a region of magnificent glaciers, big lakes (one of them even named Big Lake), forests, fertile river valleys, and many of the tallest mountains in North America. Brown (grizzly) bears, moose, Dall sheep, mountain goats, and wolves thrive hereabouts, and, happily, you'll find no small number of hiking trails and vehicular back roads that offer access for viewing these creatures in their native terrain.

Fact is, there are more miles of asphalt highways, marine highways, byways, airways, and railways in Southcentral than in any other portion of the state. In square miles the region occupies perhaps a fifth of the mainland mass of Alaska. In shape Southcentral Alaska is a roughly 250-mile-deep arc of land and waters bordered on the south by the Gulf of Alaska, on the north and west by the curving arc of the Alaska mountain range, and on the east by the Canadian border—except at the very bottom, where the Southeast Alaska panhandle comes up to join the main body of Alaska.

Before the arrival of Europeans in the eighteenth century, this region and Alaska's interior were the domain of mostly Athabascan Indians, a tough, resourceful people who lived by

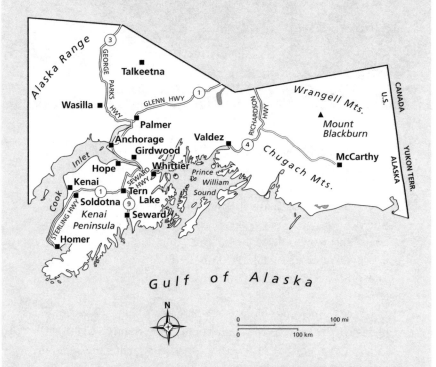

hunting moose, caribou, and bears as well as lesser game and birds. They harvested fish from saltwater shores and freshwater streams. Among their many skills was working in leather, sometimes richly adorned with beads fashioned from hollow porcupine quills and other natural materials. Those skills survive today, especially in the form of colorful decorative beadwork—greatly prized by visitors and residents alike—sewn onto moccasins, vests, and other leather goods.

Southcentral's modern history began in 1741 with the arrival of Russians sailing for the czars (Vitus Bering and Alexei Chirikov), followed by the English (Captains James Cook and George Vancouver) and other Europeans in the 1800s. After the Alaska Purchase of 1867, Americans came sporadically to the region seeking gold and other resources. But it was not until 1915 and the beginning of construction of the Alaska Railroad from Seward to Fairbanks that the area began to come into its own. Anchorage—a city created as construction and managing headquarters for the line—came into being. It later boomed, especially during and after World War II, when military installations swelled the population. In recent years the development of Alaska's petroleum resources has created additional growth in Anchorage and other communities.

Visitors find the weather surprisingly mild in this region of Alaska. Around Anchorage, for instance, summertime temperatures range in the comfortable mid-sixties and seventies. Thanks to the sheltering heights of the Alaska Range, wintertime temperatures usually hover between ten and twenty-five degrees—above zero—although they occasionally plunge to twenty or more degrees below. Whenever you come, be prepared for an extraordinary vacation in this part of Alaska. It teems with opportunities both on and off its major roadways.

TOP 10 PLACES IN SOUTHCENTRAL ALASKA

Captain Cook State Recreation Area	Matanuska Glacier
Halibut Cove	Prince William Sound
Homer	Resurrection Pass Trail
Independence Mine State Historical Park	Swanson River Canoe Trail
Kennecott	Tony Knowles Coastal Trail

horage

Since **Anchorage** is the transportation hub of Southcentral Alaska, this chapter treats it as the hub for planning trips in the region. After first detailing the city and its immediate environs, the chapter describes the water world and marine highway routes of Prince William Sound to the southeast, the more southerly highways (including the Seward and the Sterling) of the Kenai Peninsula, then the highways (George Parks, Glenn, and Richardson) that head northerly toward Denali National Park and Preserve and other points in Interior Alaska.

Anchorage is Alaska's "Big Apple," a large (for Alaska) metropolitan, cosmopolitan community of oil executives, college professors and students, business and transportation managers, tradespersons, artists, and no small number of working stiffs who keep the wheels of all this commerce turning. Curiously, Anchorage is Alaska's largest Native village as well; thousands of Indian, Eskimo, and Aleut Natives have chosen to live and work in Alaska's largest city.

southcentral alaskatrivia

The first hint of Alaska's rich gold reserves was uncovered by Russian mining engineer Peter Doroshin, who discovered gold on the Kenai Peninsula in 1850.

Anchorage is also the transportation hub of Alaska. At Ted Stevens–Anchorage International Airport, jet flights depart to and arrive from every region in Alaska, from the other states of the United States, and from Asia and Europe. The state-owned Alaska Railroad headquarters here and extends southerly to Seward, on Resurrection Bay, and Whittier, in Prince William Sound, and north to Denali National Park and Fairbanks. Three major state highways begin in or near Anchorage: the Seward Highway to the Kenai Peninsula, the Glenn Highway to Tok and the Canadian border, and the George Parks Highway to Denali National Park and Fairbanks. Off these arterials you'll find lesser roads that lead to remote villages, near-ghost towns, backwoods lodges, and lots of wilderness terrain for exploring, fishing, photography, and fun.

First, within Anchorage itself: Number-one stop on any offbeat traveler's itinerary should be the **Alaska Public Lands Information Center,** at Fourth Avenue and F Street downtown (907–271–2737; www.nps.gov/aplic). Housed in the old Anchorage Federal Building, circa 1939, the center contains scores of really helpful state and federal exhibits, videos, wildlife mounts, transportation displays, and even a trip-planning computer to assist in organizing your travels. Once you have finished there, head diagonally across the street to the **Anchorage Visitor and Convention Bureau's Log Cabin Visitor Infor-**

TOP ANNUAL EVENTS IN SOUTHCENTRAL ALASKA

Anchorage Fur Rendezvous:
This yearly February winter event in Anchorage gets cabin-weary Alaskans out and about. Featuring sled dog races, carnival rides (yup, even in the winter), and canning, cooking, baking, brewing, arts-and-crafts competitions, and more. For information contact (907) 274-1177 or visit www.furrondy.net.

Iditarod Trail Sled Dog Race:
As Alaska's state sport, dog mushing is celebrated with the premier sled dog race, the Iditarod, the first weekend of every March. The ceremonial start to this 1,049-mile-plus race begins in Anchorage. For information contact (907) 376-5155 or visit www.iditarod.com.

Kachemak Bay Wooden Boat Festival and Kachemak Bay Shorebird Festival:
Usually held in conjunction with each other, these May festivals showcase two groups common to Homer: varied and beautiful birds and handcrafted and well-kept wooden boats. The boat festival is held on Homer's spit, while the bird-watching takes place across the community. For information contact (907) 235-7740 or visit www.homeralaska.org.

Mount Marathon Race:
Spend July Fourth in Seward watching the best of the best race to the top of Seward's backdrop, Mount Marathon, then back down again in this grueling, tough-as-nails event. Accompanied by festival booths, food, and fireworks. For information contact (907) 224-8051 or visit www.sewardak.org.

Alaska State Fair:
The state's largest fair in the heart of farm country, Palmer, in the Matanuska Valley. From late August to Labor Day, the fair includes carnival rides, arts-and-crafts booths, animal exhibits, giant vegetables, quilting and canning competitions, and more. For information contact (907) 745-4827; or visit www.alaska.statefair.org.

mation Center (907–274–3531). Within the cabin's main room, as well as in the adjacent downtown center, you'll find friendly local volunteers and tons of printed material to assist you in planning your stay in the city. Visit the Web site at www.anchorage.net.

By all means, ask for the bureau's excellent free visitor's guide, which contains more than one hundred pages of tourist information, including a better-than-average walking tour of the downtown vicinity. Among more than two dozen sites noted are the *Alaska Railroad Depot* and old locomotive *Engine Number 1,* built in the early 1900s and used in constructing the Panama Canal as well as the Alaska Railroad; *Elderberry Park* and the *Oscar Anderson House,* the city's first (1915) wood-frame home, open for viewing; and *Oomingmak Musk Ox Producer's Coop,* where you can see and purchase garments made from Arctic musk ox qiviut (pronounced KEE-vee-ute), the softest yet warmest wool-like material on earth.

Anchorage is a great place to be if you're an aviation buff. At 4721 Aircraft Drive, near the Ted Stevens–Anchorage International Airport, is the **Alaska Aviation Heritage Museum,** which includes twenty-five rare, historical bush planes and dozens of photographs and exhibits. While there, you can watch aircraft being restored, view a bush-plane pioneer film, and check out bush pilot memorabilia. This also is an excellent place to watch Anchorage's many seaplane pilots come and go from the largest floatplane base in the world, **Lake Hood.** Admission is $10 for adults, $8 for seniors, and $6 for children. For more information call (907) 248–5325 or visit www.alaskaairmuseum.com.

The **Tony Knowles Coastal Trail** (named after former Anchorage mayor and former Alaska governor Tony Knowles) merits special mention. This wide asphalt trail starts at the west end of Second Avenue and follows the meandering shore of Cook Inlet for 11 scenic miles around woods, inlets, and lakes to **Kincaid Park.** Best of all, the coastal trail connects along the way with other segments of Anchorage's outstanding 120-mile network of bike and pedestrian paths. Ask for a trail system map at the visitor center.

Although downtown Anchorage is brimming with shops touting the best buys and most unique pieces in Alaska Native arts, the best place to find truly artistic works of art is at the gift shop at **Alaska Native Medical Center,** off the corner of Tudor Road and Bragaw Street. It's not within walking distance of downtown, but a trip there will be worth the time and effort. Native artists sell their wares from 10:00 A.M. to 2:00 P.M. Monday through Friday and the first and third Saturday of every month. The medical center itself is a work of art; peruse the hallways for a free art tour. Call (907) 729–1122 for more information.

The **Anchorage Museum of History and Art,** at Seventh Avenue and A Street, also has a small shop with tasteful, authentic art objects for sale. The gift shop number is (907) 343–6139. The museum is one of Anchorage's showcases, so it's not very off the beaten path, but a visit to the city isn't complete without a look-see. The museum's exhibits on Alaska history, flora, and fauna, as well as its art exhibits, rival those of metropolitan areas. Admission is $6.50 for adults. For more information about the museum, call (907) 343–4326 or visit www.anchoragemuseum.org.

Another very Alaskan shopping opportunity exists in the open-air **Downtown Saturday and Sunday Market,** staged each weekend in summer at the Lower Bowl parking lot at the corner of Third Avenue and E Street. You can pick up made-in-Alaska arts and crafts, antiques, fresh produce, fish, and garage sale items. Hours run approximately 10:00 A.M. to 6:00 P.M. each day. No charge for admission.

The *Elmendorf Wildlife Museum,* north of the city, has 200 game and bird species. It opens its doors to the public at 8481 Nineteenth Street on Elmendorf Air Force Base. To reach the base turn north on Reeve Boulevard from the Glenn Highway, about ⁷⁄₁₀ mile from the highway's start at Medfra Street. Turn right on Post Road and proceed to the base entrance. The hours are noon to 4:45 P.M. Friday and 3:00 to 4:45 P.M. Tuesday through Thursday and Saturday. For information call (907) 552–2282.

One of the best things the Alaska legislature ever did was to set aside *Chugach State Park,* nearly half a million acres of wild and wondrous mountain valleys and alpine country, right smack-dab next to Anchorage. From numerous gateways along city roads and state highways, you'll find access to gentle and tough trails to hike, lakes to fish, rivers to kayak or canoe, and wildlife to see and photograph. Among the latter are moose, Dall sheep, mountain goats, plus brown (grizzly) and black bears. For maps and more information, call (907) 345–5014.

You'll find Anchorage one of the most pleasant communities in Alaska to be hungry in. For dinner it's almost impossible to beat *Marx Brothers,* located downtown in one of Anchorage's oldest houses, at 627 West Third Avenue. It can be pricey (entrees range from $15 to $35), but where else will you find the likes of Alaska halibut in macadamia nut crust with coconut curry and mango chutney? Phone (907) 278–2133. If your taste buds run to Italian cuisine, try the *Ristorante Orso,* downtown at Fifth Avenue and G Street (907–222–3232).

You can devour great hamburgers at the *Arctic Roadrunner* from two locations: 2477 Arctic Boulevard (907–279–7311) and 5300 Old Seward Highway (907–561–1245). For chicken done fast and right, the *Lucky Wishbone,* at 1033 East Fifth Avenue (907–272–3454), is a favorite among Anchorage folk and is one of Anchorage's oldest restaurants.

You absolutely, positively, cannot miss the best pizza this side of the Mississippi at Anchorage's *Moose's Tooth Pub & Pizzeria,* named after one of Denali's more treacherous-looking ridges. You can order everything from a halibut pie to a Popeye, a spinach-laden special, to a traditional meat-lover's

southcentral alaskafacts

About 251,000, or 40 percent, of the population of Alaska lives in Southcentral Alaska.

Some of the largest tidal ranges in the world, 38.9 feet, take place in Upper Cook Inlet near Anchorage.

Anchorage is the state's largest city, but Southeast Alaska's Juneau is the state capital.

The strongest earthquake ever recorded in North America struck Anchorage on March 27, 1964. It was given a magnitude of 9.2 on the Richter scale.

favorite. The Caesar salad is especially delicious, the pizza's fresh, the beer is homebrewed, and the atmosphere is kid friendly yet adult oriented. This is a favorite among locals, and it's usually crowded at peak times, so come early if you can. The restaurant is in a tricky location, at 3300 Old Seward Highway, but it's worth the trip. For more information call (907) 258–2537 or visit www .moosestooth.net.

Gwennie's Old Alaska Restaurant is sort of outrageous, but it, too, is a favorite among locals for breakfast, lunch, and dinner. The big, rambling structure displays lots of historical photos and relics on the walls and its menu features Alaskan reindeer omelets, smoked salmon, and king crab. Prices are moderate. It's located at 4333 Spenard Road. Phone (907) 243–2090.

southcentral alaskatrivia

Anchorage's Lake Hood is the busiest seaplane base in the world. During summer as many as 800 takeoffs and landings can occur in a single day.

Pop singer Jewel grew up on her family's homestead near Homer, on Kachemak Bay.

Visitors often feel intimidated by the place and pass it by, but if you want to rub elbows (literally) with Alaskans in a frontier saloon setting, drop by *Chilkoot Charlie's,* Anchorage's best-known watering hole. Called Koot's by the locals, it's located at 2435 Spenard Road. Forget reservations. Just come out, and they'll shoehorn you in somehow. Phone (907) 272–1010 or check out www.koots.com.

Alaska state and federal employees stretch their per diem dollars in Anchorage by staying at the small (thirty-eight room) *Voyager Hotel* downtown, at 501 K Street. The ample rooms each have a queen-size bed and a couch that makes up into a twin, full kitchen facilities, and TV. They serve fresh complimentary coffee in the lobby each morning. To stay at the Voyager, you'll need reservations almost any time of year. Prices range from $89 in winter to $179 in the summer. Call (800) 247–9070 or (907) 277–9501 or visit www.voyagerhotel.com.

In the alternative-lodging category, you'll find no shortage of options in the Anchorage area. Here are a few of the best choices:

Alaskan Frontier Gardens Bed and Breakfast in South Anchorage is breathtakingly beautiful in the summer. This spacious cedarwood home offers comfortable rooms, a full breakfast, an eight-person hot tub, and lots of Alaska artifacts to look at in the main living room. The landscaping on this three-acre pine-studded lot looks like it came out of a magazine. Hanging baskets adorn the large porches, and colorful gardens embellish the lawn. Hostess Rita Gittins promises that you'll love your stay. Rooms start at $125 in the summer. For more information check out www.alaskafrontiergardens.com. Phone (907) 345–6556.

Downtown is the wonderful *Earth Bed and Breakfast,* operated by long-time Alaskans Lori Lambert and Angel Bunger. The rooms are comfortable and the rates are reasonable, starting at $99 in the summer. There's also a special climber's adventure rate starting at $45 if you don't mind sharing a room. The sunny garden is tastefully landscaped, and the bed-and-breakfast is conveniently located close to the downtown area and bike paths. The owners also operate *Earth Tours,* an agency with an emphasis on hiking, canoeing, and camping. Call (907) 279–9907 or visit www.earthbb.com.

Anchorage International Hostel, at Seventh Avenue and H Street (practically downtown), is quite large for Alaska, but since Anchorage is the travel hub for most of the state, its ninety-five beds fill up early. Reservations are a must; request them by mail from 700 H Street, Anchorage 99501. Bring your own sleeping bag if you have one; otherwise you can rent one. There are showers, a kitchen, sitting rooms, storage, and phones. The hostel is wheelchair accessible. The rate is $20 per night for members; $23 for nonmembers. For information call (907) 276–3635 or visit www.anchorageinternationalhostel .org.

Two other hostels operate out of Anchorage: the *International Back-packers Inn/Hostel,* at 308 Mumford Street (907–274–3870), and *Spenard Hostel International,* at 2845 West Forty-second Place (907–248–5036; www .alaskahostel.org). Reservations are recommended at both places.

And now, for one of the most unique places to stay and, I might add, most fun, try Angie and Tom Hamill's *Birch Trails Bed and Breakfast* at 22719 Robinson Road in the Anchorage bedroom community of Chugiak. I say "most fun" because at the Hamill place you can meet dogs—lots of dogs, Alaskan huskies, in fact, true sled dogs. The Hamills offer their entire downstairs to guests, and it is complete with private entrance, two bedrooms, shared bath, stocked kitchenette, library, and deck with hot tub and views of the Chugach Mountains. Besides great meals they also offer hiking, bird-watching, and Swedish or therapeutic massage. Summer rates start at $95 per night. Call (907) 688–5713 or visit http://home.gci.net/~birchtrails.

If you're looking for an exceptional fly-out experience in Southcentral Alaska, check out the *Within the Wild Adventure Company* (907–274–2710; www.withinthewild.com). Karl and Kirsten Dixon have created remote experiences for guests from all over the world at their handcrafted Winterlake and Redoubt Lodges. Bear viewing, hiking, canoeing, heli-skiing, and fishing are among myriad activities that await. Or you can simply sit back on the porch, revel in the view, and marvel at the gracious simplicity of life out here. Kirsten's gourmet cooking classes using home-grown foods are an unexpected delight, as are the elegant but hearty meals she and her chefs prepare.

Remember the Tony Knowles Coastal Trail that was mentioned earlier? One of the best ways to see the trail is by bicycle, and one of the best places to rent a bicycle is right downtown, only 5 blocks from the trail. **Downtown Bicycle Rental** offers hybrid, mountain, touring, and children's bikes at hourly and day rates, depending upon the bike. You'll get a free lock, helmet, and map of Anchorage's extensive trail system. The shop is at Fourth Avenue between C and D Streets. Phone (907) 279–5293 or visit www.alaska-bike-rentals.com.

Here's another quality bike tour, this one offered by **Alaskan Bicycle Adventures.** They call it Bicycle Alaska, and it is an eight-day, eight-night adventure through some of Alaska's most beautiful country. There are six days of cycling, with an average of 65 miles per day, and the trip is topped off with a cruise in the glacier-studded Prince William Sound. The cost for this adventure is $2,895. If you want a little less pedaling and a little more variety, try the seven-day Alaskan Adventure package, priced at $2,795. In this trip you'll take daily hikes, canoe trips, or sea-kayaking adventures, and you'll cycle an average of 30 miles per day. This trip, too, is topped off with a Prince William Sound cruise. For more information on this and other options, call (800) 770–7242 or (907) 245–2175 or visit www.alaskabike.com.

If you're a winter fan, Anchorage can be particularly fun. Organized sled dog races take place virtually every January and February weekend at the Tozier Sled Dog Track on Tudor Road. And nobody, but nobody, fails to feel the excitement when the biggest winter sled dog racing events of the year roll around in February and March.

First is the **Anchorage Fur Rendezvous,** staged in mid-February. This "Mardi Gras of the North" runs through two weekends and includes the **World Championship Sled Dog Race,** which begins and ends right downtown on Fourth Avenue. Literally thousands of cheering Alaskans line the way. The "Rondy" also features some rather outrageous activities among its hundreds of scheduled events, including an outhouse race, featuring privies being pushed and pulled on skids. Of special interest is the Fur Rondy Multi-Tribal Gathering, featuring dancing, drumming, and storytelling by Native people from Alaska and the Lower Forty-eight. There are also snowshoe softball games, snow-machine races, snow-sculpting competitions, Eskimo-blanket tosses, a grand parade, dances, Native crafts fairs, and outdoor fur auctions. Call (907) 274–1177 or visit www.furrondy.net for more details.

Alaska's premier sled dog race takes place the first weekend of every March in Anchorage and draws thousands upon thousands of Alaskans and visitors alike to the state's largest city. The **Iditarod Trail Sled Dog Race** runs from Anchorage some 1,049 miles to Nome in Northwest Alaska, and features some of the world's finest mushers. The ceremonial start takes place in downtown Anchorage, where hundreds of Alaskan huskies lunge and howl and jump their way from the start to the first checkpoint 20 miles to the north.

The best way to view all the excitement is to simply head downtown on the Saturday morning of the race. Race enthusiasts can follow the mushers' progress via the Iditarod Web site at www.iditarod.com.

If you're really into seeing the race, though, you need to take to the air. **Rust's Flying Service** offers an Iditarod package, ferrying you to one of the early checkpoints at Finger Lake and back again. The package starts at $450 per person, including a picnic-style lunch and beverages. One of the oldest and most reputable flying services in Anchorage, Rust's offers flight-seeing, bear viewing, and fly-in fishing packages during the summer, too. One popular option is their Mount McKinley/Denali National Park floatplane tour, starting at $295 per person. Call (907) 243–1595 or visit www.flyrusts.com.

Prince William Sound

Curious thing about **Prince William Sound.** It took the nation's all-time awful oil spill—the *Exxon Valdez* disaster of 1989—for most people to learn about one of the continent's most gorgeously pristine regions. The vessel, you'll recall, went aground on Bligh Reef, ruptured its hull, and spilled more than 11.3 million gallons of North Slope crude oil onto more than 1,500 miles of coastline. The deadly pollution, killing uncounted thousands of birds and sea mammals in its path, extended as far as the Alaska Peninsula, 600 miles away. Yet there's some good news. Although the sound will continue to suffer from subsurface oil contamination for decades to come, from a visual perspective it has largely recovered. Myriad glaciers, islands, and mountains await visitors aboard huge cruise ships, tiny kayaks, day boats, and state ferries. Whales of several species spout, roll, and sound in the waterways. Hundreds of thousands of birds again inhabit the trees and cliffside rookeries throughout the region. Bears wander along otherwise deserted beaches. Mountain goats frolic high (but visibly) on the peaks overhead.

As in Southeast Alaska, most of Prince William Sound's communities are not connected by road, but many who live there consider that a virtue. Actually, you can drive to the sound by first taking the Seward Highway from Anchorage to Portage, then driving, for a fee, along the road and tunnel to Whittier. Or you can drive on portions of the Glenn and Richardson Highways to Valdez. Cordova, the third of Prince William Sound's three principal communities, can't be reached by regular highway, but the state ferry regularly calls there as well as at Whittier and Valdez. Call (800) 642–0066 or visit www.ferryalaska.com for more information.

Here's a rundown on these towns: **Whittier** is principally a jumping-off (rather, a sailing-off) place. The community, in reality, contains an excellent dock and wharf area, a few waterfront buildings, and—dominating the scene— two very tall and prominent buildings (skyscrapers by Alaska standards) called Begich Towers and the Buckner Building. The U.S. Army built the structures during World War II to house servicemen and their families stationed at the site. Today the fourteen-story Begich Towers has been converted into condos and about half the population of Whittier lives there. The Buckner Building is now vacant. Another building, Whittier Manor, houses a good share of the rest of Whittier's residents.

The Alaska Marine Highway System operates a ferry between Whittier and Valdez during the summer. Rates vary depending upon the length of your vehicle. Passenger rates can be obtained by calling (800) 642–0066 or by visiting www.ferryalaska.com. *Take note:* Grab a book and a cup of coffee when making this call. The phone is forever tied up, and "the next available operator will be with you momentarily." Try to arrange these reservations well in advance. Commercial tour operators also operate between the two communities, or better yet, make reservations online. It will be much quicker.

Prince William Sound Cruises and Tours is one of the long-established day-cruise operators out of Whittier (877–777–4054; www.princewilliamsound.com). Its Wilderness Explorer cruise ($129) lasts six hours and tours active tidewater glaciers in the area. The four-hour Glacier Adventure cruise is $99; it explores Blackstone Bay and has an educational element for those eager for a learning experience.

If you don't plan to drive your car aboard the ferry for Valdez, don't bring it to Whittier. There's really no place for you to drive it there. On the other hand, if you'd enjoy a really different circle trip from Anchorage, drive your car through the new tunnel/road, bring it aboard the ferry to Valdez, then disembark for a drive up the Richardson and Glenn Highways back to Anchorage, or stay on the Richardson all the way to Fairbanks. If time permits, take the ferry all the way

southcentral alaskafacts

Between 1911 and 1938, one billion tons of copper were mined from the Kennecott Copper Mine.

The northernmost rain forest in Alaska is in Girdwood, about 26 miles south of Anchorage on the Seward Highway.

The largest king salmon taken with sportfishing tackle weighed 97 pounds 4 ounces, and was caught by Les Anderson in the Kenai River in 1985.

The highest mountain in the Chugach Mountains range is Mount Marcus Baker at 13,176 feet. It is located at the tips of Matanuska and Knik Glaciers.

to Cordova before disembarking at Valdez. The highway ferry trip, of course, works either direction.

Major Marine Tours is another Whittier cruising option. Cruises from Whittier to Blackstone Glacier and back are $99 per person. On the cruise you'll see active glaciers and icebergs, with narration provided by a Chugach National Forest interpreter. You can enjoy a salmon and prime rib buffet for an extra $15. Ask about their Surf and Turf packages, which include rail travel and the meal along with the cruise. Call (800) 764–7300 for information or visit www.majormarine .com.

southcentral alaskatrivia

Prince William Sound has twenty active tidewater glaciers—the largest concentration in North America.

Another great option is the Twenty-six-Glacier Cruise. See the write-up later in this chapter in the "Seward Highway: Anchorage to Tern Lake Junction" section.

For an alternative to the usual day cruise, you can rent your own personal watercraft to explore the sound. **Starbound Alaskan Adventures** (866–764– 7354; http://starboundalaskanadventures.com) provides personal watercraft, dry suits, and guides. Overnight trips with camping are an option as well, with Starbound providing the tents and cooking gear. Rates start at $500 per day, and group rates are available upon request.

Now about **Cordova.** For travelers who enjoy "untouristy" destinations, it is a great little place for poking around, mixing with the locals, exploring on one's own. Now mostly a fishing and fish-processing town, Cordova had its start as the saltwater port for shipping copper ore brought down on the Copper River & Northwestern Railway from the Kennecott mines.

You can drive about 50 miles to the face of one of Alaska's most accessible drive-up glaciers, **Childs Glacier,** on the Copper River Highway, east of town. You can also cross the historic **Million Dollar Bridge** (if you're game; it's been only "temporarily" fixed and sort of slanty ever since the 1964 Alaska earthquake) for a view of **Miles Glacier** as well. Childs Glacier, separated by a stream from the elevated, excellent USDA Forest Service interpretive center there, is extremely active. If you wander down to the stream level and the glacier calves off a big hunk of ice, run for higher ground. The surge wave can be sizable and dangerous. On the drive out from town, keep your eyes alert for bears. Other sights along the way: beaver dams, picturesque marshlands, lakes and mountain vistas, silver-salmon spawning streams, and trumpeter swans.

The **Cordova Rose Lodge** is a good choice for accommodations, with its expansive views across the water to Hawkins Island, Spike Island, and the city harbor. Some rooms are fancier than others, so feel free to have a look and see which ones you like best. The good thing, though, is that the prices are right by Alaska travel standards. Simpler rooms are $99.50 with a full breakfast, and the fancy rooms go for $135.00 with a full breakfast. Call (907) 424–7673 or visit www.cordovarose.com.

Cruises aren't too hard to come by when you're in a coastal community; the key is finding the one that's perfect for you. And if you happen to be a birder, a whale watcher, or just an all-around adventurer, one of the cruises offered by Coast Guard–certified **Discovery Voyages** will be just right. Dean Rand, captain-naturalist of the twelve-passenger, 65-foot yacht *Discovery,* offers one of the finest, albeit expensive, wilderness cruises in Alaska. His was the first wilderness cruise to be offered in Prince William Sound, and it remains a popular ecotourism-oriented adventure today. The *Discovery* originally was built for the Presbyterian Missions service to the Native communities in Southeast Alaska and today is fully renovated to house passengers comfortably and enjoyably. Trips aboard the *Discovery* range from an eleven-day spring birding expedition for $3,600 per person to an eight-day fall whale-watching tour for $3,850. These are great times of the year to travel, Rand says, because you'll have the water practically to yourself—as long you don't mind sharing with thousands of seabirds, shorebirds, and whales. Rand also offers custom charters. He carries kayaks and skiffs for landing parties, and the yacht is complete with private rooms, hot showers, and sumptuous food (including fresh seafood harvested on the trip). For more details call (800) 324–7602 or visit www.discoveryvoyages.com.

The city of **Valdez** (Alaskans say "Val-DEEZ") calls itself the Switzerland of Alaska. Actually that's not too far off the mark. The range of Chugach Mountains that arch behind and around the city are certainly in a class with the Alps. But Valdez has at least one attribute the Swiss can only dream of—an ocean view of fish-filled waters and forested islands.

The town boasts at least one additional distinction. The 800-mile **Trans-Alaska Pipeline** from Prudhoe Bay, in the Arctic, terminates here in a major, 1,000-acre terminal operated by **Alyeska Pipeline Service Company.** Alyeska loads more than a million gallons of crude oil daily onto huge oceangoing tankers docked at the site.

A good starting point for any visit to Valdez is the **visitor information center** (907–835–4636; www.valdezalaska.org) at 200 Fairbanks Drive downtown. You can view films about the 1964 Good Friday earthquake, which all but destroyed much of the old town near the water, and you can pick up a map showing the present location of historic homes from Old Valdez. Many were relocated when it was determined the old sites were no longer safe for occupancy. Nearby, at Chenega Street and Egan Drive, is the **Valdez Museum**

(907–835–2764; www.valdezmuseum.org), where exhibits range from slot machines to gold rush gear and a restored 1907 fire engine.

There are several day tour and adventure options out of Valdez, and one of the longtime favorites is operated by Captain Stan Stephens, whose experience in the industry is unparalleled. His company, **Stan Stephens Cruises,** has been plying the waters of Prince William Sound for nearly thirty years. The company offers a six-and-a-half-hour cruise to Columbia Glacier and surrounding areas, as well as a nine-and-a-half-hour Columbia and Meares Glaciers trip that takes in the entire area. Be on the lookout for sea lions, puffins, whales, and even the occasional bear. Prices are $95 for the shorter cruise, and $130 for the all-day tour. Call (866) 867–1297 or visit www.stanstephenscruises.com.

If you're into people-powered water sightseeing, **Anadyr Adventures** of Valdez (800–865–2925; www.anadyradventures.com) provides deluxe charter boat–supported kayaking trips to remote and awesome parts of Prince William Sound. Trips range from one to ten days and can accommodate novices as well as expert paddlers. Three-hour local trips start at $55 a person, two-day excursions at $350, and weeklong camping expeditions at $1,645, including gear and meals.

If you've traveled this far into Alaska and still haven't taken a river rafting trip, this may be the place to do it. Valdez-based **Keystone Raft and Kayak Adventures** (907–835–2606; www.alaskawhitewater.com) provides five trips daily down the nearby Lowe River through high-walled Keystone Canyon. The company also offers one-day floats through Class III and Class IV white water on the Tonsina River, four days on the Talkeetna River, five on the Chitina and Copper Rivers in the Wrangell Mountains, and kayak trips on waters around the state. Rates vary from $50 on the Lowe River to $1,500 for four to five days on the Tana River.

The Kenai Peninsula

Deep in the bowels of the Alaska Historical Library in Juneau resides a rare and treasured second edition of Jonathan Swift's *Gulliver's Travels,* an account written in 1726 about fictional Lemuel Gulliver's adventures in Lilliput, a nation of little people, and in Brobdingnag, the land of giants. What is especially intriguing about the book for Alaskans is Swift's map of Brobdingnag—a huge landmass extending westward from northern North America.

Remember that Vitus Bering and Alexei Shelikof, the men who discovered Alaska while sailing for the Russian czars, did so in 1741. The second edition of Swift's book is dated MDCCXXVII—1727, fourteen years before the Russian voyages of discovery. Yet Swift's map bears a resemblance (some say a close resemblance; others say, not really) to Alaska, complete with a little stretch of land that could be the Kenai Peninsula, extending from Southcentral Brobdingnag.

The comparison becomes more intriguing still when you realize that in modern Brobdingnag/Alaska roam many of North America's "most giant-size" creatures, including record-size brown (grizzly) bears, even bigger polar bears, and large concentrations of mammoth whales and walrus in adjacent seas. In addition, on the peninsula noted both in Swift's book and in modern guides, you can see and photograph huge moose.

The Kenai, probably more than any other locale, is where Alaskans themselves play and recreate. Lake, river, and saltwater fishing is superlative. Hiking trails are widespread and wide ranging. Moderate-size and tiny communities offer traditional homespun Alaskan hospitality. Access is easy by highway, rail, and air from Anchorage.

Because the Kenai is much used by Alaskans, particularly from Anchorage, it's wise to avoid weekend and holiday visits, when traffic on the only road access from Anchorage, the Seward Highway, can be horrendous. Most of the time, however, the 127-mile asphalt road is more than pleasurable as it skirts saltwater inlets, circles around big and little lakes, and penetrates thick, vast forest expanses. It richly deserves its prestigious designation by the USDA Forest Service as a National Forest Scenic Byway.

The Seward Highway: Anchorage to Tern Lake Junction

Following are some of the sightseeing opportunities along the several highways that serve the Kenai Peninsula, starting with the 127-mile *Seward Highway,* south of Anchorage. The Seward Highway mileposts you see along the side of the road, incidentally, measure the distance from Seward. So the parking area at Potter Marsh at mile 117.4, for instance, is 117$\frac{4}{10}$ miles from Seward and 9$\frac{6}{10}$ miles from Anchorage.

All along the highway be on the lookout for wildlife, especially moose. The Kenai is home to a national wildlife refuge, and the abundant moose population is the reason for it. At mile 117.4 and at mile 116 you'll see turnoffs for *Potter Marsh,* a state wildlife refuge where you can view extensive waterfowl, shorebirds, arctic terns, and American bald eagles plus king, pink, and silver salmon in the creeks that flow into the marsh. A boardwalk crosses the marsh. Between mileposts 106 and 110 on the Seward Highway, look frequently to the craggy tops of the rocky cliffs that rise from the road. If you look carefully, more often than not you'll spot mama Dall sheep and their youngsters staring curiously down at you. Do not, of course, stop your car on the highway; there are several turnoffs where you can safely stop and then walk back for easy viewing. In fact, if you are on the road for sightseeing purposes, please respect your fellow travelers and obey the frequent signs asking slower vehicles to pull over. It is the law to pull over if more than five vehicles are behind you.

If you collect unusual critters to log in your life book of wild animals, stop at **Beluga Point,** at mile 110.3. Here, if you're just a little bit lucky, you may see the small white beluga whales that congregate in these waters. The best viewing is probably around high tide. At low tide the point is a good place to witness a tidal bore (more on this phenomenon in a moment).

Bird Creek State Campground, just past mile 101, is not only a pleasant place to camp or picnic, it also provides one of the better vistas for watching one of Alaska's more spectacular natural phenomena—the **Turnagain Tidal Bore** that comes rushing through Turnagain Arm at low tide daily. Get a tide book (free at many service stations, sporting goods stores, and banks), and check the times for low tide at Anchorage. Then, to get the correct time for the Bird Creek overlook, add about two hours and fifteen minutes to whatever time is listed. What you'll see is a frothing, foaming wall of seawater—sometimes as high as 6 feet—that comes surging into the constricted inlet. Don't, by the way, even think of wading out onto the mudflats that are exposed in these and other Cook Inlet areas. The mud is like quicksand. Foolish waders have drowned during incoming tides after becoming mired in the muck.

At mile 90 the Seward Highway connects with the 3-mile Alyeska access road to **Girdwood, Alyeska Resort,** and **Crow Creek Mine.** Girdwood is less a city

southcentral alaskatrivia

The popular skiing town of Girdwood was named for miner James E. Girdwood, who came to the area in 1896.

and more a still-woodsy gathering place of some 2,000 Alaskans, most of whom love to ski (usually at adjacent Alyeska Resort) and many of whom work at shops, stores, or eateries either at the resort (800–880–3880; www .alyeskaresort.com), in Girdwood, or nearby. Many Anchoragites have condominiums here. The community isn't exactly planned or laid out, but it's small enough to be easy to wander around in. The residents are more than friendly and accommodating. At the resort (a world-class ski area in the winter months), you can take a tram ride ($16, cheaper if you're a hotel guest) 2,300 feet up the mountain for hiking or for gourmet dining in the $16 to $25 range at **Seven Glaciers Restaurant** (907–754–2248), or for just taking in the sweeping view of Turnagain Arm. A perk of eating at the restaurant—the tram ride is free.

At the **Crow Creek Mine** (907–278–8060; www.crowcreekgoldmine .com), you can pan for gold along creek beds still rich with the precious metal. The managers will even teach you how and point out likely areas for prospecting. Sure, it's sort of touristy, but there really is plenty of gold along these creek banks. Many Alaskans come here on weekends for recreational panning. Of course, you get to keep all the "color" you find. When you're through, you can refuel the body with sourdough pancakes or sandwiches in the **Bake Shop** (907–783–2831; www.thebakeshop.com) near Alyeska Resort or partake of the eclectic **Jack Sprat Cafe,** with meals both "fat" and "lean." Call (907) 783–JACK or visit www.jacksprat.net. The **Double Musky** (907–783–2822; www.doublemuskyinn.com), with its huge (fourteen- to twenty-ounce) French pepper steak, is another favorite among locals and visiting Alaskans. Arrive early or be ready to wait. The Musky is popular, and they don't take reservations.

If you're overnighting in Girdwood, consider the **Carriage House Bed & Breakfast and Stables,** a beautiful timber-frame house on California Creek. You'll enjoy the river-rock fireplace, hardwood floors with radiant heat, massive post and beam construction, and arched windows. Three rooms are available, two with private baths. Summer rates start at $115 per night. For more information call (907) 783–9464 or (888) 961–9464 or visit www.thecarriage housebandb.com.

Another good choice is **Hidden Creek Bed and Breakfast** on Vail Drive (907–783–5557; www.hiddencreekbb.com). There are three deluxe rooms, all with private baths, as well as cable TV, DVD, wireless Internet, private phone, robes and slippers, and hot tub access. Summer rates start at $175 and include a gourmet breakfast.

Hostel enthusiasts can check out the **Alyeska Home Hostel** about $\frac{3}{10}$ mile from the Alyeska Resort. This is a small, cozy house with eight dorm bunks, a private room, and a seasonal cabin. Kitchen and shower facilities are shared. The charge is $20 per person or $50 for a private room for two. To get there drive the Alyeska Road past Glacier Creek, make a right turn on Timberline Drive, then the fourth right on Alta for about ¼ mile. The hostel is on the left; you'll see the sign. For reservations call (907) 783–2222 or visit www.alyeska hostel.com.

Back on the Seward Highway: At mile 79 you can take a driving tour of **Alaska Wildlife Conservation Center** (907–783–2025; www.alaskawildlife .org), the state's only drive-through wildlife park, to view moose, elk, buffalo, musk oxen, caribou, and other North Country creatures from your own vehi-

Active Ice

There is something innately rewarding about climbing on ice in the middle of summer. I was raised in the South, where in the summer ice cubes in your tea melt within minutes. But here in Alaska, the ice remains, even in the summer. And while the ice is slowly receding, the deep-blue glaciers that cover a good portion of this state remain a presence.

Glaciers are so common, in fact, that you can literally touch them, even walk on them if you'd like. Six well-known glaciers are accessible by road in Southcentral Alaska.

Head south from Anchorage on the Seward Highway; 50 miles later you'll find the turnoff to Portage Glacier. Although you can no longer see the glacier from the visitor center, you can take a narrated boat tour to view it up close. Or you can hike to the nearby Byron Glacier—smaller, but equally impressive—if you want to actually touch the ice. (*Warning:* The ice is in constant motion, and giant pieces have been known to break off, injuring or even killing unsuspecting people. Be very careful of this, as well as crevasses that you could slip into.)

Keep driving on the Seward Highway; two hours later you'll find yourself in the town of Seward, which is the jump-off point for some of the best glacier viewing in the state in Kenai Fjords National Park. Exit Glacier is accessible by road. Just drive the access road and walk to the edge of the glacier. Again, be careful. Large chunks of ice frequently calve from the glacier.

My favorite glacier among those accessible by road is Matanuska Glacier, 46 miles northeast of Palmer, off the Glenn Highway, in the Chugach Mountains. My husband and I took my brother here once, and we spent a breezy afternoon exploring the glacier's terminus, climbing carefully across the ice.

For information on any of the other glaciers abundant in Southcentral Alaska, just ask at the Anchorage Visitor and Convention Bureau's Log Cabin Visitor Information Center in downtown Anchorage. They'll get you pointed in the right direction.

—Melissa DeVaughn

cle. The nonprofit wildlife center cares for orphaned and injured animals. Admission is $7.50 for adults and $5.00 for children.

If you're heading for the port of **Whittier,** on fabled Prince William Sound, the **Anton Anderson Memorial Tunnel** (907–472–2584; www.dot.state.ak.us/creg/whittiertunnel) is the way to go. The tunnel is located on Portage Glacier Road and connects Whittier and Prince William Sound to the Seward Highway and the rest of Southcentral Alaska. It is the longest highway tunnel in North America at 2.5 miles, and the longest combined rail-highway–use tunnel in North America (the Alaska Railroad operates to and from Whittier as well). The round-trip toll for driving the tunnel is $12 for general traffic.

Another option is to take the Alaska Railroad from Anchorage, which departs daily and costs $72 round-trip or $58 one way. Visit the Alaska Railroad Web site at www.alaskarailroad.com for more information or call (800) 544–0552 or (907) 265–2494 in Anchorage.

From Whittier, one of your best options is to hop aboard the Klondike Express for a *Twenty-six-Glacier Cruise.* Operated by *Phillips Cruises and Tours* (800–544–0529; www.26glaciers.com), a sleek, comfortable catamaran will take you on a 135-mile adventure into College and Harriman Fjords, where you'll likely see whales, sea otters, eagles, and harbor seals in addition to calving glaciers. Fun and fact-filled narration by the friendly crew, a hearty halibut snack, complimentary coffee, and a guaranteed smooth ride make this a fabulous experience. Check out their seasonal rail/cruise special at $139 round-trip.

Also located on the 5½-mile Portage Glacier Road is Alaska's most visited travel attraction, *Portage Glacier,* and perhaps Alaska's least known wildlife species, the glacier iceworm.

At the glacier the USDA Forest Service operates *Begich-Boggs Visitor Center* where, in good weather or foul, you can view the frequently iceberg-clogged lake that the ice river flows into and all kinds of interesting glacial exhibits. Though the glacier is no longer visible from here, each day a huge chunk of glacier ice is hauled into the center, where you can touch, rub, and pose with ice that began as snow on the glacier perhaps a century ago. Incredibly, there are tiny but visible organisms, popularly called iceworms, that live in glacial ice. On Friday in the summer you can head out with forest service naturalists daily for an iceworm safari (no charge) to track down some of Alaska's littlest creatures. The center is open daily in summer 9:00 A.M. to 6:00 P.M. Call (907) 783–2326.

The Gray Line of Alaska's sightseeing vessel **Ptarmigan** makes frequent one-hour excursions from lakeshore to within ¼ mile of Portage Glacier's glistening face. This is Alaska's most economical ($29) glacier cruise. Forest service naturalists accompany each trip. For information and reservations call (888) 452–1737 or visit www.graylineofalaska.com.

At Seward Highway's mile 56.2 you have two somewhat confusing choices. If you're coming from Anchorage, turn right to access the Hope Highway; stay left to stay on the road to Seward. The Hope alternative is well worth exploring. The road leads to the community of *Hope* and one of Alaska's most celebrated backpacking experiences.

First, about the road and the community: At the turnout just beyond mile 2, you have at least a chance of seeing moose in the Sixmile Creek valley below. Just past mile 11 there's a big, paved turnoff with a view of Turnagain Arm. At mile 16.5, turn on Hope Road for "downtown" Hope, a tiny pictur-

A Fall Ritual

Like putting up wood for the winter or giving the house a twice-over in the spring, hiking the Resurrection Pass Trail is a fall rite of passage for this Alaskan. There is nothing like walking through a wilderness crisp with fallen leaves and pungent with overripe blueberries—and then getting to sleep right in the middle of it.

I make the annual trip in early September, when the blueberries are sure to be abundant. I bring a couple extra water bottles and fill them with berries while making my way along the 38-mile trail over the course of a weekend. The trail itself is unbeatable, only a couple hours' drive from Anchorage on the Kenai Peninsula. Within a half an hour of hiking—save for the maintained trail—you feel as though you're the only person to have been here.

The last time I was on the Resurrection Trail, I traveled with my friend Anne. We reveled in the late summer scenery and were treated to a rare "bat" sighting at the end of a long first day.

Another time, my husband and I were treated to wildlife sightings at just about every bend. We watched from our tent site as a porcupine made its way up a tree. The next day we stood stark still after hearing a brown bear grunting in frustration; then, thankfully, we saw it run up over a ridge and disappear. On the last day we counted moose as if checking off out-of-state license plates on a road trip.

Same trail, different experiences. You can be sure I'll be back this fall.

—Melissa DeVaughn

esque community of year-round homes for a handful of residents and getaway cabins used by urban Alaskans. The road leads past the post office, then to the waterfront, a popular site for anglers. The town had its start as a mining center in 1896. Today it offers a secluded base for hiking, fishing, and just getting away from it all. Learn more about Hope by accessing www.adven alaska.com/Hope.

Just past mile 16 and before you get to Hope, turn south on Resurrection Creek Road for the trailhead of the ***Resurrection Pass Trail,*** one of Alaska's finest backcountry hiking routes. I make a point of hiking this trail every fall, when the blueberries are ripe, but summer hiking is nice, too. It ends 38 miles later at about mile 53 on the Sterling Highway. In between, trekkers experience alpine ridges and lakes, scenic valleys, and vast panoramas plus the opportunity to observe moose, Dall sheep, mountain goats, and bears. Spaced about a half-day's hiking distance apart are seven USDA Forest Service rental cabins. (For information call 907–271–2599 locally or 877–444–6777 toll-free. The Web reservation site is at www.recreation.gov.)

Back on the Seward Highway, between miles 47.5 and 44.5, you'll find numerous turnoffs that offer excellent photo ops for pictures of Upper and Lower Summit Lakes and the spectacular mountains that rise behind them. If you're driving from Anchorage to Seward in one day, the log cabin *Summit Lake Lodge,* at mile 45.8, offers a good refreshment stop with moderately priced old-fashioned eggs-meat-and-potatoes breakfasts plus full lunch and dinner menus. And if you like pie, this is the best place ever to get the pie of your choice. You name it, they make it.

Just before mile 38, you come to *Tern Lake Junction,* where the Seward Highway connects with the Sterling Highway. If you're Seward-bound, continue straight ahead on Alaska Highway Route 9. If you're headed for Soldotna, Homer, and other Sterling Highway points, turn right on Route 1.

The Seward Highway: Tern Lake Junction to Seward

Moose Pass, at mile 29.4, would be easy to miss if you blinked. It's an interesting little town (population about 206) and has a motel, general store, and restaurant. At *Estes Brothers Grocery* there's a big waterwheel that turns a working grindstone. If you collect pictures of unique signs, the one here reads MOOSE PASS IS A PEACEFUL TOWN. IF YOU HAVE AN 'AXE TO GRIND' DO IT HERE. If you're looking for an interesting spot to stretch your legs, there's a 1³⁄₁₀-mile paved biking and walking trail that skirts the edge of Trail Lake. *Trail Lake Lodge* (888–395–3624 or 907–288–3101; www.traillakelodge.com) offers a lakeside salmon bake plus a menu of steaks and seafood.

At Nash Road junction (mile 3.2 on the Seward Highway), turn left off the highway, then left again on Salmon Creek Road to find the *Farm Bed and Breakfast.* Host Jack Hoogland calls the rooms here elegantly casual. They come with private baths, decks, kitchenettes, and entrances. The setting is one of trees and greenery. Rates are $75 for a shared bath to $105 for a private bath; call (907) 224–5691 or visit www.thefarmbedandbreakfast .com.

The highway ends at mile 0 and the city of *Seward.* The community is relatively old by Alaska standards, having had its start in 1903, when railroad surveyors selected this site at the head of *Resurrection Bay* as an ocean terminal and supply center. Actually, there was a small Russian settlement there prior to 1903. Since 1923 the town has served as the farthest-south point on the 470-mile route of the Alaska Railroad and prides itself today on being the gateway to *Kenai Fjords National Park.*

The four-hour Alaska Railroad trip from Anchorage to Seward, incid
is one of the North Country's most rewarding excursions for $109 round-trip.
The journey departs Anchorage at 6:45 A.M. each morning in summer and
leaves Seward at 6:00 P.M. for the return trip. Sights along the way include the
dramatic coast of Cook Inlet, major lakes and streams, forest country, deep
gulches and gullies, and (at least every time I've made the trip) abundant
wildlife, including moose and bears. For information about rail-only travel or
rail/yacht combination tours that include cruising Resurrection Bay and Kenai
Fjords National Park, call (800) 544–0552 or visit www.alaskarailroad.com.

To get a quick glimpse of old downtown Seward, the small boat harbor, and
all the history in between, hop aboard the **Seward Trolley.** This sightseeing bus
departs from the railroad station and other points every half hour daily in summer. The fare is only $5 for an all-day pass ($3 for children). It may be the
cheapest tour in Alaska.

Two hiking destinations, among many others, are especially notable. From
a trailhead at about mile 2 on the Lowell Point Road, you can walk, at low tide,
along a 4½-mile forest and beach trail to **Caines Head State Recreation Area,**
where World War II bunkers and gun emplacements serve as reminders of
Alaska's strategic location during a time when a Japanese invasion of North
America seemed plausible.

Mount Marathon, which rises from the community's edge from just
above sea level to 3,022 feet, offers another satisfying trek. But if you don't like
crowds, avoid the peak on Independence Day. On July 4 each year the town
continues a tradition begun in 1909 with a wager between two "sourdoughs."
The bet: whether or not a person could run from midtown to the top of the
mountain and back in less than an hour. The outcome: Yes, it can be done—
so far in a record time of forty-three minutes, twenty-three seconds. These days
competitors come from other towns, states, and even nations to scramble to
the summit, then run, leap, slide, and fall during the helter-skelter descent wit-
nessed by cheering crowds of spectators along the route.

A small but informative **National Park Service visitor center** in
Seward (907–224–7500; www.nps.gov/kefj) with information on nearby Kenai
Fjords National Park is located at 1212 Fourth Avenue, on the Seward waterfront. It sits among structures that house sightseeing, charter, fishing, and
souvenir shops. The center operates 8:00 A.M. until 7:00 P.M. daily in the summer, offering short slide shows, interpretive programs, other exhibits, and
short walks.

You really won't find any hideaway eating places in Seward, but for lunch
and dinner, locals and visiting Alaskans often choose **Ray's Waterfront,** at
1316 Fourth Avenue at the small boat harbor (907–224–5606), especially for

fish and seafood. Prices are in the $8 to $12 range for lunch, $15 to $25 for dinner. Seats by the window are a must.

Newer on the dining and lodging front in Seward, but no less appetizing, is the **Seward Windsong Lodge** and accompanying **Resurrection Roadhouse** (907–224–7116) overlooking the Resurrection River on the way to Exit Glacier. The rooms are comfortable and secluded, and the food, well, let's just say the food rivals the views you'll see out the roadhouse's windows. Try the white mushroom pizza—you won't regret it. For more information on lodging, call (877) 777–4079 or (907) 224–7116 or visit www.sewardwindsong.com.

And for coffee lovers, if you're wandering the streets of downtown Seward, be sure to stop at what looks like a church but actually is **Resurrect Art Coffee House Gallery,** on Third Avenue (907–224–7161). The name is a mouthful, but so are the tasty treats and espresso. This is a relaxing place to read a newspaper, visit with locals, or just admire the artwork that adorns the former church's walls.

Exit Glacier is one of the few glaciers in the North Country whose face you can actually approach on foot. It's located at the end of Exit Glacier Road, which junctions at mile 3.7 on the Seward Highway. En route to the glacier, you initially pass by small clusters of homes, then drive through thick forests and a steep-walled valley for about 8 miles to a National Park Service visitor parking area. A series of paths and trails lead to the snout of the 3-mile-long ice river. *Caution:* You'll see whole groups walking right up to the ice to pose for photos; that's a foolish thing to do. Huge pieces of ice can fall at any time. Stay safely back; you can still get some great pictures. If you're a hiker, you'll find options from short nature trails to an all-day trek to the Harding Icefield. There are bears and moose in the area, and, as at Portage Glacier, you can find iceworms in the ice. Look for them in the early evening; they avoid the sun.

Of course, to really appreciate Kenai Fjords National Park, you need to see the fjords from the water. Several excellent day-cruise operators offer half-day or longer narrated excursions through Resurrection Bay to see whales, sea otters, a sea lion rookery, puffins, eagles, glaciers, mountains, and other features of the magnificent Kenai Fjords landscape. Times and rates vary.

You'll be surprised at the number of cruise-ship operators in Seward, and their names are all so similar sounding that it's easy to get confused. You probably won't go wrong with any of these operators—they're all pretty reputable. But I've taken many a visiting relative on these various cruises, and there are two that I think really stand out.

Major Marine Tours offers a great half-day wildlife and glacier tour for $59 that is narrated by a National Park Service ranger. You'll have a chance to

see puffins, sea otters, eagles, and all sorts of massive glaciers. For anou.
you can partake in the delicious all-you-can-eat salmon and prime rib buffet.
Other tours, including all-day tours, are offered. Call (800) 764–7300 or visit
www.majormarine.com.

Kenai Fjords Tours also offers a popular all-day trip, this one including
a stop at Fox Island for a buffet lunch of grilled salmon. The cruise departs the
Seward boat harbor at 10:00 A.M. during season and takes in the national park's
wildlife and tidewater glaciers, with a midday break for lunch. The cost is $129
for adults and $62 for children under age twelve. Call (877) 777–4051 or (907)
224–8068, or visit www.kenaifjords.com.

Clearly, the best way to see the natural beauty of this area is to be up close
and personal. Resurrection Bay, and its surrounding smaller bays, offers some
of the best kayaking the state has to offer. There are no shortage of kayak
rental and tour companies to help you plan a memorable trip.

Sunny Cove Sea Kayaking Company offers afternoon tours to eight-
day guided sea-kayaking and camping expeditions. The price ranges from
$125 for a day trip to $1,299 for a six-day kayaking-camping trek. For more
information call (800) 770–9119 or (907) 224–8810 or visit www.sunnycove
.com.

For accommodations plus kayaking tours and rentals in a beautiful,
secluded setting, contact *Kayaker's Cove,* where rustic lodging will take you
way off the beaten path and daily kayaking will invigorate your spirit. The lodge
is located on Resurrection Bay, 12 miles from Seward. Cabins rent for $60 a
night, and rooms in the lodge are $20. Kayaks are available for $45 for singles
and $55 for doubles. Call (907) 224–5739 or (866) 541–5739 or visit
www.millerslanding ak.com/kayaking_cove.htm.

Now, back to terra firma. It isn't off the beaten path—in fact, it's one of
the largest buildings in Seward—but the *Alaska SeaLife Center* is certainly
not to be missed. The facility, the crown jewel of this waterfront community,
houses some of Alaska's most interesting animal life. A trip to this research
and education center is $15 for adults, and there you'll be able to see puffins,
sea lions, seals, and other marine wildlife up close. There are daily films, a
viewing platform overlooking the bay, and all sorts of exhibits. For information call the center at (800) 224–2525 or visit www.alaskasealife.org.

If you'd enjoy sleeping in a National Historic Site, book yourself into the
Van Gilder Hotel, a small but comfortable hotel in the older business district in downtown Seward. It was built in 1916 as an office building but
became a hotel in 1921. The rates begin at $109 for a room with shared bath
and $195 for a suite. Call (907) 224–3079 or (800) 204–6835 or visit www.van
gilderhotel.com.

The Sterling Highway:
Tern Lake to Homer

Seward is as far as you can go by road on the Seward Highway, which covers the eastern side of the Kenai Peninsula. At its Tern Lake junction with the Seward Highway at mile 37, however, the paved Sterling Highway heads west, then south along the western side of the Kenai. Strangely, the mileposts along the Sterling Highway measure distances from Seward, even though the road doesn't go there. The road ends at its southernmost point, at the tip of the Homer Spit at mile 179.5.

For the traveler who enjoys luxuries while traveling, the rustic but regal **Kenai Princess Lodge** (800–426–0500; www.princessalaskalodges.com) is accessible from the road at mile 47.7. Activities include horseback riding, river rafting, flight-seeing, hiking, fishing, and touring from the lodge throughout the rest of the peninsula. Or just relax in a hot tub. Note the chandelier in the lobby made from deer antlers. Rates begin at $79 off-season, $239 during peak season. The adjacent **Kenai Princess RV Park** (also 800–426–0500) provides one of the nicest private campgrounds in the state.

The small town of **Cooper Landing,** spread out along the road before and after mile 48, offers various visitor facilities, including guided fishing trips, cabins, and shops. Cooper Landing is an outdoorsperson's heaven. There are countless trails to explore, an aquamarine lake to admire, and a fish-packed river waiting to be fished. For those who want to explore deeper into the woods, stop by Alex Kime's **Alaska Horsemen Trail Adventures** and sign up for a day or overnight trip into the Chugach Mountains. Kime, a quintessential cowboy with a constant grin on his face, is eager to share his world with guests atop the backs of one of his twenty-eight or so horses. Two-hour valley rides are $90, and day trips are $170 to $225, depending on your destination. Rates for those who want to experience horsepacking and camping in a cowboy camp begin at $1,200. Contact Alex at (907) 595–1806 or (800) 595–1806 or visit www.alaskahorsemen.com.

Alaska Wildland Adventures offers quality river trips from a launch site at mile 50.1. If you're looking for a bit of adventure, ask about their seven-hour Kenai Canyon Raft Trip through a remote, nonmotorized section of the Kenai River. It includes some spirited Class III rapids and a lunch on the shores of pristine Skilak Lake. The cost is $135. In case you prefer a more peaceful trip, the company offers a Kenai River Scenic Float through a portion of the **Kenai National Wildlife Refuge,** where there are frequent sightings of moose, eagles, Dall sheep, waterfowl, signs of beaver, and sockeye salmon. The cost is $49.

Alaska Wildland also packages half- or full-day Kenai River Sportfishing trips, on which you can angle for salmon, rainbow trout, and Dolly Varden. These trips are packaged with comfortable accommodations at *Kenai River Sportfishing Lodge.* Costs vary from $1,450 for three nights to $4,050 for eight nights and include everything from transportation from Anchorage to meals and gear. For details call (800) 478–4100 or visit www.alaskawildland.com.

Just down the road, at mile 50, Gary and Carol Galbraith's family-operated *Alaska Rivers Company* offers a half-day scenic float excursion for $49 or a full-day scenic, sometimes splashy, canyon experience for $122. Both trips include homemade picnic lunches, professional guides, and excellent wildlife viewing prospects. The Galbraiths also do guided hikes and have traditional Alaska log cabins—rustic but very comfortable—for rent on the shore of the Kenai River. The cost is $200 for parties of six, $150 for parties of four, and $135 for doubles. The River House sleeps four and rents for $225 per night. Call (907) 595–1226 or visit www.alaskariverscompany.com.

At mile 58 you have a choice to make and a *U.S. Fish and Wildlife Service Information Station* to help you make it. You can continue on the paved Sterling Highway westerly to mile 75.2, or you can take the southerly 19-mile gravel Skilak Lake Loop Road to its junction with the Sterling at mile 75.2. We recommend the latter. The gravel road isn't bad, and opportunities for photography, fishing, hiking, and wildlife spotting are excellent.

Hidden Lake, along the gravel road, is a particular delight, with a first-class *U.S. Fish and Wildlife Service* campground that features paved roads, campfire programs at an amphitheater, and a deck for spotting wildlife. *A warning note:* Beautiful *Skilak Lake,* like many of the large lakes on the Kenai, can be extremely dangerous. Horrific winds can arise suddenly on the water. If you plan to take out a small boat, stay close to shore and wear a life jacket.

After Skilak Loop Road connects with the Sterling Highway at mile 75.2, the Sterling Highway continues westerly to mile 83.4, where you have another off-highway choice. If you're transporting a canoe, the choice is an easy yes. The Swanson River and Swan Lake Roads head north, then east, for nearly 30 miles, accessing two of the most highly acclaimed canoeing routes in the North Country. The *Swanson River Canoe Trail* is 80 miles long and connects more than forty lakes with 46 miles of the Swanson River. Portages between lakes are short, less than a mile over relatively easy terrain. The *Swan Lake Canoe Trail,* separate from the Swanson River route, covers 60 miles and connects thirty lakes with forks of the Moose River. Both trails lie within the Kenai National Wildlife Refuge.

The opportunities for viewing wildlife—especially moose, eagles, trumpeter swans, and tundra swans—are enormous. For maps and additional information, call the refuge manager at the **Kenai National Wildlife Refuge** (907–262–7021) or follow the maps link under canoeing at the Web site (http://kenai.fws.gov). Information is also available at the forest service cabin at mile 58, the Kenai National Wildlife Refuge Information Center in Soldotna, and at local information centers in Kenai and Soldotna.

At mile 94.2 you face still another vexing little decision. This time your options are three. You can continue westerly on the Sterling Highway to Soldotna (the city center is only a mile down the road), then keep driving southerly on the Sterling toward the end of the road in Homer. Or you can turn northerly at what is called the Soldotna Y on the Kenai Spur Highway to the city of Kenai, then drive on to **Captain Cook State Recreation Area.** The third choice is to drive on to Soldotna, visit that city, then backtrack the short distance to the Kenai Spur Highway. After you've finished exploring the spur road and the city of Kenai, you can then bypass Soldotna and drive southerly on Kalifornsky Beach Road to rejoin the Sterling at mile 108.8. I recommend the third choice.

First, about **Soldotna:** If you want to fish the Kenai River for king salmon and other species, this community of about 3,700 offers a large number of charter-boat fishing services. You can also fish on your own from the shores of the river; many do. Among the sights to see is the **Soldotna Historical Society Museum,** which includes a small "village" of historic log buildings, among them the 1958 territorial school, the last one built in Alaska before statehood. Damon Hall, at the village site, contains an excellent display of Alaska wildlife mounts. Still other mounted wildlife displays can be seen at the **Kenai National Wildlife Refuge Visitor Center** (907–262–7021; http://kenai .fws.gov), at the top of Ski Hill Road. This is a prime location to get information about canoeing, hiking, camping, or just sightseeing in the refuge, which was established by President Franklin D. Roosevelt in 1941 as the Kenai National Moose Range.

Now retrace your steps back to the Y at mile 94.2 on the Sterling Highway, where the Kenai Spur Highway heads northerly. The city of Kenai lies about 11 miles up this road.

It's probably best to start a **Kenai** visit at the **Kenai Visitors and Cultural Center** (907–283–1991; www.visitkenai.com) near Main Street and the Kenai Spur Highway. There you'll find a cultural museum and wildlife displays as well as friendly staff to give directions around the far-flung community. Admission to the museum section is $3 for adults.

Kenai, you'll find, is one of those curious cities that doesn't really seem to have a downtown, yet this is a site where Native peoples and Russian fur traders settled in centuries past. The Russian heritage is dramatically expressed in the

Holy Assumption of the Virgin Mary Russian Orthodox Church, not far from the visitor center. The original church was founded in 1846 by a Russian monk, Egumen Nicolai. The present three-domed structure was built a half century later and is one of the oldest Russian Orthodox houses of worship in Alaska. Tours are available, and in the summer you can usually walk right in. The nearby *St. Nicholas Chapel* was constructed in 1906 and covers the grave of the founding monk. In the same vicinity is *Fort Kenay,* a log structure built during the 1967 Alaska Purchase Centennial to commemorate the original 1869 U.S. Army installation. It housed some one hundred men and officers. Check at the visitor center for a copy of a self-guided walking tour.

Walk to *Beluga Lookout,* at the end of Main Street, for possible sightings of the white beluga whales that visit these waters. Fishing for lunker king salmon, monster-size halibut, and other species is, for many visitors, what Kenai is all about. As in Soldotna, a large number of guides and charter boats call Kenai home.

Perhaps the best way to see the Kenai Peninsula and its surroundings is by plane, and the person to call for unique (and safe) flying is Michael Litzen of *Litzen Guide Service* (907–776–5868). Litzen specializes in custom packages, from guided hunt trips to fishing trips to, especially, ecotourism-oriented remote cabin drop-offs for those just wanting to get away from it all. And Litzen, who also uses his planes to do wildlife counts and radio tracking for state fish and game biologists, knows where the animals are for superb wildlife viewing that doesn't disturb the animals. A one-and-a-half-hour flight-seeing tour starts at about $350.

The Captain Cook State Recreation Area, at the very end of the Kenai Spur Highway, is one of Alaska's unsung and relatively undiscovered state parklands—probably because it's at the end of a single road. But especially if you're a camper, it's well worth the drive. *Discovery Campground,* near the end of the road, merits special mention. Here you'll find a locale of rolling hills, wooded spruce plateaus, and beautiful vistas of the Alaska Range across Cook Inlet. The volcanic peaks Mount Spurr, Mount Redoubt, and especially Mount Iliamna stand out across the water (as do thirteen oil platforms).

Three warnings: First, on the tidelands, observe the warnings and don't let an incoming tide catch you off guard. Second, delicious berries are thick in the area, and they are there for the picking, but avoid the bright red or white poisonous baneberry. And third, if you get into a standoff with a bear, leave the site and the berries to the animal. Don't even think of trying to shoo the bruin away.

After you've "done" the Kenai Spur Highway, you can retrace your travel to Kenai and the Soldotna Y at mile 94 on the Sterling Highway, then continue south down the Sterling. The more scenic choice, though, is to head west, then southerly on Kalifornsky Beach Road down the coast to Kasilof, at mile 108.8 on the Sterling Highway.

The view alone at *Alaska's Inn Between Bed and Breakfast and Cabins* is reason enough to stay at this charming home on the bluff in Kasilof. But the people are nice, too, and that makes it even more special. The inn offers two cabins, one that sleeps four and one that sleeps six. Rooms all have shared baths and cost $90 each, with breakfast after 7:30 A.M. The cabins rent for $140. One sleeps six and the other sleeps four; both have full bathrooms and kitchenettes. Call (907) 335–2769 or visit www.alaskainnbetween.com.

If you're neither a hunter nor an angler, but you'd still like to do something very Alaskan, stop at mile 117.4 and head for *Clam Gulch State Recreation Area* (where there are 116 campsites) to join hundreds of locals on the shore for the grand old Alaska sport of razor clam digging. *Three caveats:* Don't drive down the extremely steep beach road to sea level unless you have a four-wheel-drive vehicle. Don't go digging without a valid Alaska sportfishing license, available at various sporting and retail establishments. And, again, don't get stuck offshore on an incoming tide. The best clamming occurs on minus tides and varies from month to month. Locals are more than happy to share their knowledge and technique. You'll find similar clamming opportunities at the Ninilchik Beach Campground, which is part of *Ninilchik State Recreation Area,* at mile 134.5.

At about mile 135 you'll come to a side road that leads to the old original *Ninilchik Village* and the beach. Take the time to explore this site, which includes a few old log buildings. A white Russian Orthodox church, still in use, overlooks the village from a photogenic hilltop setting. Modern *Ninilchik* stretches down the road from roughly mile 135.5. If you don't like crowds, avoid the area on Memorial Day and other holidays, when thousands converge for the fishing thereabouts.

At mile 157 on the Sterling Highway, the collector of superlatives will want to turn off the main highway and drive on the Old Sterling Highway past the Anchor River to another turnoff, this one on the Anchor River Beach Road. At the end of this road lies the *Anchor Point State Recreation Site.* There, on an overlook platform facing Cook Inlet, stands a big sign that reads NORTH AMERICA'S MOST WESTERLY HIGHWAY POINT. You can't drive your car anyplace west of this point on the connected highways of the United States and Canada. Incidentally, more than a million razor clams are taken each year on the beaches between Anchor Point and Kasilof up the highway.

You come to *Homer,* my all-time favorite place in Alaska, at mile 172 and beyond, crossing onto the Homer Spit at mile 175. The Sterling Highway ends here just short of 142 miles from its beginning at Tern Lake Junction and nearly 233 miles from Anchorage.

The community, you'll find, enjoys mild and usually pleasant wea throughout the year. It's small enough to be cozy but large enough to have everything you need. The hiking, fishing, photography, and nature-watching opportunities are enormous. There's lots of Alaska history (and prehistory) here, and the people—though individualistic to the core—are as open and friendly as you'll find anywhere.

First, a little orientation: Most residences, city services (hospital, fire department, library, city hall), and government offices are located in what you might call Homer proper. Nearby, the ***Pratt Museum*** (907–235–8635; www.pratt museum.org), which emphasizes natural and cultural diversity on the Kenai Peninsula, has a marine "touch tank" aquarium, a botanical garden, and a museum store. It's located at 3779 Bartlett Street in downtown Homer. Admission is $6, and children under age six are free. The hours are 10:00 A.M. to 6:00 P.M. daily during the summer.

For a true off-the-beaten path shopping location, skip the touristy-looking shops and go to ***Jars of Clay*** at 3857 Main Street behind the theater. There,

Homer away from Home

I had just returned from an outdoor writing workshop on the shores of Tutka Bay in Southcentral Alaska. The ferry had delivered the workshop participants to the dock at Homer, where our cars or our rides awaited us. I was in no hurry to leave, though. The sun was shining, the water was sparkling, and Homer, as I'd discovered soon after moving to Alaska, was my favorite place on earth.

I decided to finally stop in at the Salty Dawg Saloon, with its telltale lighthouse tower and low log cabin. I'd heard so much about it but had never actually seen it. The Salty Dawg is a working man's place full of wiry-framed fishermen, unkempt deckhands, and rugged-looking old-timers. It's a locals' bar, too, despite its location smack on the gift-shop-strewn Homer Spit.

Despite its reputation, we workshop participants—Alaskans but not locals—were not shooed away. The barkeep was friendly and people smiled. Wood shavings covered the floor and old dollar bills plastered the walls. It was dark and the ceiling was low. It felt like nighttime even though it was the middle of an Alaska August summer day.

The Salty Dawg has a rich history. It opened its doors in 1957. It changed hands in the '60s, '70s, and '80s, and it survived a near-miss when a nearby general store caught fire in 1994. It has been added onto, revamped, and remodeled.

But still it remains the same uniquely Alaskan place that it was when it first went up. This tough little Alaska bar, like the tough Alaskans who frequent it, will be here for years to come. And I'll make a point of being there every now and again myself.

—Melissa DeVaughn

within her home, artist Ruby Haigh sells some beautiful handmade pot-
.y—both useful and decorative. The prices are reasonable, too. The shop is
open 11:00 A.M. to 6:00 P.M. Monday through Saturday. Reach her at (907)
235–8533 or check out her Web site at www.jarsofclaypottery.com.

Most visitor attractions and services are located on the 5-mile narrow gravel
bar called the **Homer Spit.** The spit, which never sat very high above sea
level, dropped 4 to 6 feet during the 1964 Alaska earthquake, but it nonetheless continues to be the site of countless visitor shops, eateries, commercial
wharfs, docks for waterborne sightseeing and fishing cruises, parking places,
campsites, and a prime port for the Alaska Marine Highway System's oceangoing ferry *Tustumena.*

The **Salty Dawg Saloon,** one of Alaska's best-known frontier bars, is
located on the spit, as is **Homer Ocean Charters,** just a few doors down.
Charter owners Roark Brown and Rick Swenson offer customized sightseeing, bird-watching, bear viewing, kayaking, and charter fishing trips throughout Homer's surrounding and scenic Kachemak Bay. Guided all-day kayak
trips start at $130 and include guide and water taxi into some of Kachemak's
more scenic finger bays. Birding excursions, which include lunch, are $60 per
person. For more information call (800) 426–6212 or visit www.homer
ocean.com.

Here's one of my favorite trips to take while in Homer: the evening **dinner ferry** aboard the beautiful wooden boat, the **Danny J,** past **Gull Island**
and on to the artist community of **Halibut Cove**, across the bay from Homer.
You'll disembark there and explore the numerous boardwalks that connect the
homes and galleries in this isolated community. On a sunny Alaska summer
evening, you'll think you've entered a postcard. The last time we were there,
we watched a seal slip in and out of the water onto a nearby dock and peer at
us quizzically, as if it were playing peekaboo. To top off your tour, you'll eat
dinner at Halibut Cove's sole restaurant, the **Saltry,** which has some of the best
food you'll eat in Alaska—period. The seafood is, obviously, fresh caught, and
the salads taste like they were just picked from a nearby garden. My husband
and I had unforgettable halibut seviche that, despite many tries, we've never
been able to replicate. The cost of the ferry is $28 per person for the evening
departures, and meals are separate. The charge for noontime daytrips is $48.
For reservations call **Central Charters** at (800) 478–7847 or visit www.central
charter.com and click on the Halibut Cove link.

If you enjoy nautical travel under your own steam, **True North Kayak
Adventures** (907–235–0708; www.truenorthkayak.com) takes small groups of
experienced and inexperienced kayakers into the wild beauty of Kachemak
Bay for full-day close encounters of the sea otter kind (plus porpoises, sea

lions, and shorebirds). Day trips start at $139 per person, and overnight trips start at $350, with family rates available.

Rainbow Tours, on Cannery Row Boardwalk on the Homer Spit (907–235–7272; www.rainbowtours.net), will book you for a guided all-day *Kachemak Bay* whale-watching tour that promises glimpses of some of the area's humpback, minke, orca, and fin whales. The 65-foot MV *Rainbow Connection* departs daily at 9:00 A.M. and returns at 6:00 P.M. for a full day of cruising Kachemak Bay and Kennedy Entrance, the entrance to Cook Inlet. The cruise also includes a visit to Gull Island, Eldred Passage, and the isolated city of *Seldovia.* Enjoy five hours of whale watching from Seldovia to Kennedy Entrance and, if the weather permits, a venture to the Barren Islands, a U.S. Fish and Wildlife National Maritime Refuge. The cost is $125 for adults, $95 for children, and includes lunch.

Rainbow Tours also offers an affordable $35 round-trip shuttle to Seldovia, the picturesque waterfront community that once billed itself as "307 Friendly People and a Few Old Crabs" on its city Web site. Seldovia originated as a Russian sea-otter hunting station and today relies on fishing, fish processing, some timber operations, and summer tourism. The city's picturesque boardwalk dates to the 1930s. Birders can collect lots of views of bald eagles here, as well as of sea- and shorebirds, and sightings of sea otters from excursion boats are common. Check out the *Buzz* (907–234–7479) coffeehouse while you're there. Not only do they make some great warm beverages, but they also have some neat gift items for sale.

If you're aiming to stay in Seldovia—which happens to be a great mountain-biking destination—a great bargain can be had at *Seldovia Seaport Cottages* (907–234–7483; www.acsalaska.net/~seaportcottages), where three separate cottages rent from $90 to $125 per night, with up to as many as five guests per cottage. Each cottage comes with a kitchenette and full bath, and mountain bikes are free for the borrowing on a first-come, first-served basis.

Homer, you'll find, abounds in charter boats, especially for halibut fishing. The town calls itself the Halibut Fishing Capital of the World. You'll see incoming anglers hang their halibut on scales at the dock and record catches in the 50-, 100-, even 200-to-300-pound classes. Check at Central Charters, mentioned earlier, for any number of charter-boat operators who will be glad to take you on your own halibut-hunting expedition.

Cranes' Crest Bed and Breakfast, at 59830 Sanford Drive (907–235–2969 or 800–613–2969; akms.com/cranes), enjoys a 1,200-foot elevated view of Kachemak Bay, Homer Spit, mountains, glaciers, and coves—not to mention sandhill cranes, wildflowers, berry bushes, and moose. Rates start at $100. For adventurous youngsters in your party, proprietor Kate Gill can provide a metal "igloo" where the young ones can camp out in their own sleeping bags for $35 per night.

Seaside Farm Hostel is many things: It's a large working homestead in the best Alaska tradition, a B&B, a campsite for tenters, a place to rent cabins— and a hostel with overnight accommodations in the main ranch house and a large cabin. There's an open-sided kitchen on-site for hostelers and campers. Hostel prices begin at $20, campsites cost $10, and cabins are $55. For reservations call (907) 235–7850 or visit www.xyz.net/~seaside.

George Parks Highway— Southern Section: Anchorage to Denali National Park

Now, back to Anchorage. Truth to tell, it's a little difficult sometimes to know exactly which highway you're traveling on in Alaska. The *George Parks Highway* between Anchorage and Fairbanks is a good example, because for the first 35 miles of the trip you're really on the Glenn Highway, which eventually takes you to Tok. The George Parks Highway starts at its junction with the Glenn at about mile 35 on the latter road, but the mileposts on both show the distance from Anchorage. To read about places to see and things to do on the first 35 miles out of Anchorage, see the discussion of the Glenn Highway–Tok Cutoff in the Glenn Highway section of this chapter.

The George Parks Highway, it should be noted, is among Alaska's best. You encounter some rough spots and frost heaves along a few portions (so keep driving speeds within safe limits), but generally it is among the wider and most modern in the state. It cuts through some of Alaska's most urbanized country as well as some of the state's wildest and most scenic. You can see Denali (Mount McKinley), North America's highest mountain, from a number of places, and the highway provides access to two of the state's most popular state and national parks.

At about mile 35.5 you can access the *Mat-Su* (for Matanuska-Susitna) *Visitors Center* (907–746–5000; www.alaskavisit.com). Especially if you plan a side trip to Palmer, a few miles east on the Glenn Highway, stop for information.

About mile 39.5 you come to the *Wasilla* city limits and shortly thereafter Wasilla's Main Street. There your choices are several: Head north a block to 323 Main Street and visit the community's *Dorothy G. Page Museum* (907–373–9071), a visitor center, and historical park. Go north as well to access the Wasilla Fishhook Road to *Independence Mine State Historical Park,* or turn south across the railroad tracks to drive along the Knik Road. Especially if you're interested in learning more about sled dog racing, head left on this road and drive for a couple of miles to the ***Iditarod Trail Committee Headquarters and Visitor Center.*** (Look for the large, colorful sign.) You can view historical mushing exhibits and films, see sled dogs, meet a musher, and shop for mushing souvenirs. The center is open daily in summer and does not charge admission. Phone (907) 376–5155. Nearly 14 miles down the road from the Parks Highway junction and about ½ mile after you come to the village of ***Knik,*** you'll find the ***Knik Museum and Sled Dog Mushers' Hall of Fame.*** In addition to mushers' portraits, mushing equipment, and Iditarod Trail historical exhibits, you can see artifacts from Knik village's gold rush (1898–1916) beginnings. The museum building itself dates to that period. Admission is $2. It's open June through mid-September from 2:00 to 6:00 P.M. Friday through Sunday. Call (907) 376–2005.

If you'd like to get up close and personal with some sled dogs and go for a spin on a sled equipped for summer travel, check out ***Dream a Dog Farm*** at mile 64.5 of the Parks Highway. Veteran musher Vern Halter opens his kennels to the public from May through September. An Iditarod presentation, kennel tour, and sled dog ride run $65 per person. If you're really in love with the sport, you can stay on as a bed-and-breakfast guest or sign up for a Mushing Adventure Camp. Call (907) 495–1198 or visit www.vernhalter.com for more information.

Another fun way to see the Valley is by horseback. ***Alaska Riding Adventures*** (907–745–8768) offers guided and unguided riding by the hour as well as overnight rides, pack trips, and ATV rentals.

Looking to overnight in the valley? ***Alaska Birch Cottages*** (907–745–0558; www.alaskabirchcottages.com) are a great option. Choose from six newer cottages conveniently located between Palmer and Wasilla, all offering fireplaces, Jacuzzi tubs, furnished kitchens, vaulted ceilings, and screened-in porches for enjoying the woods without the bugs. Kitchens are stocked with homemade wheat rolls, free-range eggs, and other breakfast goodies for your first night's stay. Rates begin at $130 per night.

Another fun, Alaskan-style place to stay is the ***Motherlode Lodge*** at mile 14 Palmer Fishhook Road (907–746–1464; www.motherlodelodge.com). The rooms are nothing fancy, and there's no television or Internet access, but that's all part of the charm. The Motherlode is a popular ski spot in the winter, and they traditionally offer Sunday with jazz music once a month. Summer rates start at $140 per night.

At mile 47, turn left on Neuser Drive for ¾ mile to the road's end at the ***Museum of Alaska Transportation and Industry.*** It features, in the words of the Mat-Su Visitors Center, "ten acres of neat ol' stuff," including airplanes, locomotives, farm and construction rigs, plus "trucks and vehicles that built Alaska." Admission is $8 for adults, $18 for families. Call (907) 376–1211 or visit www.alaska.net/~rmorris/mati1.htm. Hours are 10:00 A.M. to 8:00 P.M.

Just past mile 52 on the George Parks Highway, the Big Lake Road leads to (you guessed it) *Big Lake* and any number of lodges, B&Bs, eateries, service stations, shops, fishing supply stores, public and private RV facilities, and several smaller lakes joined to the big one. If you're interested in a different kind of overnight experience, consider *Big Lake Houseboat Rental,* which will lease you a six-guest houseboat on which you can cruise more than 50 miles of shoreline. Contact (907) 892–9187. *Suggestion:* Big Lake is one of Anchorage folks' favorite weekend getaway locales. Plan your own Big Lake visit Monday through Thursday to miss the madding crowd.

Nearing mile 99 from Anchorage, you come to a 14½-mile spur road to *Talkeetna,* one of several Alaska communities often compared to the once-popular mythical TV town of Cicely on *Northern Exposure.* There's a visitor center right at the Parks Highway junction. Busloads of tourists stop to check out this quaint Alaskan town, but if you want a real Alaskan view of the community, attend one of Talkeetna's quirky festivals. The famous Wilderness Woman Contest and Bachelor Auction event is looking for a new sponsor, but the Moose Dropping Festival in July and the Talkeetna Bluegrass Festival in August still attract visitors from around the state. For more information visit www.talkeetnachamber.org.

Near the end of the spur road, stop in at the *Talkeetna Historical Society Museum,* located on the village airstrip, which is almost in the middle of town. Formerly a schoolhouse built in the mid-1930s, the museum contains displays and information from its gold-mining past as well as items commemorating the life of famed bush pilot Don Sheldon. Talkeetna is definitely a walk-around town, so pick up a walking tour map at the museum, then wander about, taking pictures of the community's WELCOME TO BEAUTIFUL DOWNTOWN TALKEETNA sign, the historic old *Talkeetna Roadhouse,* the old *Fairview Inn,* and various other log and clapboard houses and structures spread along Talkeetna's streets and paths.

Steve Mahay's *Mahay's Riverboat Service* offers two very different sightseeing options out of Talkeetna: the Wilderness Jetboat Adventure, priced at $55 for adults, and the Three Rivers Tour for $95. The former is a leisurely two-hour, 10-mile adventure in which you will see how trappers lived at the turn of the twentieth century and visit an authentic trapper's cabin with its rustic furnishings. Your guide will display raw furs from the local area and demonstrate trapping methods. Naturalists will acquaint you with the wildflowers and plants that grow in abundance along the river system. The latter trip is three-and-a-half hours long and offers much the same as the first trip, only this one, Mahay says, is your best opportunity to see bears. Mahay operates two boats, the fifty-five-passenger *McKinley Queen* and the fifty-passenger *Talkeetna Queen*. Call (800) 736–2210 or visit www.mahaysriverboat.com.

When they're not busy airlifting climbers to base camps on Denali (Mount McKinley) in the spring and early summer, Talkeetna's several excellent bush flight services take visitors on airborne flight-seeing forays around North America's tallest mountain, sometimes even landing on a glacier's icy surface. Among the companies offering such services is Talkeetna-based **K2 Aviation** (800–764–2291 or 907–733–2291; www.flyk2.com), which offers statewide air tours and a variety of Denali Park air tour options. Prices for flight-seeing out of Talkeetna start as low as $180. The appropriately named McKinley Climber Tour takes you to 20,000 feet for a dramatic view of McKinley and Denali National Park and views of the Alaska Range extending north and west to the horizons. The one-and-a-half-hour tour is $275 per person.

Talkeetna's longest-operating (since 1946) air taxi service is Cliff Hudson's **Hudson Air Service** (800–478–2321; www.hudsonair.com). The second generations of Hudsons can take you on scenic flights, land you on Denali's glaciers, and provide wildlife viewing excursions. Talkeetna, incidentally, is also accessible by daily summer Alaska Railroad train service from Anchorage or Fairbanks. Call (800) 544–0552 for information or visit www.alaskarailroad.com.

Denali National Park and Preserve, of course, gets lots of attention, and properly so. But there's another Denali Park, **Denali State Park,** which deserves more mention than it gets. You enter this park at mile 132 on the Parks Highway, and you're within its boundaries until mile 169. In between, you can enjoy fine dining or lodging with indescribable views of Denali at **Mary's McKinley View Lodge** ($90, double occupancy) at mile 134.5 (907–733–1555). Or you can pitch a camp in the stellar lake, stream, and forest country at **Byers Lake Campground** at mile 147. The overnight fee is $10. *Caution:* Especially if you go hiking in the woods there, make noise. Grizzlies roamed the area last time we camped at this site.

At roughly mile 210 on the Parks Highway you arrive at **Cantwell** and the junction of the Parks and Denali Highways. Before hurrying on to Denali National Park, spend a little time around this small community, which many pass by. (For details see the section on the Denali Highway in the chapter on Interior Alaska.)

The entrance to Denali National Park and Preserve lies just past mile 237. For information about exploring and enjoying this grand national parkland, see the following chapter on Interior Alaska.

Glenn Highway:
Anchorage to Glennallen

The **Glenn Highway** is one of the most traveled routes in Alaska. It's also one of the most scenic. The sky-piercing Mentasta and Wrangell Mountains abut this route. It dissects long, wide valleys of spruce, alder, and birch forests, and in the Matanuska and Susitna Valleys it courses through Alaska's principal agricultural districts. The Glenn provides the principal access between Anchorage and Tok on the Alaska Highway.

Alaskans often talk about the Anchorage–Tok link as if it were one road. (And, indeed, the state Department of Highways designates it, plus part of the Seward Highway and all of the Sterling, as Alaska Route 1.) To be accurate, however, we should note that the 328-mile route actually consists of two separate highways and part of a third—the Glenn itself, which extends 189 miles from Anchorage to Glennallen; a 14-mile portion of the Richardson Highway, from Glennallen to Gakona; and the 125-mile Tok Cutoff, extending from Gakona to Tok, where it connects with the Alaska Highway.

southcentral alaskatrivia

Eagle River, which flows 9 miles north of Anchorage, heads at Eagle Glacier and was named in 1916. Before that, miners and trappers called it Glacier River and Sitk Creek. Before that, Alaska Natives called it Yukla-ina. Today a thriving community lies along the banks of Eagle River, about 15 miles north of Anchorage.

We'll explore the Glenn and Richardson sections of the highway in this Southcentral Alaska section of the book; you'll find the Tok Cutoff portion in the following chapter on Interior Alaska.

Leaving Anchorage on the Glenn, you pass access roads to Elmendorf Air Force Base and Fort Richardson, and about 13 miles out, you come to a community called **Eagle River,** most of whose residents work in Anchorage. (By the way, if you happen to like sushi, skip all the choices in Anchorage and make the drive out to Eagle River. A great little place, called **Shine's Sushi,** has excellent sashimi and plenty of inventive rolls from which to choose. Call 907–622–8889.) From downtown Eagle River, drive 12.5 miles easterly on the Eagle River Road to Chugach State Park and the nonprofit **Eagle River Nature Center.** There's lots of good information to be picked up here, including hiking maps and updates on recreation sites in one of Alaska's and America's largest state parks. Take a short hike on nearby trails, and check out nature walks and other get-togethers offered by area naturalists. The center also rents out a public-use cabin and two yurts for $65 a night each; it's the perfect overnight getaway if you're not prepared for a long trek. The cabin, built in 1998, is only a little more than a mile down the trail behind the nature center. The yurt is a few minutes away from the cabin. Both have woodstoves, firewood, and sleeping platforms. Just bring yourself and a taste for the wilderness. *A bit of a warning:* Bears are sighted here often, so be on the lookout and give way to the bruins at all times. Also, make your reservations early. The sites are popular and book up fast. Parking at the center is $5, unless you're staying at the cabin or yurt, in which case it is complimentary. For more information call (907) 694–2108 or visit www.ernc.org.

Eklutna Village and ***Eklutna Historical Park,*** 26 miles from Anchorage, is another of those priceless little places that many pass by in their rush to get from Anchorage to some more publicized travel attraction. Through historical records, oral history, and archaeology, the Athabascan village can trace its occupancy of this area back an astonishing 350 years. To get to the park, exit left off the Glenn Highway at Eklutna. The road leads to the nearby park. A half-hour tour starts with an orientation in the Heritage House, which has art displays and lifestyle exhibits. The tour then leads, on a guided gentle walk, to a tiny little Russian Orthodox church built in the 1830s. Visitors then move on to a more modern church and, finally to the village cemetery, where the dead lie buried beneath small, colorfully painted spirit houses. Admission is $5. Phone (907) 688–6026 or visit www.alaskaone.com/eklutna.

A great getaway is just a few miles away at ***Eklutna Lake,*** where you can rent a kayak and paddle beneath the vistas of Twin Peaks. Mountain-bike rentals also are available. Call ***Lifetime Adventures*** at (907) 746–4644 or visit www.lifetimeadventures.net.

Just before mile 30 on the Glenn, you have the opportunity to turn right onto the Old Glenn Highway. Both the Glenn and the Old Glenn end up in Palmer, but the older route offers options such as a view of ***Bodenburg Butte,***

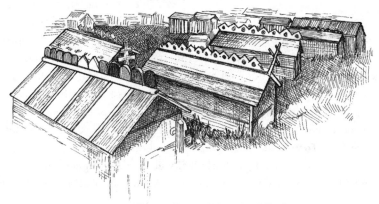

Spirit houses at Eklutna Historical Park

access to a nice view of Knik Glacier, and the opportunity to see original Matanuska Valley colony farms. At the **Williams Reindeer Farm** on Bodenburg Loop Road (which begins at mile 11.5 on the Old Glenn) you can see, pet, and even feed reindeer. The farm also now boasts a moose, elk, buffalo, and Sitka black-tailed deer. Admission charge is $6. Call (907) 745–4000 or point your Web browser to www.reindeerfarm.com.

At the end of the Old Glenn Highway, and at mile 42 on the Glenn, lies **Palmer,** borough seat for the Matanuska Susitna Borough and a major hub for trade and agriculture in the Mat-Su Valley. It's also the site during the eleven days preceding Labor Day each year of the **Alaska State Fair** (www.alaska statefair.org). (Actually, other celebrations in the state share that designation, but none other is so large and well attended.) It's here, incidentally, that you can see and photograph the valley's huge and famous vegetables, including cabbages that sometimes reach close to one hundred pounds. There are lots of other food and animal exhibits as well as carnival-type rides and—perhaps most fun of all—political booths filled with Alaskan activists gathering petition signatures and giving out information about whatever is politically hot at the moment.

southcentral alaskatrivia

Though the Alaska summer is short, the long daylight hours produce incredibly large vegetables. Each August, gardeners bring their biggest to the Alaska State Fair in Palmer, where the produce is weighed in. The largest cabbage wins its grower $2,000. The record holder is a 105-pounder.

Just beyond Palmer, the partly paved, partly gravel **Fishhook Road** at mile 49.5 on the Glenn Highway offers a delightful side trip to wide-open spaces and vistas. The main attraction along the road, however, is fascinating **Independence Mine State Historical Park,** about 17 miles from the Glenn Highway junction. The cost is $3 for a tour, plus $5 to park. Call (907) 745–2827. There's no charge for gold panning in the park, and rangers at the visitor center (the old mine manager's house) will direct you to the best prospects. Located on a private inholding within the 761-acre park is the A-framed **Hatcher Pass Lodge,** perched at a 3,000-foot elevation and offering cabins, rooms, and meals. The rate is $99 per night for a room, $165 for the cabins. Call (907) 745–5897 or visit www.hatcherpass lodge.com. Some great biking can be had around Hatcher Pass for those who like fat-tire cycling. **Alaska Backcountry Bike Tours** can guide you on an all-day or multiday adventure in the area and beyond. Owner Tony Berberich will share his years of mountain-biking experience with experts and novices alike. An all-day bike ride at Eklutna Lake

State Recreation Area is $109. For those with more experience, a ride along Johnson Pass is $129. Multiday trips range from $395 for three days and two nights to $1,195 for seven days and six nights. Ask about rates for a Hatcher Pass excursion, which can be arranged individually. Call (866) 354–2453 or visit www.mountainbikealaska.com.

Eventually the 49-mile Fishhook Road joins with the George Parks Highway at Willow—or you can backtrack to the Glenn Highway. Just off the Glenn Highway at about mile 50, a former farm from the old colony days now houses the *Musk Ox Farm* in Palmer, the only one of its kind in the country. About seventy of the animals (sort of a scaled-down water buffalo with long hair) live there. Their highly prized qiviut wool is knitted (only by Alaska Natives) into hats, scarves, and other items. An ounce of qiviut is eight times warmer than an equal amount of sheep's wool. The farm is open to the public 10:00 A.M. to 6:00 P.M. May through September. Admission is $8. For information call (907) 745–4151 or visit www.muskoxfarm.org.

If you'd like to walk on a glacier—minus the expense of a high-priced helicopter tour—the *Matanuska Glacier* offers a rare opportunity to do so. Turn off the Glenn Highway at mile 102 and take the gravel road to *Glacier Park Resort* (888–253–4480; www.matanuskaglacier.com), which is perhaps a rather grand description for a pretty basic camping and tenting area plus gift shop, laundry, showers, liquor store, and snack foods. It nonetheless merits its $8.00 admission fee for adults ($4.50 for children) because from the parking lot you can stroll right up onto the glacier. If you use common sense, it's safe, but be cautious on the ice. It can be slick. And be on the lookout for crevasses that can run deep and cold. Camping at the resort is $15. Other ways and places to view the glacier include the *Matanuska Glacier State Recreation Site* and camping area ($10 per site) at mile 101, the state highway pullout just past mile 101.5, and Majestic Valley Wilderness Lodge at mile 114.9, which, according to one of our faithful readers, is immaculately well kept and with a comfortable family room for reading and rooms starting at $105. Make reservations ahead of time and the owner will make a wonderful home-cooked meal for $12 to $28. For more information call (907) 746–2930 or visit www .majesticvalleylodge.com.

At mile 113.5 lies *Sheep Mountain Lodge* (877–645–5121 or 907–745–5121; www.sheepmountain.com), established nearly a half century ago. If you can tear yourself away from the lodge's hot tub and sauna, there's great sheep viewing by telescope as well as excellent hiking and skiing in the area. From the lodge you can head out on over 12 miles of cleared trails leading into the mountains. Visit in late summer or early fall and you may come away with a great stash of wild berries. Rates start at $149 for two in a cabin and $60 for up to four people in the bunkhouse.

Another worthwhile side trip, just short of 20 miles each way, takes you to **Lake Louise** via the Lake Louise Road, which begins just before mile 160 on the Glenn Highway. Several fine fishing and outdoor lodges as well as a state recreation area and campgrounds are located on this lake in one of the North Country's premier water/mountain/glacier settings.

Evergreen Lodge is located on beautiful Lake Louise and provides lodging and B&B accommodations starting at $100 per night. The long-established lodge (907–822–3250; www.alaskaevergreenlodge.com) also operates flight-seeing tours and guided fly-out fishing. After a hearty breakfast, guests can enjoy boating, swimming, and hiking in and around the lake. If you're lucky you'll catch a glimpse of a moose, caribou, or bald eagle. Dinner at the lodge must be arranged in advance. **Lake Louise Lodge** (907–822–3311 or 877–878–3311; www.lakelouiselodge.com) also offers year-round accommodations, including rustic cabins and rooms with decks overlooking the lake. To fully enjoy the lake, paddle out in the canoe included with your stay. Rates start at $100 per night.

If you're tenting or driving an RV, **Tolsona Wilderness Campground** lies ¾ mile north of the noise and traffic of the highway at mile 173 and is set in the forest beside Tolsona Creek. One of its attractions is a primitive 1-mile hiking trail to an active mud spring, where gases bubbling up from lower Cretaceous and upper Jurassic formations carry fine particles of silt to the surface to form a 2,075-foot hill from which the spring emerges. The spring itself flows year-round and is a source of water for wildlife, especially in the cold and frozen months of the year. Also, be sure to check out the proprietor's varied collection of turn-of-the-twentieth-century artifacts. It's a museum tour—for free! The fee for tenters is $20, for RV hook-up campsites $28. Call (907) 822–3865 or visit www.tolsona.com.

The Glenn and Richardson Highways meet and blend at Glennallen. Beyond this community, for 14 miles you're really traveling on the Richardson Highway and therefore the mileposts indicate miles from its start at Valdez. Then, at Gakona Junction, the Richardson continues north to Delta Junction and Fairbanks, while the **Tok Cutoff,** on the Anchorage–Tok route we're discussing here, courses northeasterly. You're right, it can be a little confusing, so be alert.

And . . . not to confuse you further, beyond Glennallen you're really traveling in Interior Alaska, so for information about the more northerly portions of this route, refer to the chapter on Interior Alaska.

The Richardson Highway—Southern Section: Valdez to Gakona Junction

When you drive on the 368-mile Richardson Highway, you're traveling along a historic gold rush route first pioneered in 1898 as the Valdez–Eagle Trail. The trail at that time, however, began with a treacherous start literally over the ice of Valdez Glacier, a fact that devastated or turned back many a would-be prospector before he ever started his trek to the gold fields. The following year Captain W. R. Abercrombie created an alternate route through Keystone Canyon and across Thompson Pass, bypassing the glacier. The route—first a sled dog and horse trail, now paved and fully modern—has been a major Alaskan land link between Prince William Sound and the Interior ever since. Today the Richardson connects Valdez with Delta Junction and Fairbanks. Now in its second century, a few of the road's pioneer (but now renovated) road-houses remain along the way, reminders of the era when warm, welcome accommodations were spaced a day's horse- or dog-team travel apart.

As you head north, check out the ***Crooked Creek Salmon Spawning Viewing Area*** at mile 0.9 of the Richardson Highway. In July and August the creek is teeming with salmon, and you can get a close look with the underwater video cam inside the U.S. Forest Service Station.

The canyon drive into or out of Valdez is one of Alaska's most spectacular, with high, steep walls and no small number of breathtaking waterfalls. The sur-rounding mountains are likewise high, rugged, and spectacular. Of special note are ***Bridal Falls*** at mile 13.8 of the Richardson Highway and ***Horsetail Falls*** at mile 12.8. These make for good photo ops, plus there's a nice interpretive plaque on gold rush history at the Bridal Falls pullout. If you have some time to stretch your legs, take the 2-mile ***Valdez Goat Trail,*** a restored section of the military pack train trail that allowed miners to bypass the more hazardous route over glacial ice.

It sounds pleasurable and it is: ***Blueberry Lake State Recreation Site,*** with loop entrances at both mile 23 and mile 24 along the Richardson, is a visual delight and a favorite campground for Alaskans. An alpine area situated above timberline, the site offers a sweeping sight of Keystone Canyon as well as close-up views of dwarf plants and other flora usually associated with northern tundra. It's also the natural habitat for Alaska's state bird, the willow ptarmigan. Flocks of dozens are not uncommon. The state camping fee is $12 per night.

At mile 26 you come to 2,678-foot ***Thompson Pass,*** where winter snow-fall totaling nearly 1,000 inches has been recorded. The long, tall poles alongside the road guide snowplows and snowblowers in the snowy season. About 2½ miles beyond the pass is *Worthington Glacier State Recreation Site,* where you'll find displays and exhibits explaining the huge river of ice. You can, if you'd like, drive up practically to the glacier.

At about mile 83 you come to the paved 35-mile Edgerton Highway to *Chitina* (pronounced CHIT-na; the second "i" is silent), which connects at the highway's end with the 60-mile gravel McCarthy Road. This road, in turn, leads over a former railroad bed to the near-ghost towns of *McCarthy* and *Kennecott* within *Wrangell–St. Elias National Park.* Take the time to drive at least to Chitina, stopping en route perhaps at *Kenny Lake Mercantile and RV Park* (at mile 7.5) to top off your gas tank or, if you're pulling a rig, to drop off your RV and proceed unencumbered. In fact, you can even leave your car and RV here if you wish. This is a pickup point for scheduled van service to McCarthy and Kennecott. Call (907) 822–3313 or visit www.kennylake.com for details. Rates are $12, $20 with electric hookup. If you enjoy collecting nature scenics, stop at mile 23.5 at bubbling, forested Liberty Creek and thunderous Liberty Falls in *Liberty Falls State Recreation Site.* The highway itself bisects rolling hills and takes in views of wide, forested valleys, grand lakes, and the imposing peaks of the Wrangells. If you're really lucky, you may even see bison herds across the Copper River.

The *Chitina National Park Service* (907–823–2205) has a ranger office, and the staff there can tell you about park and local attractions as well as conditions on the McCarthy Road, which begins where the Edgerton ends. Picturesque Chitina is almost a ghost town—just ask the locals, who have painted humorous, ghostly pictures on a few of the town's abandoned turn-of-the-twentieth-century structures. Hand-hewn log cabins, western-style stores, and rusting old cars, trucks, and wagons give testimony to the town's gold rush past.

If you're game, by all means continue beyond Chitina on the McCarthy Road, but be advised that it can be a slow, bumpy, and narrow. It can also be pretty muddy in the rain. Still, the rewards are many when you make it to the road's end at the Kennicott River and, after all, this is off-the-beaten-path travel at its best. McCarthy, the town for which the road is named, lies across the river and you can access it easily by a footbridge across the water.

About two dozen hardy souls call McCarthy home, including the owners of *McCarthy Lodge Restaurant and Saloon* as well as the *Ma Johnson Hotel* (circa 1916). Visitor rooms, all of which are located in the hotel, are in the early-twentieth-century tradition, long and slender and furnished in Victorian decor. The hotel does, however, offer modern shared baths. The $159 rate for two includes custom bathrobes and slippers for use at the hotel. Call (907) 554–4402 or visit www.mccarthylodge.com. The same friendly folks run *Lancaster's Backpacker Hotel,* with rates starting at $48 per person.

The *McCarthy Museum,* housed in the old railway depot, displays items and photographs from the community's mining glory days. Five miles down the road (van pickup is available) lies the abandoned town and copper mine of *Kennecott* plus *Kennicott Glacier Lodge,* a thoroughly modern, thoroughly elegant thirty-six-room lodge, most of it built in the style and decor of the surrounding old structures. Rates for the Kennicott Glacier Lodge, including transport from McCarthy and three meals a day, begin at $152.50 per person per night, double occupancy. Call (800) 582–5128 or visit www.kennicottlodge .com for details. There's lots of exploring and poking around to be done in this National Historic Landmark community.

I before E, unless You're a Miner

Is it Kennecott with an "e" or Kennicott with an "i"? The river and glacier, deep in the Wrangell Mountains, are Kennicott, named for Robert Kennicott. The much-photographed mine, with its deep-red buildings, is known today as Kennecott due to a misspelling made in 1906.

The Kennecott Mines Co. established a camp and offices on the bank of National Creek, meaning to take its name from the Kennicott Glacier 3 miles to the north. But inadvertently its owners dropped the "i" and added an "e." It stuck. In 1908 the U.S. Postal Service established the post office of Kennecott. The town, which grew to a population of 494 by 1920, took its name from the mining company. During its heyday the Kennecott mined more than 590,000 tons of copper ore, making it the richest copper mine in the world. By 1938 copper prices had crashed and the company closed the mine.

To visit the mine you must make a sometimes harrowing drive to the town of McCarthy. From Glennallen follow the Edgerton Highway 66 miles to the hamlet of Chitina, population 49. After crossing the steel-span bridge over the Copper River, you're on the McCarthy Road, which follows the old Copper River and Northwestern Railway built between 1907 and 1911 to carry copper to the town of Cordova on Prince William Sound.

The 60-mile-long McCarthy Road is unpaved and often bumpy. In dry weather it's dusty. In rainy weather it's muddy. Top speed on the road is 20 mph.

For years the final stage of the journey to McCarthy and Kennecott was the hand-pulled cable car used by locals and visitors alike to cross the braided Kennicott River. In 1997 safety concerns finally forced the construction of a railed footbridge to replace the cable car.

Abandoned Kennecott Copper Mine

Two bush flight services based in McCarthy offer a wide variety of flight-seeing, hiker drop-off, and transportation services, including flights to Kennecott and Kennicott Glacier Lodge. **Wrangell Mountain Air** (800–478–1160; www.wrangell mountainair.com) and **McCarthy Air** (907–554–4440; www.mccarthy air.com) can serve you from McCarthy or from Chitina as well as from Glennallen or even Anchorage. Sample rates: Wrangell Mountain Air will ferry you from Chitina to McCarthy (thus relieving you of a long bumpy ride) for $199 round-trip; McCarthy Air tours include backcountry drop-off as well as flight-seeing for $60 to $160, depending upon where you want to be dropped off. Wrangell Mountain Air offers flight-seeing tours as well as hiking, rafting, and glacier-trek fly-ins starting at $90.

St. Elias Alpine Guides (907–554–4445 or 888–933–5427; www.stelias guides.com) offers a wide selection of options, including a Root Glacier Hike for $60 per person. This four- to six-hour trek allows you, while wearing crampons of course, to explore the ice formations, waterfalls, and blue-water pools that make glaciers so exotic. Other day-trek adventure options include river rafting, learn-to-climb instruction, fly-in hikes, history tours, and backcountry skills seminars. Multiday rafting and mountaineering adventures are available. Call for current price information.

Back on the Richardson Highway, you come to the turnoff for **Copper Center** just beyond mile 100. The highway officially bypasses this community, which grew out of a nineteenth-century trading post, but *you* shouldn't. Turn right onto the *Old* Richardson just past mile 100. The historic old **Copper Center Lodge,** still serving travelers as it has since 1897, is today fully modern but well preserved. Rates start at $125 for double occupancy. Call (907) 822–3245 or visit www.coppercenterlodge.com. The lodge's restaurant serves sourdough pancakes made with a starter that can be traced back more than a century. Next door, in a small log cabin, you'll find one of two small but worthwhile stops for history buffs. The **George Ashby Memorial Museum** houses mining, trapping, Indian, and pioneer relics and displays. Half the cabin is an authentic old log bunkhouse. And within the museum you can walk through the actual iron doors of the old Copper Center Jailhouse. There is no charge, but donations are accepted. The other (relatively recent) historical stop is the log *Chapel on the Hill,* at mile 101 on the Old Richardson Highway, constructed in the early forties by U.S. Army servicemen. Daily free slide shows give visitors a visual look at Copper Valley and its features.

Driving north from Copper Center, the old segment of the Richardson Highway connects with the north end of the bypass at mile 106, and you're officially back on the Richardson.

The park headquarters and visitor center for the *Wrangell–St. Elias National Park and Preserve* (the nation's largest, at 13.2 million acres) is located at mile 106.8 on the Old Richardson Highway, just north of Copper Center. The park, which is the size of six Yellowstones, contains nine of the sixteen highest peaks in the nation—not to mention countless glaciers, forested valleys, and many species of wildlife. The headquarters is your source of information about park hiking, camping, road access (extremely limited), and attractions. Call (907) 822–5234.

At mile 115 the highway meets at *Glennallen* with the Glenn Highway from Anchorage. For the next 14 miles, the Richardson Highway and the Glenn Highway–Tok Cutoff route are the same. Near mile 129 and Gakona Junction, the Tok Cutoff heads northeast, while the Richardson continues north to Delta Junction and Fairbanks.

And now, although there's no official boundary between Southcentral Alaska and the Interior, this is probably a good place to separate the two regions. For information about the northern portion of the Richardson Highway, see the next chapter on Interior Alaska.

Places to Stay in Southcentral Alaska

ANCHORAGE

Anchorage Hotel,
330 E Street;
(907) 272–4553.

Hotel Captain Cook,
Fourth Avenue and K Street;
(907) 276–6000.

CHUGIAK

Birch Trails B&B,
22719 Robinson Road;
(907) 688–5713,
http://home.gci.net/~birch
trails/

CORDOVA

Cordova Rose Lodge;
(907) 424–7673,
www.cordovarose.com

GIRDWOOD

Alyeska Resort,
1000 Arlberg Avenue;
(907) 754–1111.
Luxury in the heart of the Girdwood skiing community.

HOMER

Land's End,
4786 Homer Spit Road;
(907) 235–2500.
At the end of the Homer Spit.

SEWARD

Seward Windsong Lodge,
Mile ½, Exit Glacier Road;
(877) 777–4079,
www.sewardwindsong.com
On the road to Exit Glacier,
just outside Seward.

SOLDOTNA

Goodnight Inn Lodge,
44715 Sterling Highway;
(907) 262–4584.
Right by the Kenai River.

Places to Eat in Southcentral Alaska

ANCHORAGE

Arctic Roadrunner,
2477 Arctic Boulevard;
(907) 279–7311;
5300 Old Seward Highway;
(907) 561–1245.

Glacier BrewHouse,
737 West Fifth Avenue;
(907) 274–2739.
Great Alaska seafood
and freshly prepared
side dishes that are both
artful and tasty.

**Gwennie's Old Alaska
Restaurant,**
4333 Spenard Road;
(907) 243–2090.

Lucky Wishbone,
1033 East Fifth Avenue;
(907) 272–3454.

Marx Brothers,
627 West Third Avenue;
(907) 278–2133.
Imaginative menu of
contemporary cuisine near
the waterfront.

**Moose's Tooth
Pub & Pizzeria,**
3300 Old
Seward Highway;
(907) 258–2537,
www.moosetooth.net
Gourmet pizza
and microbrew.

Ristorante Orso,
Fifth Avenue and G Street;
(907) 222–3232.

Snow City Cafe,
1034 West Fourth Avenue;
(907) 272–CITY.
Creative breakfasts and
lunches in slightly Bohemian
atmosphere. Wonderful
weekend brunches.

EAGLE RIVER

Shine's Sushi,
Eagle River Shopping Center
Old Glenn Highway;
(907) 622–8889.
Extensive menu of sushi,
sashimi, and cooked
Japanese fare.

HOMER

Cafe Cups,
162 West
Pioneer Avenue;
(907) 235–8330.
Eclectic combination of
vegetarian, prime seafood,
and meat in an artistic,
relaxed setting.

The Saltry,
on the dock at Halibut Cove,
across from Homer on
Kachemak Bay;
(907) 296–2223.
Fresh-caught Alaska
seafood.

SEWARD

**Resurrection Bay
Roadhouse,**
mile ½, Exit Glacier Road;
(877) 777–4079,
www.sewardwindsong.com
Just outside of Seward.
Broad menu, but the pizza is
the best.

Interior Alaska

From one point in Alaska's interior region—the summit of Denali (Mount McKinley)—climbers can literally look down on every other mountaintop, hill, ridge, valley, and plain in North America. (Although McKinley is the name the federal government officially recognizes for the continent's highest peak, Alaskans, noting that President William McKinley, of Ohio, never once laid eyes on even a little mountain in Alaska, greatly prefer to use the beautiful Athabascan Indian name for the peak, *Denali,* which means "the high one." Entreaties from the Alaska legislature and Alaska's delegation in Congress to officially change the name, however, have fallen on deaf ears.) The view from Denali may explain why Interior Alaskans speak in such expansive terms about their region of sky-piercing mountains, rolling hills, long and mighty rivers, subarctic tundra lands, and vast taiga forests. This is gold-mining country and has been since Felix Pedro's 1902 strike near present-day Fairbanks. It's oil country as well, at least in the sense that a large share of the 800-mile Trans-Alaska Pipeline passes through the Interior on its way from Prudhoe Bay to the coast at Valdez.

And the Interior is grand traveling country. It's a land of long roads and riverways and remote fly-in lodges and cabins.

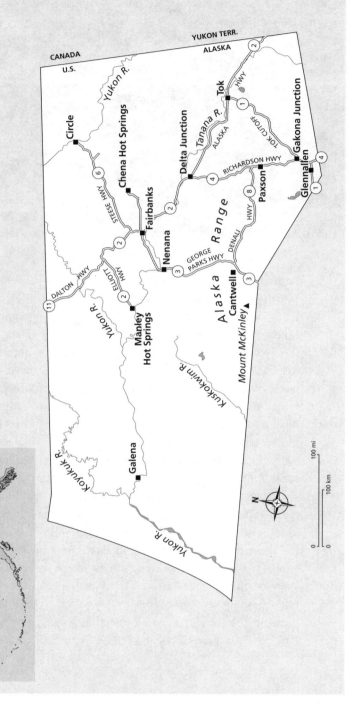

INTERIOR ALASKA

YUKON TERR.
ALASKA
CANADA
U.S.

Yukon R.

Circle

Chena Hot Springs

STEESE HWY

6

Fairbanks

2

Nenana

2

ELLIOTT HWY

2

Manley Hot Springs

DALTON HWY

11

Yukon R.

Koyukuk R.

Galena

Kuskokwim R.

Yukon R.

Delta Junction

Tanana R.

Tok

ALASKA HWY

1

TOK CUTOFF

Gakona Junction

4

Glennallen

1

RICHARDSON HWY

4

Paxson

8

DENALI HWY

GEORGE PARKS HWY

3

Cantwell

Mount McKinley

A l a s k a   R a n g e

3

N

0   100 mi
0   100 km

It is a place with a rich Athabascan Native culture, and a place of grizzlies, moose, caribou, wolves, and scores of smaller species. It's a warm and balmy region in the summer, though temperatures can plummet to sixty *below* in the winter.

Fairbanks, about 300 miles from the Canadian border and the second-largest community in Alaska, serves as transportation and travel hub for the region, and for that reason we describe the many facets of Fairbanks at the beginning of this chapter. We then deal with pleasurable things to see and do along Interior Alaska's roads and highways, most of which (but not all) lead to or from Fairbanks. We will examine the Interior portions of the state's four multiregion highways in the same order in which they appeared in earlier chapters. Specifically we'll describe the Alaska Highway from the border (where we left off in the Yukon chapter) to the highway's end at Delta Junction. We'll examine the northern portions of the George Parks Highway connecting Anchorage and Fairbanks and the Glenn Highway–Tok Cutoff route, which runs from Anchorage to Tok. And of course we will cover the northern portion of the Richardson Highway that begins at Valdez and ends in Fairbanks. We'll look, too, at the Steese Highway from Fairbanks to Circle City on the Yukon River. Not to be omitted in these pages are the smaller and often-overlooked Denali Highway and the Elliott Highway.

Fairbanks

A bustling, busy, dynamic city is *Fairbanks,* on the banks of the Chena River. Fairbanksans call it the Golden Heart of Alaska, and it was indeed gold in the early years of the century that brought about the founding of the town.

When in 1901 Captain E. T. Barnette set out from St. Michael, at the mouth of the Yukon River, aboard the stern-wheeler *Lavelle Young,* he intended to

TOP 10 PLACES IN INTERIOR ALASKA

Camp Denali and North Face Lodge	Husky Homestead at Goose Lake Kennels
Chena Hot Springs Resort	
	Rika's Roadhouse
Cleft of the Rock Bed and Breakfast/Alaska Biking Adventures	Tangle Lakes Lodge
Denali National Park and Preserve	A Taste of Alaska Lodge
Denali West Lodge	University of Alaska Museum of the North

Denali's Wife

Traveling through Alaska, you'll notice reference to a mountain called Foraker, a 17,400-foot peak at the head of Foraker Glacier in Denali National Park and Preserve. It was named in 1899 for Joseph Benson Foraker, a U.S. Senator from Ohio. It wasn't uncommon at the time to name mountains, valleys, and towns after political officials, even if they had never stepped foot on Alaska soil.

But Foraker wasn't always singled out. When Russian explorers first discovered North America's highest peak, officially called Mount McKinley after President William McKinley, they saw Foraker in its shadow and thought it to be part of the same mountain. They called the two, collectively, Bolshaya Gora, or "Big Mountain." Likewise, before the Russians, the Tanana Indians of the Susitna River Valley also considered Foraker and McKinley one mountain, calling the massif *Denali,* meaning "the great one" or "the high one."

However, the Tanana Indians in the Lake Minchumena area had a broadside view of the massif and could differentiate the two peaks. They referred to Foraker as *Sultana,* the "woman," or *Menlale,* meaning "Denali's wife."

establish a trading post in the gold prospecting area at Tanana Crossing, about halfway between Valdez and Eagle. He didn't get that far, however. The ship couldn't navigate the shallow Chena River beyond present-day Fairbanks, so he established his post there. And a fortunate choice it turned out to be. Felix Pedro, an Italian prospector, discovered gold in the area a year later, and a "rush" to Fairbanks soon followed.

The *Fairbanks Convention and Visitor Bureau Information Center* (907–456–5774; www.explorefairbanks.com), right downtown on the banks of the Chena River at 550 First Avenue, provides lots of up-to-date information on things to see and do, places to go, restaurants, and overnight options. For a free visitor's guide to the Golden Heart City, call (800) 327–5774. In the summer of 2008, the Fairbanks Convention and Visitor Bureau Information Center moves to the new Morris Thompson Cultural and Visitor Center at 101 Dunkel Street. For the traveler seeking offbeat options, an even more important resource is the *Alaska Public Lands Information Center,* which you'll find on the lower level of Courthouse Square, at Cushman Street and Third Avenue. Here you'll see displays, wildlife mounts, cultural artifacts, and basic information about the Interior's outdoor touring, camping, and recreational opportunities. There is no admission charge. Call (907) 456–0527 or visit www.nps.gov/aplic/center.

The *Riverboat* **Discovery** *Cruise* is Fairbanks' most popular tour, yet it's also very much an off-the-beaten-path and educational experience. Twice daily, at 8:45 A.M. and 2:00 P.M., the vessel departs from its docks at 1975 Discovery Drive (southwest of downtown) for a cruise down the Chena and Tanana Rivers. En route, as the hustle and hurry of Fairbanks fades farther and farther behind, passengers learn about the Native Athabascan peoples of this area—some of whom are onboard as guides—as well as the history of gold rushes and oil booms and homesteading hereabouts. They watch as huge fish wheels, powered by stream currents, scoop fish into large holding baskets from the rivers they're cruising. If they're lucky they even see moose in the woods along the shore. Finally the vessel stops at a river island for a visit at *Old Chena Indian Village.* As visitors wander from site to site on the island, they see how Athabascan Indians and Eskimos from farther north smoke fish, tan wildlife hides, sew leather, bead garments, and live in a harsh but bountiful environment. Sled dog mushing demonstrations, often including visits with pups, are part of the fun. The cost is $49.95. Call (907) 479–6673 or (866) 479–6673 or visit www.riverboatdiscovery.com.

If you're interested in birds, *Creamer's Field Migratory Waterfowl Refuge,* only 1 mile from downtown, provides great viewing of huge flocks of ducks and geese in the spring and fall and sandhill cranes during the summer months. Toward the end of August, when up to 3,000 cranes may grace the fields at any given time, you can enjoy the festivities at the annual *Sandhill Crane Festival,* featuring a guest speaker, guided nature walks, workshops, and dinner. At other times you can walk along a 2-mile self-guided nature trail and visit the restored farmhouse that now serves as visitor center. The start of the trail is located at 1300 College Road. College Road is one of Fairbanks's principal east-west thoroughfares. Donations are accepted. Call (907) 452–5162.

> **interior**
> alaskatrivia
>
> Between 1926 and 1957 the Fairbanks Exploration Company mined approximately $70 million worth of gold from the Fairbanks area.

Close by Creamer's Field, at 2600 College Road, you can shop at the *Tanana Valley Farmer's Market* (906–456–3276; www.tvfmarket.com) for fresh veggies, meats, bakery items, flowers, and craft goods on Wednesday from 11:00 A.M. to 4:00 P.M.; Saturday from 9:00 A.M. until 4:00 P.M. It's the only market of its kind in Interior Alaska, open during the summer months only.

At the *University of Alaska Museum of the North,* on the UA Fairbanks campus, northwest of downtown, you can view natural and historical exhibits, such as an incredible 36,000-year-old Steppe bison that was almost perfectly preserved in Alaska's permafrost until its discovery in the twentieth century. Also on display are contemporary wildlife mounts (including a really humungous brown bear), the state's largest exhibit of gold, Native art, plus an exhibit on the aurora borealis (northern lights). The $42 million museum building is by far the most dramatic architecture in Fairbanks. In the new art gallery, you'll see the full spectrum of Alaskan art, from primitive carvings to contemporary pieces. Don't miss the photo opportunity in the "designer outhouse," crafted from found items that offer a whimsical take on local culture. Plan at least two to four hours for your visit, especially if you're going to take in one of the twice-daily multimedia presentations on the aurora and winter activities (cost for the presentations is $7). Museum admission is $10, $9 for seniors, and $5 for children ages seven to seventeen; children under six are free. The museum is open daily. Call (907) 474–7505 or visit www.uaf.edu/museum.

For your photo collection of strange beasties of the Arctic, tour the university's considerably less visited *Large Animal Research Station* (907–474–7207; www.uaf.edu/lars), off Yankovich Road north of the main campus. Half-hour and one-hour tours are offered during the summer, at prices ranging from $6 to $10. There, among other animals, you'll find the shaggy, horned musk ox, once hunted to extinction within Alaska. With the help of imported animals from Canada, the species is making a comeback. UAF also offers Wednesday afternoon tours of the *Geophysical Institute* (907–474–7558), where scholars ferret out knowledge of the earth's deepest regions and the heaven's northern

TOP ANNUAL EVENTS IN INTERIOR ALASKA

Chatanika Days Outhouse Races:
Here's something different in the Interior community of Chatanika off the Steese Highway. Held each March, this winter festival also includes a long-johns contest and snow-machine tug-of-war. (907) 389–2164

Ice Art Competition:
Held each March in Fairbanks, this world-class competition features the world's best ice carvers, who make intricate ice sculptures. (907) 451–8250; www.icealaska.com

World Eskimo-Indian Olympics:
Held every July in Fairbanks. (907) 452–6646; www.weio.org

Mainstreet Alaska Sourdough Potlach:
In Tok each August. www.tokalaskainfo.com

Tanana Valley State Fair:
Summer brings all sorts of state fairs to Alaska, but this one in Fairbanks is the largest in the Interior. The fair begins in early August and features Alaska's famous giant vegetables along with a large midway, live entertainment, and animal exhibits. (907) 452–3750; www.tananavalleyfair.org

This Is Sled Dog Country

The yapping of dogs on a usually busy downtown street in Fairbanks drew me to the crowd of spectators. I am a dog lover, an animal lover actually, so it was only natural that I check out what was going on. I was greeted with the North American Sled Dog races, one of the most competitive sprint sled dog races in the world. I watched in awe as teams of twenty or more dogs were hooked up to one little wooden sled with one musher standing at the runners, and I wondered how in the world these people can control so many excited, yanking, lunging dogs.

When I first moved to Alaska and got into the sport of mushing, I'm sure I was like most novices. I thought it would be fun, like taking a ride on a snow machine and having complete control. Well, it's not that way at all. I ran eight dogs the first time I took to the runners of a sled, and in retrospect I realize that was about six too many for a beginner. But my mushing buddy was confident in my ability (or he just wanted to get a good laugh!) and he told me this: "No matter what, don't let go of the sled."

We took off out of the dog yard, and I immediately felt out of control. The sled whipped and bumped, and the dogs were absolutely intent on running as fast as they possibly could. Within a half mile, the sled slid out from under me on a turn, and I was being dragged and bounced along behind it—but still holding on. The dogs never looked back. I somehow righted the sled as we continued, and I brushed myself off. Five minutes later I repeated my antics, still clinging desperately to the handlebow, and righted myself just in time to see Gus, with his team ahead of me, looking back to check my progress.

In Fairbanks I watched the North American teams cross the finish line. It took more than a simple snow hook to brake these dogs. Groups of men and women came from the finish-line crowd and lunged at each sled as it crossed, helping to slow the dogs, while the musher stood with all his or her weight on the brake. The dogs looked no slower coming in than they had leaving the starting chute.

Today, with my own small team, I can truly appreciate what I saw that day in Fairbanks, which serves as a sort of hub for Interior mushers. I never underestimate a dog's power, I never assume a run will go perfectly, and, no matter what, I never let go of the sled.

—Melissa DeVaughn

lights. And for the botanically inclined, the university will give you a guided visit to the Agricultural and Forestry Experiment Station's *Georgeson Botanical Garden.* Call (907) 474–1944. Guided tours are on Friday afternoon. Admission is $1.

In 1967, wanting to commemorate the one hundredth anniversary of Alaska's purchase from Russia in a lasting way, the people of Fairbanks and the State of Alaska created a forty-four-acre pioneer theme park called Alaska 67. Later renamed Alaskaland, now it's called *Pioneer Park* (907–459–1087) and

interior
alaskatrivia

Sled dogs, like wolves, foxes, and coyotes, curl up to protect less heavily furred parts of their bodies from extreme cold. Often these sleeping canines will allow falling or drifting snow to cover them, providing more insulation from the cold air.

continues in business on Airport Way. There's no admission charge to enter Pioneer Park, but there are fees to visit some portions of the park. Among various things to see and do, especially during the summer months, you'll find a genuine sternwheeler riverboat (the SS *Nenana,* a National Historic Landmark), the Gold Rush Town of relocated and restored homes and stores from Fairbanks's early days, the frontier Palace Theatre and Saloon, a miniature mining valley, a pioneer air museum of early aircraft, plus one of the two best salmon bakes/barbecues in Alaska. (The other is in Juneau.) Circling it all is the ***Crooked Creek & Whiskey Island Railroad,*** not terribly authentic, perhaps, but it is fun and a good way to get the lay of the land before you start wandering around the acreage.

For the culturally curious, one of Pioneer Park's most interesting locales is the ***Native Village,*** where Athabascan Indian young people proudly entertain and educate visitors with stories and ancient dances. In the village museum, where you'll note a pleasant faint scent of cottonwood-smoked animal skins, you'll see artifacts, tools, weapons (such as a bear-killing spear), and art, including masterful beadwork. The young people share legends, history, and their techniques of survival in one of the harshest environments on earth. There's also an Athabascan *kashim,* a log house with sod roof, as well as a traditional underground sod home of the type once used by Alaska's Eskimo peoples. There is a modest admission fee to the village.

Here's a chance to collect another Alaska superlative. If you're a golfer and want to play some really far-out golf, be aware that two courses in Fairbanks lay claim to being the farthest north golf course in the world. Friends in the city tell me that the ***North Star Golf Club*** is actually a tad more northerly (though on the opposite side of the city) than the ***Fairbanks Golf and Country Club—*** but who's measuring? The thing to do is play them both. You'll find North Star northeast of town off Old Steese Highway on Golf Club Drive. Call (907) 457–4653 or visit www.northstar golf.com for tee times. The Fairbanks Golf and Country Club is located northwest, near the intersection of Farmers Loop Road and Ballaine Road. Phone (907) 479–6555.

You can relive some of Fairbanks's gold heritage at a working gold mine and visitor operation called ***El Dorado Gold Mine,*** about 9 miles northwest of Fairbanks on the Elliott Highway. You'll be treated to a short train ride on a tour of old and new "diggin's" at the mine, then a demonstration of how sluic-ing and panning for gold work. Once you're ready, they turn you loose with a pan of your own and some ore that's guaranteed to contain "color." You can keep all you find. The experience runs $34.95. Call (907) 479–6673 or (866) 479–6673 or visit www.eldoradogoldmine.com.

Historic **Gold Dredge Number 8,** at mile 9 on the Old Steese Highway, is a restored relic from an important mining era in Alaska's gold country. Between 1928 and 1959 this huge, floating hulk, five decks high and 250 feet long, scooped $3 billion worth of gold from creeks near Fairbanks. You can take a guided tour of the now-inoperative dredge for $25, which includes the tour, a video presentation of the dredge in action, and gold panning. Seven tours are operated daily in the summer beginning at 9:30 A.M. Time your visit between 11:00 A.M. and 3:00 P.M.; lunch is served in the dining hall for $9.75 for adults. Call (907) 457–6058.

If you get to Alaska and wish you had brought your bike or canoe or what have you, be sure to stop by **Alaska Outdoor Rentals and Guides LLC** near the Peger Road entrance to Pioneer Park. The com-pany has thirty years of experience in rent-ing out just the thing you'll need for your outdoor experience. Call them at (907) 457–2453 or visit www.2paddle1.com.

Among the smaller Alaska-based tour companies operating out of Fairbanks is **Trans-Arctic Circle Treks Ltd.** (800–336–8735 or 907–479–5451; www.arctic treks.com). Trans-Arctic Circle Treks offers one- to four-day adventures across the northern portion of the state. An overnight Chechako special to the Arctic Circle will take you from Fairbanks to the Arctic Cir-cle in the comfort of a fifteen-passenger van. The cost is $149.

interior
alaskafacts

The geographic center of Alaska lies 60 miles northwest of Mount McKinley (Denali), at 63 degrees-50 north, 152 degrees west.

The Yukon River is Alaska's longest river. It runs 1,400 miles from Canada to the Bering Sea.

The first oil pumped through the 800-mile Trans-Alaska Pipeline took thirty-eight days, twelve hours, and fifty-four minutes to arrive in Valdez.

Anaktuvuk Pass is the last remaining settlement of Nunamiut Eskimos, the inland Inupiat whose ancestors date to 500 B.C.

The Brooks Range includes nine groups of mountains, but not Mount McKinley, which is in the Alaska Range.

Alaska is one of those places where, even if you don't imbibe, you really ought to visit a few of the more colorful frontier saloons. In Fairbanks at least three watering holes match that description: the **Palace Theatre and Saloon** at Pioneer Park (907–456–5960); the **Dog Sled Saloon** (907–452–1888) in the

Malemute Saloon, Fairbanks

Captain Bartlett Inn, itself rather a colorful log motel, at 1411 Airport Way; and the *Malemute Saloon,* at the Ester Gold Camp (907–479–2500) just off mile 351.7 on the George Parks Highway. The last is one of those atmospheric places frequented by locals as well as visitors where patrons throw peanut shells on the sawdust floor and gawk at the artifacts and the art junk on the walls. Both the Palace and the Malemute offer great shows in the summer; call for details.

Anaktuvuk Pass north of the Arctic Circle on the northern edge of the Brooks Range is a place worth seeing. The pass is both a geographic location and a Nunamiut ("People of the Land") Eskimo village. Your surroundings are the majestic peaks encompassed in Gates of the Arctic National Park. Its villagers still live a largely subsistence caribou-hunting and fishing lifestyle.

Warbelow's Air Ventures, Inc. (907–474–0518; www.warbelows.com), a family-owned business with forty-plus years of flying, offers year-round tours of outlying villages at rates ranging from $149 to $649 per person. The Bush Flight Experience includes pilot briefing and a one-hour flight over the Trans-Alaska Pipeline and along historic Goldstream Valley. Or hop aboard a flight to Fort Yukon, where you'll travel with a Native guide along the Yukon or Porcupine River, with stops at a Native fish camp and a chance to catch feisty northern pike. Another popular tour goes to Gates of the Arctic National Park and the Nunamiut Eskimo village of Anaktuvuk Pass. Additional options include the Bush Mail Flight, Journey Above the Arctic Circle, and Koyukuk National Wildlife Refuge fishing expedition.

Here's a unique way to see the "land of the midnight sun," as Alaska is often referred to in the summer: by hot air balloon. *Midnight Sun Balloon Tours* in Fairbanks can take you floating over the land in its colorful, 106,000-cubic-foot hot air balloons. See the Tanana Valley, watch for sandhill cranes as they migrate, and keep a keen eye open for moose and bears. The balloon is so quiet it can sneak up on animals in their natural habitat without scaring them off. Call (907) 456–3028 or visit www.alaskaballoontours.com.

Koyukuk National Wildlife Refuge, which totals almost four million acres, is home to excellent birding ventures, but access can be a challenge. The area encompasses a vast floodplain containing fourteen rivers, hundreds of streams, and thousands of lakes. More than 400,000 ducks and geese migrate south from the refuge each year. Check with local air taxi services for access to the area, or call the refuge headquarters in Galena at (907) 656–1231.

interior alaskatrivia

The town of Glennallen derives its name from the combined last names of Captain Edwin Forbes Glenn and Lieutenant Henry T. Allen, who explored the Copper River region in the late 1800s.

If you're looking for a classic, woodsy Alaska wilderness–type lodge located twenty minutes from downtown, *A Taste of Alaska Lodge* at 551 Eberhart Road off Chena Hot Springs Road (907–488–7855; www.atasteofalaska.com) is the answer to your quest. The main lodge is a 7,000-square-foot natural log structure featuring six guest rooms and two suites, all with private baths. Other accommodations on the 280-acre spread include a two-bedroom log house with private hot tub, a one-bedroom frame house, and a five-person hot tub building. Guests enjoy views of Mount McKinley, the Alaska Range, and the Trans-Alaska Pipeline. Year-round rates range from $175 to $225 per night for single or double occupancy; there is a charge of $25 per night for additional guests. The rates include a full breakfast, cable TV and wireless Internet, and access to gold panning at a private claim.

Set on Chena Ridge among towering spruce with panoramic views of the Tanana Valley, the Alaska Range, and Fairbanks is *Aurora Express* (1540 Chena Ridge Road; 800–221–0073 or 907–474–0949; www.fairbanksbedand breakfast.com). Owners Mike and Susan Wilson have made a business of renovating railcars to use as attractive rooms for guests. Among their lodging options are the National Emblem, which has two bathrooms and sleeps up to five people—a good choice for families; the Arlene, a private car with two bedrooms; the National Domain, four rooms, each with private entries and private baths; and the Golden Nelly, a special room in the caboose (the locomotive is there just for looks). Rooms range from $115 to $250. Breakfasts are beyond the description of "full," and are more like a Sunday brunch every day. Don't be surprised to find king crab Muenster crepes, fruit tortes, and any number of elegant offerings. Breakfasts are buffet-style in the Diner Car, which also houses satellite TV and phone service for all guests.

ror standard Alaska fare that is prepared nicely, try the **Pumphouse Restaurant,** at 796 Chena Pump Road. The seafood is particularly good. Phone (907) 479–8452 or visit www.pumphouse.com. **Pikes Landing,** on the Chena riverbanks, at 4438 Airport Way, is another favorite. We usually choose the casual outdoor setting on the large deck (907–479–6500). Or try the **Two Rivers Lodge** (907–488–6815), at mile 16 on the Chena Hot Springs Road, where your choices range from seafood to steaks and Cajun cuisine.

The Alaska Highway: U.S. Border to Delta Junction

Now, back to the Alaska Highway, where, in the Yukon chapter, we left off at the U.S.–Canada border. Your first stop in Interior Alaska, mandatory if you're coming in from Canada on the Alaska Highway, is the U.S. Customs and Immigration Station at mile 1,221.8, right at the international boundary. The station sits sort of out in the middle of nowhere, with no large community nearby.

At mile 1,229, similarly situated, the U.S. Fish and Wildlife Service maintains a log cabin visitor center with an observation deck and outdoor exhibits about Alaska's wildlife. There's more of the same indoors, along with animal mounts and lots of good information about Alaska's fish, birds, and other wild critters.

At mile 1,302 you come to the Tetlin Junction, a meeting of the Alaska Highway and the Taylor Highway, which extends north to Eagle. The Taylor, in turn, provides access to the Canadian Yukon Territory's Top of the World Highway to Dawson City, Yukon. For information about these roads, see the sections after Dawson City in the chapter "Canada's Yukon."

You'll come to the next major highway junction at mile 1,314, right in the middle of **Tok** (rhymes with joke), where the Alaska Highway, heading sort of west, meets the Tok Cutoff–Glenn Highway from southwesterly Anchorage. Just before the junction you'll see the **Alaska Public Lands Information Center** (907–883–5667; www.commerce.state.ak.us/oed), where you can get tons of information about state and federal lands, waters, and outdoor recreation. Audiovisual aids, wildlife mounts, and helpful staff will provide you with the latest about places and things to do both on and off the beaten path. Also worth a visit is **Alaska's Mainstreet Visitor Center** (907–883–5775; www.tok alaskainfo.com), operated by Tok's chamber of commerce. The center, also at the above-mentioned junction, is located in the largest one-story log structure in the state. It features a number of mounted wildlife and birdlife dioramas. The visitor center opens in May and offers free trip-planning services to walk-ins.

For a quiet retreat after days on the road, check out **Tok Line Camp Bed and Breakfast.** Tucked in the woods are two 16-by-20-foot cabins with indoor plumbing, kitchenette, double bed, and futon in each. Rates are $100 per night, and the kitchen is stocked with the fixings for a continental breakfast. Call (907) 883–5506.

If you're interested in gold and great local lore, check out the **Jack Wade Gold Company and Mining Museum.** Owner Diane Achman will show you all sorts of artifacts from two family mines dating from the 1880s, including a mammoth tooth with roots, musical instruments, and photos of mining then and now. Don't miss the collection of gold nuggets, including a hefty five-pounder. You can get information here on places to pan for gold, but if you're not willing to count on

> ## interior alaskatrivia
>
> The lowest body temperature recorded in a living mammal is minus 2.9 degrees Celsius in hibernating arctic ground squirrels. A high sugar condition may keep the animals' blood from freezing.

your luck, check out the gold jewelry for sale in the shop. It's all made by Diane from gold mined in the Forty-Mile District. The shop and museum are located in the Snowshoe Motel at mile 1314 of the Alaska Highway. Call (907) 883–5887.

Here in Tok the locals take sled dog racing, Alaska's official state sport, very seriously. You can see mushing equipment and puppies at the **Burnt Paw Gift Shop and Cabins** (907–883–4121; www.burntpawcabins.com), mile 1,314.3 on the Alaska Highway, or stay overnight and get to spend quality time with the animals. **Westmark Hotel** (907–883–5174 or 800–544–0970; www.westmarkhotels.com), near the Alaska Highway–Tok Cutoff junction, is another lodging option. You can ride a dogsled pulled by an ATV at **Mukluk Land Theme Park,** at mile 1,317. Call (907) 883–2571 for more information. Admission is $5.

Speaking of sled dog racing, winter visitors can see mushers and their dogs almost any weekend working out or racing on the **Tok Dog Mushers Association Trail,** which starts at their log headquarters building at mile 1,312.8 on the Alaska Highway. Spectators can view the 20-mile course from many points along the highway.

If you'd like to start your day and your visit in a thoroughly Alaskan way, try the all-you-can-eat sourdough pancake breakfast with Alaska reindeer sausage at the **Sourdough Campground,** 1½ miles south of the junction on the Tok Cutoff. The cost is $7. During tourist season, dinner is served nightly at 6:00 P.M. in the pavilion. Your meal comes complete with fresh pie and homemade ice cream. After dinner there's free live entertainment featuring

Alaskan performers. Sourdough is a full-service campground, with laundry, wireless Internet, car and RV wash, and gift shop. Phone (907) 883–5543.

For a tasty end to your day, try *Tok Gateway Salmon Bake,* at about mile 1,313, which features outdoor grilled king salmon, halibut, ribs, and reindeer sausage. It's open 11:00 A.M. to 9:00 P.M. every day except Sunday, when it opens at 4:00 P.M. Phone (907) 883–5555 or visit www.tokalaska.com. Prices start at $11.95.

Perhaps your best lodging option in Tok is John and Jill Rusyniak's *Cleft of the Rock Bed and Breakfast,* 1½ miles down Sundog Trail and 3 miles northwest of Tok. The Rusyniaks have guest rooms and suites as well as Alaska log cabins, with rates ranging from $85 to $125. A hot breakfast is served each morning. The B&B is situated in a black spruce forest with bike trails nearby, which is convenient since the Rusyniaks also own *Alaska Biking Adventures.* They offer bike rentals and guided wilderness tours ranging from two hours to all day. Guided trips are $25 to $65. Bike rentals start at $5 an hour, but guests get a nice discount. To access either business call (907) 883–5775 or visit www.cleftoftherock.net.

interior
alaskafacts

The three highest mountain peaks in North America are in Alaska: the South Peak of Denali (20,320 feet), the North Peak of Denali (19,470 feet), and Mount St. Elias (18,008 feet).

At six million acres, Denali National Park and Preserve is about the size of Massachusetts.

Collared pikas, tiny members of the rabbit family, can be found in both the southern Brooks Range and the Alaska Range.

Fairbanks is the state's second largest city, with a population of nearly 86,000 in the greater Fairbanks area.

The earliest recorded breakup date and time for the Nenana Ice Classic was April 20, 1940, at 3:27 P.M. The latest breakup occurred May 20, 1964, at 11:41 A.M.

If you're traveling by RV or roughing it in a tent, *Tok RV Village* (907–883–5877) at mile 1313.4 of the Alaska Highway is a good choice. They offer 160 sites with showers, vehicle wash, TV and Internet terminals, pull-throughs, and double pull-outs. There's also a gift shop on-site.

Flight-seeing can be had through *40-Mile Air,* which will take you over the Alaska Range to see glistening glaciers. The fifty-minute flights offer you a chance to see moose, bears, and Dall sheep. Call (907) 883–5191.

When you get to *Delta Junction,* at mile 1,422, you've come to the end of the Alaska Highway. From that point on north, the road to Fairbanks is the Richardson Highway, and the mileposts beside the road indicate distance from

Valdez. Delta Junction's Richardson Highway milepost is 266. For infor[...] about the Richardson from Delta Junction north, see the section in this c[...] on the Richardson Highway.

The George Parks Highway— Northern Section: Denali to Fairbanks

The George Parks Highway, you'll recall, runs for nearly 360 miles from near Anchorage on the shores of Cook Inlet, to Fairbanks. In our Southcentral chapter, we followed the course of this excellent highway to Denali National Park and Preserve, where this section picks up this road once more.

For many, Denali National Park and Preserve is the high point of an Alaska vacation. (No pun was intended, but as a matter of fact, the top of Denali Mountain, at 20,320 feet, is the highest point in North America.) And in the surrounding parklands, visitors may well see more game—moose, grizzly bears, caribou, Dall sheep, perhaps even wolves plus any number of smaller creatures and birds—than anywhere else they travel in the state.

It should be noted, however, that much of the park and its environs are by no means off the beaten path. In particular, the strip along the George Parks Highway near the mile 237 park entrance overwhelms with hotels, lodges, motels, cabins, RV parks, and varied visitor services. Most of the overnight accommodations there are roomy, nice, and comfortable, like *Denali's Crow's Nest Log Cabins,* at mile 238.5 (907–683–2723 or 888–917–8130; www.denali crowsnest.com). Some of them, such as the *Denali Princess Wilderness Lodge* (800–426–0500; www.princesslodges.com) and *Grand Denali Lodge* (907–683–5100 or 800–276–7234; www.denalinationalpark.com) properties, are quite superior. But the sheer numbers of such places provide ample evidence that many thousands of visitors beat down this path every summer. So where, if you're a dedicated offbeat traveler, can you stay? And what can you do away from the crowds?

Actually you have options, not the least of which is to pitch a tent or park your RV at one of seven National Park Service campgrounds within the park itself, then hike in the backcountry hills, valleys, mountain slopes, and open spaces in splendid isolation. Isolation, that is, from the human sort. During the nine-day backcountry trek I went on with a friend a few years back, we were greeted face-to-face by a curious grizzly bear just moments after making a short river crossing. Needless to say, when you're this far off the beaten path, you can expect something like that to happen. Be aware, however, that overnight backcountry hikes require a permit, and the number of backcountry users permitted in a given area is limited. *Another caution:* Campsites within the park are often hard to come by, so it's wise to reserve months ahead if you can by calling the reservations line, (800) 622–7275 (in Anchorage call 907–272–7275). If all advance-reservation camping slots have been assigned for the days you plan to visit, you may be able to reserve space up to two days in advance on a first-come, first-served basis at the Denali Park Service Visitor Center on the main park road, ½ mile inside the park boundary. Thirty percent of the sites are set aside for these walk-in reservations.

If you enjoy day hikes, check the bulletin boards and with the ranger on duty at the information center for the times, location, and degree of hiking skills required for various ranger-escorted treks not only in the park entrance

"Bearly" Escaped

The big brown bear walked deliberately toward me, and I hustled to hoist my pack on my shoulders and start backing away. The instructions of the Denali National Park and Preserve rangers rushed through my mind in a jumble, and I couldn't keep the order straight—drop and play dead or wait until the big bruin charges, stand my ground and shout the thing off (yeah, right . . .), or, despite their warnings, follow my own instincts and turn tail and run as fast as I can with the fifty-pound pack on my back? My hiking partner shouldered her pack and we stood side by side. In a collective but unspoken agreement we began shouting "Go away, bear! Hey, bear! Get out of here, bear!" We waved our walking sticks and tried to make ourselves look ominous, too big of a problem for the bear to mess with.

Still, it walked toward us. At about 7 feet, I turned to Michele. "Do we drop now?" I asked. Michele didn't answer and just kept shouting at the bear. It wasn't being aggressive, no need to play dead. We stayed put, two 125-pound women versus a 450-pound grizzly bear. It came even closer—6 feet, 5 feet, now 4 feet. I could hear my heart pounding and willed it to quiet down for fear of aggravating the bear.

I've been scared before, so scared that the rush of adrenaline set my hands to quivering and my heart to beating extrafast. It's happened during a near miss of a head-on collision, when I almost fell down the steps with my newborn in my arms, when my husband jumped from behind a door to "startle" me. But never have I been more frightened than I was that day in Denali National Park during a nine-day backcountry trek into trailless wilderness.

The bear seemed more curious than aggressive. It stuck its dark, pointed nose in the air and stuck out a cotton-candy-pink tongue. It licked the air, tasting our scent. It herded us a few more feet backward. And it turned and walked away. We stood motionless on the river bar, our sticks still in the air, our mouths set tight with tension. The bear ambled into the brush and was gone.

—Melissa DeVaughn

area but at bus-accessible points along the single road that bisects the park and at the *Eielson Visitor Center* and *Wonder Lake,* near the road's end.

If you're not a camper, consider spending a few days at award-winning *Camp Denali and North Face Lodge,* at the western end of the park road, just outside the National Park Service boundary. This is one of Alaska's best-loved backcountry ecotourism lodges and has been since its founding nearly a half century ago. Guests enjoy breathtaking views of Denali and other peaks of the Alaska Range from hillside log cabins. Meals are served family-style in the main lodge building. Short walks and wildlife-viewing hikes, guided by experienced wilderness interpreters, provide fascinating insight into the nature of things. Canoeing, biking, rafting, flight-seeing, gold panning, and evening natural history talks provide further options. Call (907) 683–2290 or visit www.campdenali.com.

Also at the far western end of the road lies *Kantishna Roadhouse* and the former gold-mining town of Kantishna, now a wilderness resort. The accommodations are in a log lodge and cabins. Attractions include the Smokey Joe Saloon, escorted nature walks, hiking, mountain biking, gold panning, and fishing. Rates, including round-trip bus transportation from Denali train depot, all meals, and most activities, start at $385 per person per night in a twin room. Call (800) 942–7420 or visit www.kantishnaroadhouse.com.

Another all-inclusive option is *Denali Backcountry Lodge,* also in Kantishna. You'll take a narrated tour through the park to reach the lodge, where all meals, lodging, and activities are included at rates starting at $315 per person for quad occupancy. Contact (800) 541–9779 or visit www.denalilodges.com.

Perhaps one of the best—but most expensive; whoever said traveling in bush Alaska is cheap?—options for out-of-the-way lodging can be had at the fly-in *Denali West Lodge,* located on the shores of breathtaking Lake Minchumina. The lodge offers summertime packages that include all food, lodging, and activities such as hiking or paddling on the lake. In the winter there are dog-mushing expeditions that will take you to the base of Mount McKinley for an experience like none other. The cost for a nine-day camping and mushing trip is $8,000, all-inclusive. Lodge-based mushing trips are $4,000 for four nights. Call (888) 607–5566 or visit www.denaliwest.com.

Within Denali Park itself, you'll spot most wildlife during bus or motor-coach tours that run daily on the single park road. Although the park service no longer offers free shuttles on the road as it once did, a program of low-cost bus rides represents a "best buy" option for frugal travelers. The price now for a trip on the road ranges from $22.50 to $43.25 per adult, depending on a visitor's destination in the park. Discounts are available for three- and six-day passes. Note that travelers can now book shuttle reservations and buy tickets through the same toll-free number they can use to reserve campsites, (800) 622–PARK, or via www.nps.gov/dena. Narrated tours in roomier coaches are offered by Denali Park Resorts (800–276–7234; www.denalinationalpark.com). The six- to eight-hour *Tundra Wilderness Tour,* priced at $93.75, travels to the Toklat River in the park and includes a naturalist guide and a boxed lunch. The $62.50 *Natural History Tour* is four to five hours, including a snack and hot beverage.

Denali National Park is one of my favorite places, and I've been there at least half a dozen times. I often wish I lived there, especially if it could be somewhere like Denali musher Jeff King's home. Four-time Iditarod Sled Dog Race champion King, his wife, Donna, their three daughters, and eighty-plus dogs live on a ridge just south of the park, and a tour of this world-class musher's dog yard is a must-see on your itinerary. Called *Husky Homestead at Goose Lake Kennels,* it offers a ninety-minute narrated kennel tour with an in-depth look at dog mushing with one of Alaska's best mushers. King knows how to get to you. As you step out of the van that will take you to his home, you'll be greeted by fluffy, soft-eared, gentle-eyed sled dog puppies—known as Alaskan huskies to those in the sport—that you can cuddle to your heart's content. You'll see summer training in action and learn about what it takes to mush dogs 1,000 miles from Anchorage to Nome. Jeff has lots of interesting stories to tell from his twenty-plus years of mushing—don't be shy, just ask him. Tours are held three times a day in the summer and cost $39 for adults. Phone (907) 683–2904 or visit www.huskyhomestead.com. By the way, Donna Gates King's wildlife art also ranks as one of the "best," in this author's opinion. Check out her work at the kennels, or visit her Goose Lake Studio just outside the park boundaries.

If you're looking for some rugged adventure but hiking's not your thing, try some four wheeling with *Denali Jeep Backcountry Safari.* Your guide and jeep will take you from the park entrance north along Stampede Road, through much of the same wilderness where Chris McCandless met his end as recounted in the book and movie *Into the Wild.* Chances are you'll see some wildlife along the way. Call (907) 561–6777 or visit www.BestofAlaska.com for more information.

Also worth a visit at mile 238 on the Parks Highway, north of the park entrance, is *Denali Raft Adventures'* two-hour Canyon Run raft trip through such exotic-sounding rapids as Cable Car, Coffee Grinder, and Ice Worm. Two- to eight-hour trips are $72 to $159, depending upon the adventure that you choose. Call (888) 683–2234 or visit www.denaliraft.com.

This kind of raft trip will work up your appetite, and if it does, skip the hungry crowds at the park entry eateries and drive south on the Parks Highway to

Who Really Climbed Denali First?

The debate rages on. Who climbed North America's highest peak, Denali, first—adventurer Frederick Cook in 1906 (not to be confused with Captain James Cook, who explored much of Alaska's coastline and named its prominent features in the late 1700s) or Hudson Stuck in 1913? Cook attempted to climb the mountain twice in 1906. He acknowledged defeat on the first attempt but claimed that he made it to the mountain's summit on the second attempt. Many people doubted him, but not having climbed the mountain themselves, they had no way to prove it.

In 1910 a group of Alaskan sourdoughs, during a discussion in a bar, decided they, too, doubted the truth of Cook's story. They decided to climb the mountain themselves and maybe make a rightful claim to fame. So off went Tom Lloyd, Charles McGonagall, Pete Anderson, and Billy Taylor, who, with little climbing experience but lots of Alaska hardscrabble toughness, reached the north peak summit—not realizing that it was actually lower than the south peak—and planted a spruce pole there to prove they had made it. So their ascent wasn't acknowledged either, but it sure gained them lots of respect.

Three years later, along comes the Reverend Hudson Stuck, Episcopal archdeacon of the Yukon, who decided he, too, would get a little closer to God and make his way up the 20,320-foot Denali. He and three other men began the ascent—Harry Karstens, Robert Tatum, and Walter Harper—and reached the summit in June 1913. Their photographs were deemed authentic, and Hudson, for the most part, has claimed this spot in history. As far as being the first man in that group to reach the summit, though, it was Harper who first stood atop the summit. And perhaps rightly so. The name Denali is an Athabascan Indian word for "the high one" or "the great one"—and Harper was an Athabascan Indian.

Today, as many as 1,000 people a year attempt to climb Denali each spring between April and June, but only a small percentage succeed.

mile 224 to **Denali Perch Resort,** a local favorite that offers great seafood and steaks in a wooded surrounding. They also run a pizza pub with hand-tossed pizza. Call (907) 683–2523 or (888) 322–2523 or visit www.denaliperchresort .com. Cabins are also available for rent for $85 per night.

The best and most peaceful lodging, just north of the park entrance, can be had at the **Earth Song Lodge,** run by Jon and Karin Nierenberg. You can stay in one of twelve tastefully built log cabins with private baths. There is a naturalist on staff and evening programs in the coffeehouse. Call (907) 683–2863 or visit www.earthsonglodge.com.

Denali Mountain Morning Hostel and Lodge, near Carlo Creek about a dozen miles south of the park, offers bunking for those with backpacks or on a budget. The cost for a bunk is $25 per person, and private rooms and cabins are available. Families might like the large, seven-person cabin, which is $85 for three. A private room is $75 for two people. Call (907) 683–7503 or visit www .hostelalaska.com.

A nice nearby camping facility is at *Carlo Creek Lodge and Campground* (907–683–2576; www.ccldenaliparkalaska.com). The covered sites are roomy and come with picnic tables and fire pits. Laundry and shower facilities also are available. Rates are $4 per person plus $12 for tents and $14 for RVs.

There are, in addition to park ranger–escorted hikes, several quality commercial firms that offer treks and climbs that vary from tender to tough. Whether you want to climb all the way to North America's highest peak—a rigorous, dangerous climb only strong and experienced mountaineers should attempt—or you want a less-demanding but equally adventurous backcountry wilderness trek, *Alaska Mountaineering School–Alaska Denali Guiding, Inc.,* provides an ample variety of hiking and climbing opportunities. The Talkeetna-based company specializes in guiding small groups to remote areas in the Denali National Park area. Prices range from a four-day, $650 off-trail backpacking experience to the most challenging of all trips—an attempt to reach Denali's summit—for $4,900. Call (907) 733–1016 or visit www.climbalaska.org.

Another fun option for getting up close and personal with Denali is to sign up for one of the small group classes, research internships, or field seminars offered each summer by the *Denali Institute.* You can check out their schedule starting in December of the preceding year by calling (888) 688–1269 or e-mailing courses@denaliinstitute.org.

interioralaskatrivia

The first land- and sea-grant university in Alaska was in Fairbanks, and it was called the Alaska Agricultural College and School of Mines. It opened in 1917 and in 1935 was renamed the University of Alaska. Today there is the University of Alaska Fairbanks, University of Alaska Anchorage, and University of Alaska Southeast, as well as feeder campuses spread across the state.

Back on the George Parks Highway, roughly 300 miles north of Anchorage, you come to *Nenana,* on the Tanana River. (Nenana is pronounced nee-NAN-a; Tanana is TA-naw-naw.) Don't breeze through without stopping at least to see the *Alaska Railroad Museum* in the 1923 railroad depot building alongside the tracks on Front Street. The old-fashioned pressed-tin ceiling is a particular curiosity, and if you happen to be a pin collector, you can pick up lapel pins commemorating not only the Alaska Railroad but various other U.S. and Canadian rail systems as well.

Also worth a look-see is the 1905 log *St. Mark's Episcopal Church,* whose altar is adorned with elaborate Athabascan beadwork. It's located at

Front and A Streets, east of the depot. At Nenana's sod-roof log *visitor center* on A Street, just off the Parks Highway, volunteers will tell you about Alaska's most popular annual statewide guessing game—the Nenana Ice Classic, in which the winner can earn more than $300,000 by predicting when the ice will break up on the Tanana River. For information call (907) 832–5446 or visit www.nenanaakiceclassics.com. If you want to overnight in Nenana, consider *Bed and Maybe Breakfast* (105 Front Street) in the old railroad depot. This structure was built specially in 1923 for then-President Harding's visit to Alaska (incidentally, he died soon after that trip). You can see the Native cemetery and the historic railroad bridge from your window. Phone (907) 832–5556.

If you work up an appetite as you head up the road, you'll want to stop at the *Monderosa Bar and Grill* (907–832–5243) at mile 309 of the Parks High-

interior
alaskatrivia

The language of the Athabascan Indians who inhabit the Interior is closely related to that of the Navajo and Apache.

Nenana means "a good place to camp between two rivers."

way. Folks have been known to drive 50 or 60 miles to order up one of the famous "mondo" burgers. They've got a beautiful natural log building along with patio dining in the summer, and they serve beer, wine, cocktails, steak, and shrimp in addition to their famous burgers.

If you turn off the highway at mile 351 and stay to your right, you'll be at the old gold mining town of Ester. Miners worked the Old F.E. (Fairbanks Exploration) Company dredges here until into the 1950s, and while most of the gold may be gone, this tiny community still shines with local color and unusual characters.

The self-proclaimed "Republic of Ester" is a hodgepodge of dirt roads, cabins, and quirky studios worked by talented artists. To rub shoulders with Esterites, stop by the Golden Eagle Saloon, where even your dog is welcome. If you fall in love with the place and want to take a bit of it with you, pick up a copy of the *Ester Republic* (907–451–9892).

Ester's also a great place to purchase truly original Alaskan arts and crafts. For your own version of what keeps Alaskans warm at forty degrees below, check out Judy Stauffer's *Ester Hatworks* (907–479–5525). Original silver jewelry featuring graceful renditions of some of Alaska's wildlife can be found at *Judie Gumm's Designs* (800–478–4568; www.judiegumm.com).

Glenn Highway–Tok Cutoff— Northern Section: Glennallen to Tok

A word of review about the Glenn Highway–Tok Cutoff from Anchorage to Tok. The route, you'll recall, is actually three segments: 189 miles of the Glenn from Anchorage to Glennallen, 14 miles on the Richardson, and a final 125 miles on the Tok Cutoff. This section begins where the section in the South-central Alaska chapter left off, at Glennallen, where the Copper Valley Chamber of Commerce operates a log cabin visitor center. The center itself is worth a stop and a picture, since plants actually grow from the cabin's sod roof. This is authentic Alaskana. Many a sourdough used this same material for insulation on log cabins in the remote bush country.

Fourteen miles farther, at the Richardson Highway's mile 128.6, the Tok Cutoff begins. *Gakona Junction* is mile 0. Tok, our destination, is located at milepost 125. At mile 2, stop at least for an evening meal (no lunches) at the *Carriage House* dining room of the *Gakona Lodge & Trading Post* (907–822–3482; www.gakonalodge.com). The lodge, built in 1905, originally served travelers on the old Richardson Trail and is now on the National Register of Historic Places.

At mile 36.5 of the Tok Cutoff, *Christochina Bed and Breakfast* offers clean, smoke-free rooms. There's a great view of Mount Sanford from the deck, and trails are nearby. Call (907) 822–3989 or visit www.christochinabed andbreakfast.com.

Just past mile 65 you come to the 45-mile Nabesna Road and one of your few opportunities to actually drive into Wrangell–St. Elias National Park, one of the wildest, most mountainous and least developed in the U.S. park system. Just beyond the junction, at *Slana,* you'll see the *Slana National Park Service Ranger Station.* Inquire about road conditions, especially the last dozen miles or so, which can be quite rough. Just before mile 4 you enter the park itself. For the dedicated backwoods aficionado, *Huck Hobbit's Homestead Campground and Retreat* has two 12-by-12-foot log cabins to rent. To get to the homestead, turn left on the side road at mile 4, drive 3 miles to the signed parking place for your vehicle, then walk an additional ½ mile of trail to Steve & Joy Hobbs's wonderful, rustic getaway. Steve will meet you at the trailhead if you feel nervous about the hike or if you have lots of gear to haul. He will also rent you camping space and a tent if you need one, has canoes available, and will point you in the direction of the best fishing and berry picking. The rates are $20 for a bed and $15 for every night after or $5 for a camping spot. Breakfast is $7. Call for reservations at (907) 822–3196. There are several other lodges and overnight accommodations toward the road, including ***End of the Road Bed and Breakfast*** (907–822–531? These are "plumbing-free" cabins, but a shower room is available and the lodge has plumbing. Driving beyond this point is usually OK in any vehicle—unless it's been raining a lot, in which case creeks can flood the road.

The Glenn–Richardson–Tok Cutoff route from Anchorage to Tok ends at mile 125. (For information about Tok, see the section in this chapter on the Alaska Highway.)

The Richardson Highway—Northern Section: Gakona Junction to Fairbanks

In this section we take a look at the northern portion of the historic Valdez-to-Fairbanks Richardson Highway, commencing at the Gakona Junction where the Richardson meets the Tok Cutoff at mile 128.5.

The terrain along the Richardson continues to reveal tall, majestic mountains, countless big and little lakes, and thick forests. You stand a good chance of seeing moose alongside the road (pay special attention to small ponds, where a huge animal may rise up and break the surface after having scoured the pond's bottom for succulent plantlife) as well as caribou and perhaps grizzly bears. The Trans-Alaska Pipeline shows itself at various times.

If you missed out on king salmon fishing either in Southeast or Southcentral Alaska, you can make up for it here on the Gulkana River. ***Gulkana Fish Guides*** offer raft trips June through July from their headquarters at mile 128.5. Also at the headquarters is ***Gakona Fish Camp Cabins,*** with cabins renting for $139 for two people and $10 additional for each extra person. Call (907) 822–3664 or e-mail gakona@gakonaak.net.

If it's time to stop for the evening, a good place to overnight is the historic ***Paxson Inn & Lodge,*** built in 1903. Call (907) 822–3330.

The Richardson Highway connects with the ***Denali Highway*** at ***Paxson*** at mile 185.5. If you don't plan to drive all 135 miles to Cantwell and Denali National Park, at least consider round-tripping some of the first 21 paved miles of the road. The panoramic views—of glaciers, lakes, and majestic, snow-covered peaks—from the tops of hills, rises, and turnoff viewing areas are just breathtaking.

At mile 266 the Richardson Highway and the Alaska Highway meet at ***Delta Junction.*** Actually, this is where the Alaska Highway ends. The Richardson continues north to Fairbanks and mileposts beside the road continue to measure distance from Valdez.

The **Delta Junction Information Center** (907–895–5068), at the junction of the two highways, is a good place to stop for visitor information and road condition updates. Especially if you had your picture taken at the Alaska Highway milepost 0 monument in Dawson Creek, British Columbia, you'll want to do the same at the highway's end monument at the information center. You can also pick up an "End of the Alaska Highway" certificate for $1.

For campers or RV travelers, there are private and state-owned campgrounds just north and south of town. **Delta State Recreation Site,** at mile 267, is a good, convenient choice that offers twenty-four sites on the banks of the Delta River with views of the Alaska Range. The campground has the basics—water, toilets, and a covered shelter with tables. And at $10 per night, it's more than affordable.

Bald Eagle Ranch Bed and Breakfast offers spacious rooms and serves up full breakfasts made to order. Expect great food and lively conversation. They have cabins and other accommodations as well as rooms in the main house. Horseback trail rides are available, but this popular option books early. Look for the B&B at mile 272 of the Richardson Highway, on the west side. Call (907) 895–5270 or visit www.baldeagleranchbb.com.

Among Alaskans, at least, Delta Junction is probably best known for its herd of 500 or so bison (American buffalo). They're the outgrowth of small numbers of the animals established there in the 1920s and roam freely over the 70,000-acre **Delta Bison Range.** Occasionally the bison spill over into adjacent barley farm fields, and farmers are not amused. If you want to see the herd, you stand a pretty good chance at the visitor viewpoint just past mile 241 on the Richardson. If you'd like to see the **Trans-Alaska Pipeline,** a terrific photo op awaits where the pipeline crosses over the Tanana River at mile 275.

interior
alaskatrivia

Caribou populate the whole of Interior Alaska. They are the only type of deer in which both sexes grow antlers. One of their characteristics is wide hooves, which enable the animal to cross snow, ice, and slippery slopes.

Not to be missed is **Rika's Roadhouse** at **Big Delta State Historical Park,** just upstream from the pipeline river crossing. The roadhouse is right out of Alaska's history. Built in 1910 and purchased by Rika Wallen in 1923, it served for decades as a major overnight stop on the Richardson wagon road and highway for travelers between Valdez and Fairbanks. Today the roadhouse has been restored, as have a sod-roofed museum building, an old U.S. Army Signal Corps station, and other historic structures. Staff in 1920s garb will guide you around the park for an informative tour that includes live farm animals. The ***Packhouse Restaurant*** is one of the best you'll find along Alaska's road system and features home-made soups as well as breads from the Alaska Baking Company on-site. There is no admission charge to visit the road-house, but tent or RV sites at the state campground run $10 per night. Phone (907) 895–4201 or visit www.rikas.com.

Harding Lake, 1½ miles off the Richardson Highway from mile 321.5, is a great place to swim, have a beach picnic, or camp overnight. Avoid it Friday night through Sunday, however. Lots of Fairbanksans drive down for the weekend, and it gets pretty crowded. The camping fee is $10 per night.

As you approach Fairbanks, don't let your desire to get there lead you to bypass the ***Chena Lakes Recreation Area,*** accessible from a 2-mile side road at mile 346.7. Whether you're RV camping or simply looking for a superb picnic spot, this place is definitely worth a look-see. (It's not to be confused, incidentally, with the Chena River State Recreation Site in Fairbanks, nor with the Chena River State Recreation Area on the Chena Hot Springs Road.) The Chena Lakes Rec Area is a sprawling, lake-oriented, 2,178-acre site with scores of campsites, lots of picnic areas, swimming beaches, even a children's playground. There's at least one island with camping and picnic facilities. Again, local Alaskans tend to use it most heavily on weekends and holidays.

Also worth a stop before you arrive in Fairbanks is ***Santa Claus House*** in (where else?) ***North Pole,*** Alaska. The large shop, located at mile 349, is packed with Christmas-type gifts, including Santa Claus letters for kids that Santa will mail and postmark from North Pole in December.

The Richardson ends at mile 364. If you started your Alaska Highway–Richardson trip in Dawson Creek, British Columbia, you've traveled 1,520 miles.

The Steese Highway:
Fairbanks to Circle City

Although it's paved for only 44 of its 162 miles from Fairbanks, the Steese Highway is one of the most satisfying among the backroads in Alaska. Along the way you see the sites of old mining camps and new ones, hot springs spas, gorgeous rolling hills and mountains, small authentic Alaska communities, some of the most intensely colorful wildflower viewing to be found anywhere, and the Chatanika and Chena River Recreation Areas. We've found midweek travel easier, with less gravel dust in the air than on weekends, when many Alaskans head for hot springs spas and good fishing along the route.

You've barely been traveling northwest along Steese Highway from its beginning at the junction of the Richardson and Parks Highways when, at mile 4.9, you come to the *Chena Hot Springs Road.* The road is paved and generally well maintained but drive carefully; it can be bumpy. For a good portion of its nearly 57 miles, the road travels through the *Chena River Recreation Area,* with lots of scenic spots for camping, picnics, fishing, and wildlife viewing.

About 20 miles or so down the road, you'll approach the Two Rivers area, which can accurately be described as sled dog country. Some of the state's most dedicated mushers come from this area. Among the offerings for sled dog adventure in the area is *Chena Dog Sled Adventures,* which can teach you how to drive your own dog team. Cabins are available if you want to spend more time with these four-legged friends. Call (907) 488–5845 or visit www .ptialaska.net/~sleddogs/index.html.

At road's end you'll find lodging, a restaurant, bar, and other facilities at *Chena Hot Springs Resort,* with its spring-fed pool, hot tub, and 2,800-square-foot redwood deck with ten-person spa. Accommodations include hotel rooms starting at $160. Activities, besides soaking, include horseback riding, canoeing, hiking, mountain biking, and hayrides. The resort also features the *Aurora Ice Museum,* the largest year-round, manmade ice structure in the world. Phone (907) 451–8104 or (800) 478–4681 or visit www.chenahot springs.com.

Back on the Steese Highway, one of the best places to see the Trans-Alaska Pipeline up close is about 10 miles north of downtown Fairbanks, just off the highway. The pipe, in fact, is elevated, so you can stand right under it and have your picture taken while countless gallons of crude oil flow over your head.

interior
alaskatrivia

Vast portions of the Interior were not glaciated during the last ice age. Therefore they remain in a state similar to that which they were during the Pleistocene era.

Also at the site is an *Alyeska Pipeline Service Company Information Center* with interpretive displays.

At the junction of the Steese and Elliott Highways lies *Fox,* a tiny town with a couple of great local hangouts. If you're looking for great prime rib and seafood, nothing beats the *Turtle Club* (907–457–3883) at mile 10 of the Steese Highway. Be sure to call ahead for reservations, unless you're content to eat in the bar. And speaking of bars, you can't visit Fox without stopping next door at the **Howling Dog S** (907–456–4695), another popular local hangout. The patrons are almost as colorful as the memorabilia, and there's usually live music and dancing on weekends.

Across the street in the old Fox Roadhouse is the **Silver Gulch Brewing Company** (907–452–2739), producing microbrews with a steady following. Check out the free tasting sessions on Friday night.

The **Old F.E. Gold Camp,** at mile 27.5 at **Chatanika,** is right out of Alaska's glory mining days. The F.E. (for Fairbanks Exploration) Company operated the camp from 1922 to 1964 and is today on the National Register of Historic Places. On-site you'll see lots of artifacts from the '40s, '30s, and earlier. The camp offers comfortable rooms in the bunkhouse for $55. Log cabins with Jacuzzis start at $75. Lunch and dinner are tasteful affairs, with seafood, steaks, prime rib, and rack of lamb on the menu. The year-round Sunday brunch also is popular. Call (907) 389–2414 or visit www.fegold camp.com.

If you happen to be traveling on the Steese Highway about the time of the summer solstice (June 20 or 21), plan to celebrate the change of seasons the way many Fairbanksans do—by driving to **Eagle Summit** (mile 108) for a midnight picnic and a view of the sun dipping close to the horizon *but not quite setting,* then rising again to start a new day and a new summer season. The summit lies south of the Arctic Circle, but this phenomena is possible because of the summit's 3,624-foot elevation. Farther down the road at mile 128, you'll find the **Steese Roadhouse** (907–520–5800), offering lodging, gas, and a general store.

The Steese Highway dead-ends at mile 162, at the picturesque community of **Circle,** a community of mostly Native Alaskan residents. The town got its name when early prospectors thought it straddled the Arctic Circle. It doesn't— the circle lies 50 miles north—but the town does sit on the banks of the Yukon River, which made it a busy transportation and trading hub during the early and middle years of the twentieth century.

Camping can be had at the end of the road on the banks of the Yukon River. There are tables, toilets, and a parking area.

An interesting spot to visit in Circle is the old **Pioneer Cemetery,** with markers dating to the 1800s. To get there walk upriver past some old machinery on a gravel road, until you reach a barricade to private property. It's OK to cross through the front yard (using good manners, obviously) to the trailhead. After about ten minutes—and a million mosquitos—you'll see the graves on the left.

Elliott Highway: Fairbanks to Manley Hot Springs

Most of the travelers you'll meet on the Elliott Highway, especially beyond the road's mile 73.1 junction with the Dalton Highway to Deadhorse, will be Alaskans. And chances are they'll be heading to or coming from one of Fairbanks's favorite getaway destinations, **Manley Hot Springs.** It's one of two popular hot springs spas in the region, the other being Chena Hot Springs at the end of an access road off the Steese Highway.

The Elliott Highway takes off from the Steese about 11 miles north of Fairbanks, and for the first 30 miles it's paved. Beyond that it's gravel, but not a bad road at all, although it gets slick in places when it rains. There are some roller-coaster rises and falls, but if you keep your speed at a reasonable rate, it's no problem.

At mile 1.2 on the Elliott, you come to El Dorado Gold Mine, a worthwhile stop that's both a commercial operation and a visitor attraction. (For a description, see the Fairbanks section.)

At mile 49.5 you can visit **Arctic Circle Trading Post,** which includes the **Wildwood General Store.** To be had here, for those of you who like interesting collectibles, are Arctic Circle Certificates and the official Arctic Circle registry. Put your name down in history as someone who's been to the Arctic Circle. The certificates are proof! The owners of the trading post encourage you to talk with the employees, who will tell you what it's like to live so far from "citified civilization." Call (907) 474–3507.

Roughly 21 miles later you come to a junction with a 2-mile access road to **Livengood.** It was a major gold camp at times in the first half of the twentieth century, but now only one hundred or so people live in the area. Just past mile 73, the Elliott meets with the Dalton Highway supply road to the North Slope, Deadhorse, and Prudhoe Bay.

At mile 94.5 you come to a generous double pullout on the south side of the road. From here you have a good view of Minto Flats, the Tanana River, and the foothills of the Alaska Range. After mile 97 keep your eyes peeled northerly for great views of Sawtooth, Wolverine, and Elephant Mountains. At mile 110 the highway joins an 11-mile access road to the Native village of **Minto** (there's a lodge that provides meals and a general store, if you're looking for a place to eat or buy snacks), and 40 miles farther down the Elliott, you come to Manley Hot Springs.

Very Alaskan, this place. **Manley Roadhouse** is one of a vanishing breed of accommodations that once were common along the sled dog and horse trails of the north. This one was built in 1906, when the community served as a trading center for mining districts in the area. The roadhouse accommodated riverboat crews, miners, and commercial travelers. Today owner Robert E. Lee offers visitors the chance to revisit those days in his roadhouse with single and double sleeping accommodations, a rustic, antiques-filled sitting room, and the Roadhouse Bar, with Alaska's largest back bar. Rooms start at $90 for a double, $100 for a cabin with no plumbing. The rate is $65 for a single. For reservations call (907) 672–3161.

Denali Highway: Paxson to Cantwell

They used to call the **Denali Highway** one of the worst roads in Alaska. It's still bumpy in places, a washboard in others, and you do have to watch for potholes. But if you keep your speed down and your eyes open, you can drive its 136 miles from Paxson on the Richardson Highway to Cantwell on the George Parks Highway without fear or foreboding. At its Cantwell end it's only a few minutes to the entrance of Denali National Park. Because of the road's relatively high elevation, right at timberline or a bit above, you can enjoy lots of high tundra views. Sights of Alaska Range peaks are frequent and fabulous.

Perhaps because the Denali's old and unsavory reputation won't quite die, the road receives surprisingly less traffic than you would expect, considering its location. And because of its sparse traffic, the highway today is much appreciated by stream and lake anglers who don't care for bumper-to-bumper "combat fishing" crowds. There are several state and private RV campgrounds along the way as well as private lodges.

Off-road vehicle enthusiasts enjoy its designated routes, and mountain bikers and hikers also regard highly its marked and unmarked trails. *A caution, though:* If you're heading far off the road, be sure to carry a compass. It's distressingly easy to get turned around in the woods, or even in open tundra, if clouds close in. From your first entry onto the road at Paxson (mile 0), keep your eye out for brown (grizzly) bears, moose, and other wild critters. They're often spotted.

The Denali is paved at its start, but the asphalt ends at mile 21. **Tangle Lakes Lodge** is located at mile 22. A fire destroyed the original lodge and bar in 1998, so the present structure was newly built to greet guests in beautiful surroundings that include one of the best arctic grayling fisheries in the state. If you're a birder, this is the place to find all sorts of species, including ptarmigan (which is Alaska's state bird, not the eagle as many people assume), arctic warblers, gyrfalcons, wandering tattlers, and many other oft-sighted species. Cabin rates are $75 per night or $200 for the large cabin, which is great for groups. If you just want a canoe, they rent for $3 an hour or $10 for three hours. For more information call (907) 688–9174.

A Denali Highway lodging option not to be missed on the other end of the road is the ***Gracious House Lodge and Flying Service.*** Butch and Carol Gratias have been hosting people at their scenic homestead since 1957, serving meals and renting rooms, as well as repairing vehicles and flying hunters and recreationalists to their destinations of choice. It's one of our favorite stops on the highway. Contact them at (907) 259–1111 (summer) or (907) 333–3148 (winter) or www.alaskaone.com/gracious.

At mile 135.5 you've arrived in ***Cantwell,*** which began life as a rail-line flag stop and continues to be served by the Alaska Railroad on its run between Anchorage and Fairbanks. Newer businesses have located near the intersection of the Denali and George Parks Highways, but if you'd like to peek into Alaska's yesteryear, stop by for a meal, lodging, or beverage at the ***Cantwell Lodge*** (907–768–2300) in the older section of town, 2 miles west of the junction. Meals (summer only) range from $8 for a hamburger and fries to $18 for a steak.

Places to Stay in Interior Alaska

CANTWELL

Cantwell Lodge,
western end of Denali Highway;
(907) 768–2300.

CENTRAL

Steese Roadhouse,
Junction of Steese Highway and Circle Hot Springs Road;
(907) 520–5800.

CHATANIKA

Old F. E. Gold Camp,
at mile 27.5 at Chatanika;
(907) 389–2414,
www.fegoldcamp.com

CHENA HOT SPRINGS

Chena Hot Springs Resort,
Chena Hot Springs Road;
(907) 452–7867,
www.chenahotsprings.com

DELTA JUNCTION

Bald Eagle Ranch Bed & Breakfast,
mile 272 Richardson Highway;
(907) 895–5270.

Delta State Campground,
mile 267 Richardson–Alaska Highway.

DENALI HIGHWAY

Gracious House
(907) 259–1111
(let it ring 10 times),
www.alaskaone.com/gracious

Tangle Lakes Lodge,
mile 22 Denali Highway;
(907) 688–9174,
www.tanglelakeslodge.com

DENALI NATIONAL PARK

Camp Denali–North Face Lodge,
western end of Park Road;
(907) 683–2290,
www.campdenali.com

Carlo Creek Lodge and Campground,
South of Denali National Park;
(907) 683–2576,
www.ccldenaliparkalaska
.com

Denali Backcountry Lodge;
(800) 541–9779,
www.denalilodges.com
All-inclusive packages.

Denali's Crow's Nest Log Cabins,
mile 238.8 George Parks Highway;
(907) 683–2773 or
(888) 917–8130,
www.denalicrowsnest.com

Denali Mountain Morning Hostel and Lodge,
near Carlo Creek about a dozen miles south of Denali National Park;
(907) 683–7503,
www.hostelalaska.com

Denali Park Resorts;
(800) 276–7234,
www.denalinationalpark.com
A booking service for three park hotels plus shuttle buses and tours in Denali National Park.

Earth Song Lodge;
(907) 683–2863,
www.earthsonglodge.com
Just north of Denali National Park in Healy.

Kantishna Roadhouse,
western end of Park Road;
(800) 942–7420,
www.kantishnaroadhouse.com

National Park Service campgrounds;
(800) 622–7275;
in Anchorage
(907) 272–7275.
Seven locations in the park.

FAIRBANKS

Aurora Express,
1540 Chena Ridge Road;
(800) 221–0073,
www.auroraexpress.com

A Taste of Alaska Lodge,
551 Eberhart Road;
(907) 488–7855,
www.atasteofalaska.com
Off Chena Hot Springs Road

GAKONA

Christochina Bed & Breakfast,
mile 36.5 Tok Cutoff;
(907) 822–3989.

Gakona Fish Camp Cabins,
mile 128.5 Richardson Highway;
(907) 822–3664.

MANLEY HOT SPRINGS

Manley Roadhouse,
mile 152 Elliot Highway;
(907) 672–3161.

NENANA

Bed and Maybe Breakfast,
105 Front Street;
(907) 832–5556.
In the old railroad depot.

PAXSON

Paxson Inn & Lodge,
mile 185.5 Richardson Highway;
(907) 822–3330.

SLANA

End of the Road Bed and Breakfast,
mile 42 Nabesna Road;
(907) 822–5312.
"Plumbing-free" cabins, showers available.

Huck Hobbit's Homestead Campground and Retreat,
mile 4 Nabesna Road;
(907) 822–3196.
Log cabins for rent.

TOK

Cleft of the Rock Bed & Breakfast,
1½ miles down Sundog Trail;
(800) 478–5646,
www.cleftoftherock.net
Three miles northwest of Tok.

Tok Line Camp Bed & Breakfast,
1.5 miles from town center;
(907) 883–5506.
Call for directions.

Westmark Hotel,
near Alaska Highway–Tok Cutoff junction;
(907) 883–5174 or
(800) 544–0970.

Places to Eat in Interior Alaska

CANTWELL

Cantwell Lodge,
western terminus of Denali Highway;
(907) 768–2300.

CHATANIKA

Old F.E. Gold Camp,
at mile 27.5 at Chatanika;
(907) 389–2414,
www.fegoldcamp.com

DELTA JUNCTION

Packhouse Restaurant,
mile 275 Richardson–Alaska Highway near Delta Junction;
(907) 895–4201.
Fresh bread and homemade soup.

DENALI HIGHWAY

Tangle Lakes Lodge,
mile 22 Denali Highway;
(907) 822–4202,
www.tanglelakeslodge.com

DENALI NATIONAL PARK

Denali Perch Resort,
mile 224 George Parks
Highway;
(907) 683–2523.
Just south of Denali National
Park and Preserve, away
from the park crowds.
Tasty fish, pasta, and steaks.

ESTER

Malemute Saloon,
at the Ester Gold Camp just
off mile 351.7
on the George Parks
Highway;
(907) 479–2500.

FAIRBANKS

Dog Sled Saloon,
1411 Airport Way;
(907) 452–1888

Pikes Landing,
4438 Airport Way;
(907) 479–7113.
Delicious Sunday buffet.
Overlooking the Chena River.

**The Pumphouse
Restaurant,**
796 Chena Pump Road;
(907) 479–8452,
www.pumphouse.com
Good seafood.

Two Rivers Lodge,
mile 16 on Chena Hot
Springs Road;
(907) 488–6815.

FOX

Turtle Club,
mile 10 Steese Highway;
(907) 457–3883.

GAKONA

Carriage House,
mile 2 Tok Cutoff;
(907) 822–3482.
Part of the Gakona Lodge &
Trading Post, a 1905 lodge
now on the National Register
of Historic Places.

TOK

Tok Gateway Salmon Bake,
mile 1,313 Alaska Highway;
(907) 883–5555,
www.tokalaska.com
Outdoor grilled king salmon,
halibut, ribs, and reindeer
sausage.

Alaska's Far North

Alaska's Far North, more than any other region, is a land of extremes. As its name implies this region lies farther north than any other in the state or nation. It's the only part of the United States lapped by the Arctic Ocean's summer waters and barricaded by its winter pack ice. At its northernmost reaches, the region enjoys the country's longest period of daylight—eighty-four continuous days of constant daylight from May 10 to August 2. In contrast, during the dark days of winter, the sun literally does not rise for sixty-seven days. At least one of the region's wildlife species, the polar bear, can be found nowhere else in the nation. And, of course, Alaska's Far North is home to one of North America's largest oil fields, Prudhoe Bay.

Although some may imagine the Far North as drab and lifeless, the tundra country can turn ablaze with wildflowers, berries, and other colorful plantlife in summer. Millions of birds migrate to the northern tundra from North and even South America each spring. Especially during flight-seeing tours, but during road trips as well, you stand a good chance of seeing grizzly bears, caribou, and moose.

Among Native peoples of the region, there are two groups of Eskimos: the Inupiat on the shores of the Alaska mainland and the Yu'pik Eskimos, who reside in Gambell and Savoonga

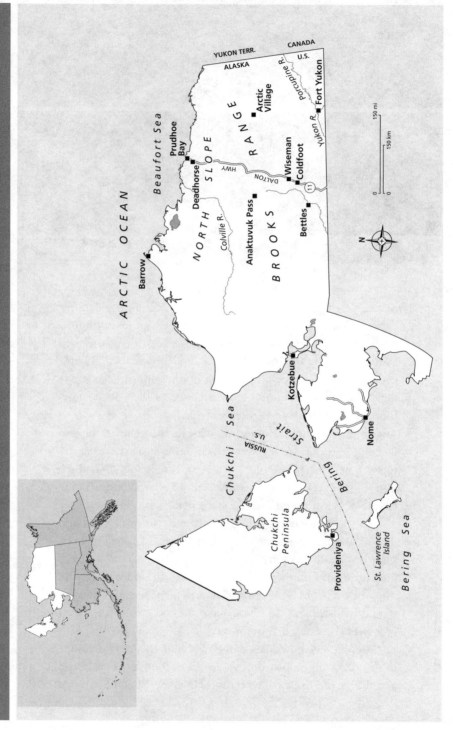

ALASKA'S FAR NORTH

on St. Lawrence Island, a large island in the Bering Sea only 40 miles from Russian Siberia. A small number of Nunamiut inland Eskimos live at Anaktuvuk Pass, about 260 miles north-northwest of Fairbanks, while Athabascan Indian communities may be found as far north as Arctic Village in the Brooks Range, 290 miles north of Fairbanks and roughly 100 miles north of Fort Yukon.

Major Communities of the Far North

Barrow is just about as far off the beaten path as you can get and still have your feet planted on U.S. soil. Located 330 miles north of the Arctic Circle, the mostly Inupiat town is, in fact, the northernmost community in the Western Hemisphere. That's only one of the superlatives you can collect during a visit here. Barrow is also the seat of government for the North Slope Borough, which, at 88,000 square miles, ranks as the largest municipality in the world. (A borough, in Alaska, is rather like a county in the Lower Forty-eight, but much of the state is not part of any municipality or borough.)

In spite of its remoteness, you can get to Barrow easily. Alaska Airlines provides daily jet service from Anchorage and Fairbanks, and once you've arrived, you'll find several ground tour organizations with one- and two-day excursions designed to maximize your time at the Top of the World. Biggest of these is *Tundra Tours,* which also operates the fully modern *Top of the World Hotel.* On Tundra's tours you'll travel beside the Arctic Ocean, pass through an old U.S. Navy research site, visit a Distant Early Warning System installation, take a short trek on the tundra for a look at an old-time traditional hunting camp, and finally reach the northernmost point your bus can take you. From there you can disembark and go beachcombing and maybe even stick your toe in the chilly *Arctic Ocean* waters. Contact Tundra Tours or the Top of the World Hotel at (907) 852–3900 or visit www.alaskaone.com/topworld. Rates at the hotel start at $190 for a double.

TOP 10 PLACES IN THE FAR NORTH

Arctic Alaska's Kiana Lodge	Great Kobuk Sand Dunes
Arctic National Wildlife Refuge	Iditarod Trail (of the Sled Dog Race)
The beaches of Nome	Northernmost tip of Point Barrow
Bettles Lodge	Pilgrim Hot Springs
Gates of the Arctic National Park	Serpentine Hot Springs

Northern Alaska Tour Company offers village tours, emphasizing the Inupiat Eskimo culture with a program of traditional dance and song plus demonstrations of skin sewing, Native games, and the Eskimo blanket toss. The tours also explore Arctic shores. One-day tours of Barrow run $469 per person, which includes airfare from Fairbanks, and overnight tours are $569 per person, based on double occupancy. Prices are slightly higher in the winter, when fewer flights leave for this far-flung community. Call (907) 474–8600 or (800) 474–1986 or visit www.alaskasarctic.com.

Once in Barrow you may want to get around on your own for some even more off-the-beaten-path destinations, and you'll need wheels to do that. Try *UIC Auto Rental* (907–852–2700). Prices are on the high side—but, hey, how else are you going to get wheels this far north?

You could put that daily car rental fee toward a good guide instead, who will do all the driving for you. Try *Arctic Tour Company* at (907) 852–4512, which will take you to the northernmost point in Alaska, literally. In military-style Hummer vehicles you'll go where the tour buses can't—to the original *Point Barrow.* Most of the time you'll even see polar bears, says Arctic Tour's owner and operator. The two-hour tour is $60 per person, with a minimum of two persons; no reservations are accepted. Just call when you get there.

By far the best hotel choice in Barrow is the *King Eider Inn,* with rooms starting at $180 per night. Call (888) 303–4337 or (907) 852–4700 or visit www .kingeider.net. King Eider also rents cars and SUVs to overnight guests.

One final superlative for Barrow: *Pepe's North of the Border* (1204 Agvik) is indisputably the farthest north Mexican restaurant in North America. By Lower Forty-eight standards it's expensive (everything has to be flown in

A Place to Celebrate

Shaped like a giant Ulu knife, the Inupiat Heritage Center in Barrow is a place for young and old Inupiat Eskimos to share their culture and pass on traditions. It cost almost $12 million to build. The building has four rooms: a 20,000-plus-volume consortium library, a room where Inupiat artists can work on their art, an exhibit room to show off some of the results of their labor, and a multipurpose room for demonstrations and lectures. The creations that can be seen at the center include umiaks (skinboats) and dogsleds, ivory carving, and skin sewing.

In building such a monument to their way of life, the Inupiats are showing they are a culture steeped in tradition. In fact, during the building's dedication, a ceremony in which strips of baleen were placed at the corners of the building symbolized the passage of the cultural traditions of the elders to the young people in the community.

from "down south"), but the food is good and you can meet the locals there. Phone (907) 852–8200.

The best eats, however, can be had at *Arctic Pizza,* which besides pizza serves seafood, Mexican, and American fare. Call (907) 852–4222.

Alaska's largest Eskimo community, *Kotzebue,* lies 26 miles north of the Arctic Circle, 550 air miles from Anchorage, and 200 miles from the shores of the Russian Far East. The Inupiat Eskimos have lived in this area for 10,000 to 15,000 years, and the village of Qikiktagruk, now called Kotzebue, served as a trading center. In 1818 German Admiral Otto Von Kotzebue, sailing for the Russian Navy, arrived in the sound. Today Kotzebue is the service center for the *Northwest Arctic Borough,* which includes areas around Kotzebue Sound, portions of the Brooks Range, and parts of the Seward Peninsula.

With a population of 7,600, 75 percent of which is Inupiat Eskimo, the borough is approximately the size of the state of Indiana. Its boundaries also encompass the Noatak and Kobuk Rivers, favorites of anglers looking for a true wilderness fishing experience. In addition, Kotzebue serves as the access point for the *Red Dog Mine,* which lies 90 miles to the north. Red Dog contains the world's largest concentrations of zinc. The metal is mined year-round and held at Kotzebue until the four-month ice-free shipping season begins in late spring.

Though many of Kotzebue's city tour operators have temporarily shut down, as have the museum and visitor center, Kotzebue is the jumping-off point for some genuine wilderness adventures. Alaska Airlines offers daily service from Anchorage, and if you plan to stay overnight, you can do so at the fully modern *Nullagvik Hotel* (300 Shore Avenue; 907–442–3331), where the rack rate for a double room is $184. By chartering out of Kotzebue, you can fly over *Selawik Wildlife Refuge,* the *Great Kobuk Sand Dunes,* and *Kobuk Valley National Park.* For more information contact LeeSea Air at (907) 475–2101.

farnorth alaskatrivia

The oldest frame building north of the Arctic Circle is the Cape Smythe Whaling and Trading Station, built in 1893 in Browerville, a whaling community near Barrow.

Serious anglers can opt for a week of remote fishing at the foot of the Brooks Range, where the folks at *Midnight Sun Adventures* say the average Dolly Varden is over seven pounds, with twenty-pound lunkers showing up every so often. Midnight Sun will pick you up in Kotzebue with one of their Piper Cubs and fly you to their rustic lodge, consisting of stove-heated bunk cabins far from the road system. The rate of $6,000 per person per week, based on double occupancy, includes round-trip transportation from Kotzebue, lodging, meals, and guided fishing. For more information contact **Fly Water Travel** at (800) 552–2729 or visit www.flywatertravel.com.

For another travel adventure, check out LaVonne Hendricks's **Arctic Circle Adventures,** whose options range from one-day area tours to five-day, customized, all-in-one packages. Each trip is an adventure in itself, but here's a sampling of what you might experience with Hendricks: tundra hiking, bird-watching, ethnic and Inupiat cultural tours, a tour of a beachfront commercial salmon fish camp about 5 miles from Kotzebue via a four-wheel-drive road, and lodging at rustic cabins nestled beneath 250-foot bluffs. Food includes family-style dinners of fish, meat, and greens harvested from the tundra—with local folks as dinner guests—and breakfasts of sourdough pancakes, reindeer sausage, fresh trout, and salmon. The rates vary depending on your length of stay and what you want to see. Call (907) 442–6013 at Hendricks's camp in the summer. In the winter call (907) 276–0976. The Arctic Circle Adventures Web site is www.fishcamp.org.

In addition to having its own worthwhile attractions, Kotzebue serves as a major jumping-off point for expeditions to the surrounding bush. From the community, you can fly **Hageland Aviation** (907–442–2936; www.hageland .com) to the nearby village of **Kiana** (the round-trip is $150) for modern lodging, hunting, fishing, and riverboat trips via Lorry and Nellie Schuerch's **Arctic Alaska's Kiana Lodge.** The couple, of Inupiat Eskimo descent, offers comfortable lodging in their wonderfully decorated and beautiful lodge, which has six guest rooms, a sauna, and, remarkably for this far out in the bush, toilets and hot showers. Their tours cover such natural wonders as **Kobuk Valley National Park,** the sand dunes, and all the wildlife you can imagine. Sheefish, arctic char, grayling, pike, and chum salmon are some of the fish that can be caught on guided and

farnorth alaskatrivia

If you're outside of the village of Kivalina, north of Kotzebue, and want to go camping, don't pitch your tent at Siniktagnelik on the right bank of the Wulik River. The Eskimo word *Siniktagnelik* means "no camping place because one cannot sleep because many years ago some people mysteriously died here."

unguided trips in the area. Packages run in the $500-a-day range and include everything you'll need for a pleasurable experience. Call (907) 475–2149 in the summer or visit www.alaskasheefishing.com.

Lower Forty-eight residents seem to know at least three things about **Nome.** First, it was the site of a lively gold stampede from 1898 through the early years of the twentieth century. Second, each year in March the 1,000-mile **Iditarod Trail** Sled Dog Race finishes there under a massive timber-burled

An Arctic Desert

Above the Arctic Circle, northwest of Kotzebue, lie the shifting sands of the Great Kobuk Sand Dunes. This, the largest active dune field in the Arctic, is composed mainly of glacial silt. Some of the dunes reach heights of 100 feet, and summer temperatures there can reach ninety degrees Fahrenheit.

The dunes are part of the Kobuk Valley National Park, a 1.7-million-acre area set aside in 1980 to protect them. During the ice age the Kobuk Valley remained ice free, providing a corridor adjoining the Bering Sea land bridge, which once linked Alaska and Siberia. Little has changed in this valley since then. The cold, dry climate remains, and plant life resembles the flora of the late Pleistocene era.

winner's arch, having started some nine days to two weeks earlier in Anchorage. And, third, Nome lies in the far, far north, well above the Arctic Circle.

Well, two out of three's not bad.

Although virtually everyone thinks of Nome as an Arctic community, it's actually a bit south of the Arctic Circle. The town does, however, experience Arctic weather, especially in the wintertime. Seas freeze solid off its shores well into late spring. Each year in March, in fact, the Nome Lions Club sponsors a *Bering Sea Ice Golf Classic,* during which shivering duffers play a six-hole, par 41 course consisting of fairways on frozen sea ice with flagged holes made from coffee cans sunk into the ice.

Nome, with a population of 3,500, more than half of them Alaska Native Eskimos, is a fair-size city by Alaska standards, but except for an occasional "far out" cruise ship, you can get there only by air. The air service, however, is excellent. Alaska Airlines jets fly to the city several times daily. And here's one of Alaska's best-kept secrets: Once you've arrived here on the shores of the Bering Sea, there are hundreds of miles of good roads to explore. Places to visit and things to see include former gold mining sites, Native villages, impressive scenic vistas, even a hot springs. Nome is also one of the few places in North America where you can take a side trip to Russia.

A little history: One unconfirmed account records that Nome got its start in 1897, when John Hummel, an aging prospector suffering from scurvy, arrived in the area to search for gold, which many had predicted would be found there. But unlike others, Hummel did his panning on the beach, more hopeful of curing his ailments in the sun and salt air than of anything else. Incredibly, while sifting the beach sands he found gold. More incredible still, as he tested up and down the shoreline, he continued to see precious metal in every pan.

TOP ANNUAL EVENT IN THE FAR NORTH

Iditarod Trail Sled Dog Race:
The main event in a monthlong
celebration in Nome. The race starts in
Anchorage on the first Satruday in
March, but mushers begin arriving any
time after the ninth day in Nome. A

Mushers and Miners Ball, a statewide
basketball tournament, and the Bering
Sea Ice Golf Classic are all held during
March; (907) 443–5535; www.nome
alaska.org

In no time the rush was on! Another more substantiated version of Nome's beginning states that "three lucky Swedes"—Jafet Lindberg, Erik Lindblom, and John Brynteson—started the rush by finding gold in Anvil Creek in 1898 and that the beach finds came a year or so later.

However the rush began, it hasn't stopped yet. Mining remains a big part of Nome's economy. These days the rush consists of tourists eager to see where all the excitement took place. When you arrive in town, your first stop should be the ***Nome Convention and Visitor Bureau's Visitor Information Center*** (907–443–6624; www.nomealaska.org), located downtown on Front Street, across from Nome City Hall. Lots of free brochures, walking maps, restaurant menus, antiques, and historic photos are available or on display Monday through Friday. Also on Front Street, in the basement of the library building, you'll find the ***Carrie McLain Museum*** (907–443–6630), with its wide variety of Alaskan artifacts and historical memorabilia. At the ***XYZ Center*** (907–443–5238), located in the north end of the city hall building, visitors can join Nome's elders for lunch and interesting conversation. Lunch costs $5 for those under sixty years of age; seniors may make a donation. The menu might include reindeer, blueberries, or other foods from the area. Any time of the year your most vivid memories of Nome may well be the gold dredges. One old and abandoned dredge is within walking distance of town. The huge lumbering behemoths once created their own ponds as they crept and floated across the tundra, scooping up ore and extracting gold. And, of course, what could be more fitting for a visit to Nome than to buy a gold pan at one of the local stores and pan for some "color" of your own on the beaches where thousands once labored for nuggets and fortunes?

About those highways: For a place you can't drive to, Nome has lots of miles to tour by auto. Three major roads offer access to wildlife viewing, rivers to fish, mining ruins to examine, plus awesome seascapes and landscapes to photograph. You have only one choice for rentals—***Stampede Ven-***

tures (907–443–3838). Cab service can be had by calling *Checker Cab* at (907) 443–5136.

The *Nome–Council Road,* which extends 72 miles east from Nome's main thoroughfare, Front Street, follows the coast for about 30 miles, then moves inland past rivers and sloping hills to the village of *Council.* About halfway out you'll come to the former community of *Solomon,* with its picturesque graveyard of old abandoned railroad engines and cars. Locals call this the Last Train to Nowhere. The 73-mile *Nome–Teller Road* leads to the village of *Teller* (population 200). You reach this highway from the west end of Front Street by turning north on Bering Street, which leads into the northwest-heading Teller Road.

A shorter driving option (about 3 miles one way) takes you to the top of *Anvil Mountain,* near an inoperative communications site. The rewarding view takes in the city of Nome, the Bering Sea, Sledge Island, and a colorful expanse of Arctic tundra.

Perhaps most rewarding, you can drive to *Pilgrim Hot Springs* on the Kougarok Road, which is accessible about 2 miles north of town by turning north off Bering Street. The experience offers a lot of natural history, mining history, and vast fields of tiny colorful flowers growing wild on the tundra. The 36-mile drive will take about forty-five minutes one way. Pack a snack to enjoy on the shores of Salmon Lake at the Bureau of Land Management campground. Farther down the road comes historic Pilgrim Hot Springs —once the site of a Catholic mission orphanage—and experimental gardens where tons of beets, carrots, turnips, cabbage, kale, rutabagas, rhubarb, onions, and potatoes were harvested from the hot springs–heated ground. Visitors

farnorth alaskafacts

The sun does not set in Barrow between May 10 and August 2 each summer, and it does not rise between November 18 and January 24 each winter.

Cape Prince of Wales, at the tip of the Seward Peninsula, is the westernmost point of mainland Alaska. Cape Mountain (2,289 feet), which rises above the Eskimo village of Wales, is the terminus of the Continental Divide.

are welcome to soak up the local atmosphere by spending quality time in a Pilgrim Hot Springs hot tub. (Bring your own towel.) There's time, as well, for birdwatching, trail hiking, and angling for trout or grayling in the Pilgrim River. During a drive north on the Kougarok Road, you'll pass through the Nome River Valley, where it's not uncommon to spot musk ox, moose, and reindeer.

If you'd prefer to have a local expert along to show you the sights, contact Richard Beneville, owner of *Nome Discovery Tours.* From beach gold panning to traveling Nome's road system to learning about the area's history, Beneville has a trip to suit your needs. Five-hour tours start at $85 per person. Phone (907) 443–2814 or visit www.nomechamber.org/discoverytours.html.

Nome Tour & Marketing (907–443–2651) has a $75 tour that takes in the history of Nome and includes a slide show of the area during the years 1898 through 1934. You also get to pan for gold and visit the kennel of Iditarod musher Mike Webber.

If you think Nome is fascinating by foot or vehicle, try seeing it from a few thousand feet above ground. *Bering Air* (907–443–5464; www.bering air.com) is one of your best options for flight-seeing, and its pilots can take you to such locales as *Bering Land Bridge National Preserve,* one of the most remote national park areas in the country and a remnant of the land bridge that connected Asia with North America more than 13,000 years ago. While there, unwind in the naturally occurring *Serpentine Hot Springs.* The majority of this land bridge, once thousands of miles wide, now lies beneath the waters of the Chukchi and Bering Seas. Call (907) 443–2522 for more information on the springs. Or try a flight-see over ancient lava beds—yup, you can find just about anything if you look hard enough in Alaska.

farnorth alaskafacts

Don't be surprised if you see Pacific walrus during a visit to Nome. They migrate between the Chukchi and Bering seas. A bull walrus can weigh up to two tons.

When you're standing at the Arctic Circle on the summer solstice, the sun never sets. And if you're standing there on the winter solstice, the sun will not rise above the horizon.

Other options include a 60-mile flight to the Native village of *Golovin.* Tickets are $108 one way or $172 round-trip.

Bering Air's Russia desk can help you plan an international excursion across the sea to Russia. Arranging flights from Nome to *Provideniya,* Russia, isn't quite as simple as booking a sightseeing tour, but flights to the former Soviet Union are possible. Upon request the airline will send literature explaining how to arrange permission from the Russian government to enter the country. Passengers traveling individually and with flexible schedules may be able to travel on a less expensive seat-fare basis on chartered planes.

Anchorage-based *Circumpolar Expeditions* (907–272–9299 or 888–567–7165; www.arctictravel.net) is another option for seeing Russia if you prefer your itinerary planned well in advance. The company offers a nine-day Whale and Walrus Tour for $4,999 that includes sightseeing of whales and walruses and other natural wonders in the Chukotka region. For ocean-bound adventure, sail with Circumpolar from Whittier to Kodiak, Katmai, Shumagin, Dutch

Harbor, the Pribilofs, through the Bering Sea, and on to Nome on the fourteen-day Voyage to the Bering Sea for $8,399 per person. **Cruise West** (888–851–8133; www.cruisewest.com) offers a similar thirteen-day excursion.

Other air tours include **Frontier Flying Service** flights to **Gambell** and **Savoonga** villages on **St. Lawrence Island,** off the coast of Siberia. Call (907) 443–2414 or visit www.frontierflyingservice.com for more information. Various carriers also offer trips to the villages of **St. Michael,** known for its grass baskets; **Shaktoolik,** where you'll find Eskimo dolls, parkas, and mukluks; and **White Mountain,** which has excellent earrings of porcupine quills, beads, and ivory.

Arranging to see Nome and its surrounding area by air is only a phone call away if you want the planning done for you. Lori and Dan Michels's **Sky Trekking Alaska** (907–357–3153; www.skytrekkingalaska.com) is based in the Southcentral community of Wasilla, but the company flies clients pretty much anywhere they want to go, including Nome. Winter travelers and Iditarod enthusiasts will enjoy one of three Sky Trekking options available for following the sled dog race from Anchorage to Nome. A three-day, $3,360 package takes you to Nome to see the winners arrive, and to enjoy the scenery and bustle of activity as the town celebrates the mushers' arrivals. The four-day adventure is $3,670 and includes a visit to an Iditarod race kennel and a chance to be a musher handler in the chute at the ceremonial start of the race. The final option includes tracking the entire race for twelve days, during which you follow mushers from checkpoint to checkpoint. For $9,350, this is the best way to see the remote terrain the dogs and mushers travel through, and it's a great way to appreciate the organization involved in putting on this world-class event.

Several hotels offer lodging and dining accommodations in Nome, including the **Nome Nugget Inn** (on Front Street; 907–443–2323 or 877–443–2323), where most of the airline tourists stay. If you like more informal surroundings, consider lifelong Nome resident Cussy Kauer's **Chateau de Cape Nome** (907–443–2083). Kauer's great-grandfather came through the Klondike gold rush and over to Nome, so her house is chock-full of history and wildlife mounts, including a bear that she shot herself. Four

farnorth alaskatrivia

Continuous permafrost reaches depths of 2,000 feet in the Far North and can wreak havoc on buildings whose heat causes partial thawing. To remedy the problem, many buildings in the Far North are built on ground that is kept frozen during the summer with refrigeration coils. It is easier to cool the ground for a few months each year than deal with the repairs caused by shifting ice and sagging structures.

rooms share two baths, and guests have kitchen access plus a view of the Bering Sea. Rooms are $100 per night year-round. Another comfortable option is the spacious **Aurora Inn and Suites** on Front Street (907–443–3838 or 800–354–4606; www.aurorainnome.com). Opt for a standard or premium room with or without kitchenette or choose an executive suite. Rates range from $130 to $220 per night. There's a guest sauna on-site as well as vehicle rentals through Stampede Rentals.

While these places offer ample creature comforts, I've got to tell you that the best way to stay in Nome—especially if you're as lucky as I've been and have crystal-clear weather—is by camping on the beach on the east side of town. Believe it or not, it's free and convenient to town. When I was there for a mountain biking trip, I'd simply ride the ½ mile or so into town for breakfast and, once my belly was full, begin the day's adventures. **Fat Freddie's,** at 305 Front Street (907–443–5899), has the best diner breakfasts in town and offers a view of the Bering Sea. Another dining option is **Milano's Pizzeria** on Front Street (907–443–2924), which, as is common in remote places, offers an interesting combination of Japanese and Italian fare. It's one of the only places I've visited where I could get a California roll, pepperoni pizza, and lobster all in one place. For more information on camping on **Nome's beaches,** call (907) 443–6624.

Life on the Beach

I lie on my sleeping bag with my head propped up, reading a book and relaxing. It's bedtime, but I can still feel the warmth of the sun through the tent fly. Of course, this is to be expected when you're camping just below the Arctic Circle in the middle of the summer. The sun barely sets this time of year. I am in Nome, Alaska, on the Bering Sea coast, and I'm camped on the beach. All I hear are the waves lapping tamely along the shore or an occasional bird that still hasn't settled for the evening.

Then I hear something different, a soft swoosh every now and then, like a stocking-footed child padding into a room. I peek outside my tent and am amazed to be surrounded by what must be at least a hundred reindeer making their way to the water's edge. These animals are part of several reindeer herds owned by Native Alaskans living in the region. The locals have told me not to be surprised to see them. They'll often visit the beaches, not for fun in the sun, but to seek refuge from the hordes of mosquitoes that plague them inland.

I'm a bit daunted by the sight of these big creatures encircling my little blue tent, but there's not much else I can do but get back under cover and hope they don't decide to stampede. In the morning I awake and they are gone, with fading impressions of their hooves left in the sand the only evidence that it wasn't a dream.

—Melissa DeVaughn

The Bush

Since 1948 the small Brooks Range bush outpost called **Bettles** has been the base of operations for **Bettles Lodge,** now registered as a National Historic Site. Longtime Alaskans Dan and Lynda Klaes have owned the lodge since 1982, with children Jamie and Tyler helping out over the years. At the lodge, open year-round, you'll find comfortable rooms and a restaurant, tavern, and tackle shop. The Klaes offer accommodations and customized tours in a part of Alaska that less than 1 percent of the state's visitors get to enjoy. Day tours run $500 per person and include airfare from Fairbanks, lunch at the lodge, a Koyukuk River boat tour, and an Arctic Circle certificate. For $740 you can add an overnight stay at the lodge and two additional meals. Fabulous fly-out fishing is one of the specialties here, with sheefish, arctic grayling, lake trout, arctic char, chum salmon, and northern pike all for the taking. In conjunction with **Bettles Air,** the Klaes and their friendly staff will arrange customized tours. For more information about Bettles Lodge and Bettles Air, call (907) 479–7018 or (800) 770–5111 or visit www.bettleslodge.com or www.bettlesair.com.

There are more options in the Brooks Range. **Alaska Discovery,** of Juneau, offers a hiking/boating adventure for $3,050 on the seldom-traveled **Kongakut River.** The trip is ten days, originating with a bush flight from Fairbanks. Another outstanding option is arctic refuge hiking in the **Gates of the Arctic National Park.** This is a great late-summer trip and a perfect time to view the fall colors and perhaps see the migrating western arctic caribou herd. You'll be just above the Arctic Circle for this adventure, which costs $2,650. Phone (800) 586–1911 or visit www.akdiscovery.com.

Another Gates of the Arctic option well worth visiting is **Peace of Selby** on Selby/Narvak Lake in the Brooks Range. Fully furnished, comfortable lodge accommodations, with meals included, are $500 a night per person. Available for $300 per person per night are cabins on Nutuvukti and Minakokosa Lakes and on the Kobuk River. Guided float trips, canoeing, day or overnight hikes, and fishing expeditions are available. This is a photographer's or bird-watcher's heaven. Also popular at Peace of Selby are winter adventures, ranging from cross-country skiing to snowshoeing to watching the caribou migration. Access, of course, is by air from Fairbanks. For more details phone (907) 672–3206 or visit www.alaskawilderness.net.

For those who enjoy bird-watching, not just to check off another species on their list but to see birds in their most natural environment, **Wilderness Birding Adventures** offers an exciting assortment of possibilities from Shuyak State Park on Kodiak Island to the far north Arctic. Among the latter are float trips of the Colville River as well as floats or base-camp adventures on a small island of mountains protruding from the Arctic coastal plain in the ***Arctic National Wildlife Refuge.*** A twelve-day float down the Marsh Fork/ Canning River on the western edge of the refuge offers a chance to see many species of birds. The company also packages tours of Gambell on St. Lawrence Island, and of Nome, where rare species fly over from Siberia. Tours are priced as low as $775 for a three-day Owls of the North excursion from Anchorage to $3,500 for a ten-day Kongakut River Rafting trip through perhaps some of the most remote wilderness in the United States. Call (907) 694–7442 or visit www.wildernessbirding.com.

farnorth alaskatrivia

Any part of Alaska that can't be reached by road is called the bush. A community that can only be reached by sled, snow machine, airplane, or boat is called a "bush village."

Another great option for Far North trekking is ***ABEC Alaska,*** which began offering wilderness adventures in the Brooks Range in 1980. Experienced guides offer personalized service on both backpacking and river trips to incredible Arctic vantage points like the Hulahula River, the Kongakut River, the Noatak River, and the Gates of the Arctic. Depending on your destination and the season, you may see herds of migrating caribou, grazing musk ox, or scrambling Dall sheep. Based out of Fairbanks, ABEC can be reached by called (877) 424–8907 or (907) 457–8907 or by visiting www.abecalaska.com. Trips range from $2,200 for six days to $4,950 for seventeen days.

Jim Campbell and Carol Kasza, husband and wife, have hiked and climbed mountains around the world, but to establish their own guiding business— ***Arctic Treks***—they selected the Brooks Range. They offer wilderness hiking, backpacking, and rafting options from seven to eleven days. Prices range from $3,050 to $4,150, including airfare from Fairbanks. They take only six to nine clients per trip. Call (907) 455–6502 or visit www.arctictreksadventures.com.

Established in 1847 by the Hudson's Bay Company, ***Fort Yukon*** is today one of Alaska's oldest settlements and the largest Athabascan Indian village in the state. The Gwich'in Athabascans have lived in this area for literally thousands of years. The town, which the people call Gwichyaa Zhee (meaning "house on the flats"), lies 8 miles north of the Arctic Circle and about 140 miles northeast of Fairbanks. You can get there by air via three scheduled carriers and four charter outfits or by boat. No roads lead to Fort Yukon.

If you enjoy buying souvenirs at the source, check out the ***Alaska Commercial Company*** store for beaded moose-skin accessories. Most visitor services are available. One of the principal visitor attractions is a ***replica of the original Fort Yukon.*** Nearby is the old Hudson's Bay cemetery. Interestingly, Hudson's Bay built the fort not for protection from the Indians but as a safeguard against the Russians who "owned" Alaska until 1867. Be sure also to see the **Old Mission School,** which is on the National Register of Historic Places. Ask to visit **St. Stephen's Territorial Episcopal Church,** where you can view exquisite and colorful Athabascan beaded embroidery on the altar cloth. The Athabascans are renowned for their beadwork designs, which decorate boots, moccasins, jackets, and gloves.

The Dalton Highway

This road—the only overland route into the Arctic from Alaska's highway network—is not for the timid or the unprepared. But the **Dalton Highway** is one of the last great adventure roads in the United States. If you have the right vehicle and plan ahead, it can be one of the most satisfying drives of a lifetime.

Alaska began construction of the 414-mile road in April 1974 and had it operational that fall in order to expedite construction of the 800-mile pipeline from Prudhoe Bay to Valdez. The Dalton today is gravel, two lanes, hilly in places, bumpy in many more, lonely (you may not see another car for hours), and has few service facilities along the way. If you break down you may not get help until an Alaska state trooper comes by on patrol. That's the bad news. The good news is that it is safely negotiable if you use common sense, and it opens up some of the most awesome northern mountain and tundra country in the world.

If you want to experience the highway but you don't want the hassle of planning, preparing, or driving the Dalton on your own, there's an easy option: Book reservations with one of several large or little tour companies that schedule motor-coach or van trips all summer long. Several of these offer drive/fly three-day itineraries during which you cruise the highway in one direction and fly between Fairbanks and Prudhoe Bay in the other. Among the companies that offer this and other options are **Gray Line of Alaska** (888–452–1737; www.graylineofalaska.com), **Northern Alaska Tour Company** (907–474–8600; www.northernalaska.com), and **Trans-Arctic Circle Treks, Ltd.** (800–479–8908 or 907–479–5451; www.arctictreks.com). Prices vary with the different companies, points of origin, and whether you're traveling in a high or "shoulder" season. Northern Alaska offers a taste of the Dalton Highway with a one-day drive/fly round-trip package from Fairbanks to Coldfoot, 60 miles north of the Arctic Circle. Grayline and Trans-Arctic Circle offer multiday packages taking you all the way to the end of the road at Prudhoe Bay.

If you decide to drive the road yourself, make sure your car is in top mechanical condition. It's a good idea to call the Alaska Department of Transportation (907–451–2210) before you leave to find out the current road conditions. To be safe, carry an extra tire and two mounted spares. Chances are you'll need at least one. Especially if you're camping out along the way (in fact, even if you're not), bring lots of bug dope. And by all means, pack plenty of film or spare batteries for your digital camera. It's a long, long drive to the nearest photo shop. If you don't plan to camp, make sure you've called ahead and reserved motel space in Coldfoot and Deadhorse. Be aware that gasoline is available along the way only at the Yukon River (mile 56), at Coldfoot (mile 175), and at Deadhorse at road's end (mile 414).

Whether you're in the family vehicle or an air-conditioned motor coach, the adventure begins when you leave the Elliott Highway past mile 73 and head north on the Dalton. Four miles later you're descending a steep incline into Lost Creek Valley, with the pipeline visible (as it frequently will be) to your right. From time to time the pipe will crisscross under the road. Sometimes the line will be buried for many miles, and you won't see it at all.

farnorth
alaskatrivia

Don't be surprised if you hear locals call the Dalton Highway the "haul" road. This 414-mile scenic but often rough road was built in 1974 as a transport road during the construction of the Trans-Alaska Pipeline, and it is still used to "haul" materials to keep the pipeline in operation.

About 48 miles out you begin your descent to the Yukon River, and at mile 55.6, there it is: the storied Yukon and an impressive 2,290-foot wood-decked bridge that rises (or falls, depending on which way you're driving) at a 6 percent grade.

Across the river on its northern bank, you can top off your fuel tank at **Yukon River Camps** (907–655–9001) as well as eat a restaurant meal and overnight in a motel. Rates are $89. None of the rooms have a private bath, but there are two bathrooms—one for women and one for men.

At mile 115.3 you can take a photo you'll be proud to hang on your living room wall. Here you will officially cross the Arctic Circle at 66 degrees, 33 minutes north latitude, and there's a big sign there to prove it.

At mile 175 you'll come to **Coldfoot,** which started life as an old-time mining camp and exists today as the major overnight spot for truckers and visitors on the Dalton Highway. The name, according to local legend, came about when early gold stampeders got this far north, then got "cold feet" and retreated south.

For accommodations try **Coldfoot Camp,** with gas, food, basic yet expensive lodging ($169 for two in a small room), and even flight-seeing. Call (907) 474–3500 or (866) 474–3400 or visit www.coldfootcamp.com.

The National Park Service maintains a *visitor center* at Coldfoot, offering road and travel updates as well as programs each night about the Arctic.

Approaching mile 189 along the highway, you join a short access road to *Wiseman.* Like many others of its kind, this community once thrived as a trading center for prospectors and miners. These days about two dozen determined souls still live there year-round, joined by others in the summer. The *Wiseman Museum* is a good place to stop and check out old mining artifacts and photos. And if you don't want to tent out, call *Arctic Getaway Bed & Breakfast* at (907) 678–4456 or visit www.arcticgetaway.com. It's not fancy, but hosts Berni and Uta Hicker will make you feel at home. Also in Wiseman is *Boreal Lodging* (907–678–4566; www.boreallodge.com). Four rooms at the lodge share two bathrooms and a kitchen, while the Boreal Cabin has a private bath.

At mile 235.3, just south of a highway turnoff, you'll see the northernmost spruce tree in Alaska. No others grow beyond this point. This is also the start of a long and very steep grade—10 percent. Be sure to give any downhill-traveling trucks you meet their full half of the road.

Another steep ascent begins just beyond mile 242 and ends at Atigun Pass, which at 4,800 feet is the highest in Alaska. Watch for Dall sheep, especially on Slope Mountain.

About 75 miles later you'll see a pingo 5 miles west of the road. These curious circular mounds, more common the closer you get to the Arctic Ocean's shores, rise dramatically from surrounding tabletop-smooth terrain. They're caused by frozen water beneath the surface.

At mile 414 you've arrived at *Deadhorse,* the gathering point where crude oil from Prudhoe Bay, Kuparuk River, and other lesser oil fields is brought in by a network of smaller pipelines and directed into the 48-inch Trans-Alaska Pipeline for transport to Valdez, 800 miles to the south.

Truth to tell, you'll probably judge Deadhorse a pretty bleak and dreary place. Some of the oil company buildings (with self-contained dorms, cafeterias, libraries, and recreation centers) are modern and bright, even cheerful, and some of the subcontractor structures and quarters are on a par with counterparts in industrial parks in the Lower Forty-eight. But a considerable number of Deadhorse's buildings and lots are unkempt, junky, littered, and strewn with unused or abandoned pipe, equipment, and building material. No one really seems to care, since almost no one lives here year-round. Virtually the entire population consists of crews and individuals who arrive or depart on periodic shift assignments. There are no church buildings, schools, movie theaters, or any of the other trappings of a bona fide community. Few if any of the workers bring spouses or family. They claim residence in Anchorage, Fairbanks, and

The Trans-Alaska Pipeline along the
Dalton Highway

even far-flung points like Dallas and Fort Worth.

So what's the attraction? Well, it may be drab, dreary, and desolate, but in a strange sort of way, it's dramatic and absorbing. There's a lot of coming-going-moving-shaking activity, and if you take one of the organized tours available, you'll learn a lot about the place and the process by which the United States at one time got a whopping 2 million barrels of crude oil a day. You can have your picture taken at **Pipeline Mile Zero.** You'll likely see wild caribou grazing virtually in the shadow of oil rigs and pipelines just outside of town, and any number of waterfowl bird species resting or nesting on the tundra. And if you don't happen to have Point Barrow on your itinerary, where else will you be able to skip a stone on the Arctic Ocean? (Or, if you're a winter or very early summer visitor, actually take a few steps out onto the Arctic ice pack.)

You can't, by the way, just mosey around Deadhorse in your car on your own as you would back home. Much of this community, including roads, is private property, and you need permission to visit many sites, including the shores of the Arctic Ocean. This is the reason many visitors choose all-inclusive van or motor-coach drive/fly tours from Fairbanks or Anchorage. If you plan to drive here in your own vehicle, you should definitely make housing reservations ahead of time. The **Prudhoe Bay Hotel** (907–659–2449; www.prudhoebayhotel.com) is open year-round and accommodates visitors as well as petroleum workers. **Arctic Caribou Inn** (907–659–2368 or 877–659–2368; www.arcticcaribouinn.com) provides rooms, tours, breakfasts, dinners, and a gas station.

If you'd like to get a bird's-eye view of the area, consider traveling with **AlaskaTours.com** (907–277–3000; www.alaskatours.com). As part of their eleven-day tour of Anchorage, Prince William Sound, Denali Park, Fairbanks, Coldfoot, Prudhoe Bay, and Barrow, they transport visitors from Prudhoe to Barrow on a Navaho single-engine bush plane. It's all part of the Alaskan experience, with prices starting at $3,937 for the package.

Prudhoe Bay Fleet Shop or the **Veco Light Vehicle Shop** will repair your car if need be, and gas can be had at either **NANA** or the Tesoro station

(907–659–3198), which is open twenty-four hours. Incidentally, no one uses street addresses here. To find something just look for signs or ask someone.

The Dalton Highway, of course, is a north–south, single-direction road. There are no loops or alternate routes back. If you're driving, when your visit ends, you simply retrace your path to the Elliott Highway and on to Fairbanks to begin your next adventure.

Places to Stay in the Far North

BARROW

King Eider Inn;
(888) 303–4337 or
(907) 852–4700,
www.kingeider.net

Top of the World Hotel,
1204 Agvik;
(907) 852–3900.
Fully modern and in town.

COLDFOOT

Coldfoot Camp;
(907) 474–3400 or
(866) 474–3400,
www.coldfootcamp.com

DEADHORSE

Arctic Caribou Inn;
(907) 659–2368 or
(877) 659–2368,
www.arcticcaribouinn.com

Prudhoe Bay Hotel;
(907) 659–2449,
www.prudhoebayhotel.com

KOTZEBUE

**Arctic Alaska's
Kiana Lodge;**
(907) 333–5866 in winter,
(907) 475–2259 in summer,
www.alaskaoutdoors
.com/Kiana

Nullagvik Hotel,
308 Shore Avenue;
(907) 442–3331,
www.nullagvik.com

NOME

Aurora Inn and Suites,
Front Street;
(907) 443–3838 or
(800) 354–4606;
www.aurorainnome.com

Chateau de Cape Nome,
1105 East Fourth Avenue;
(907) 443–2083.

Nome Nugget Inn,
Front Street;
(907) 443–2323.

SELBY/NARVAK LAKE

Peace of Selby,
within Gates of the Arctic
National Park and Noatak
National Preserve;
(907) 672–3206,
www.alaskawilderness.net
It's out there, but certainly
peaceful.

WISEMAN

**Arctic Getaway Bed and
Breakfast,**
mile 189 Dalton Highway;
(907) 678–4456,
www.arcticgetaway.com

Boreal Lodging;
(907) 678–4566,
www.boreallodge.com

Places to Eat in the Far North

BARROW

Arctic Pizza;
(907) 852–4422.

Pepe's North of the Border,
1204 Agvik;
(907) 852–8200.
Mexican cuisine.

KOTZEBUE

Nullagvik Restaurant;
(907) 442–3331.
Reindeer stew and sausage,
fresh local fish, and other
tasty fare.

NOME

Fat Freddie's,
563 Front Street;
(907) 443–5899.
Not fancy, but tasty and
filling diner food.

Milano's Pizzeria;
(907) 443–2924.

Southwestern Alaska

Strange opportunity you have in Southwestern Alaska. If you really want to, you can travel farther off the beaten path in this region than in any other in the nation. Farther west and—here's the strange part—farther *east*.

The Aleutian Islands, as you probably know, stretch from the end of the Alaska Peninsula almost to Japan. The westernmost point in the United States lies on one of those islands, Amatignak, at longitude 179°10' west.

Now about the easternmost point. Just across the 180th meridian that separates the earth's Western Hemisphere from the Eastern Hemisphere (and exactly halfway around the world from the prime meridian at Greenwich, England) is Semisopochnoi Island's Pochnoi Point, at longitude 179°46' east. Thus the nation's most northern (at Point Barrow), western, and eastern real estate is located in Alaska. (The most southern, if you're curious, is on the southern side of the Big Island of Hawaii.)

Here are some other Alaska-size statistics about this region: You can visit Alaska's largest island, Kodiak, and in the process see the nation's biggest land omnivore, the Kodiak brown bear. You can photograph the biggest moose in Alaska on the Alaska Peninsula. Some of North America's most volatile volcanoes

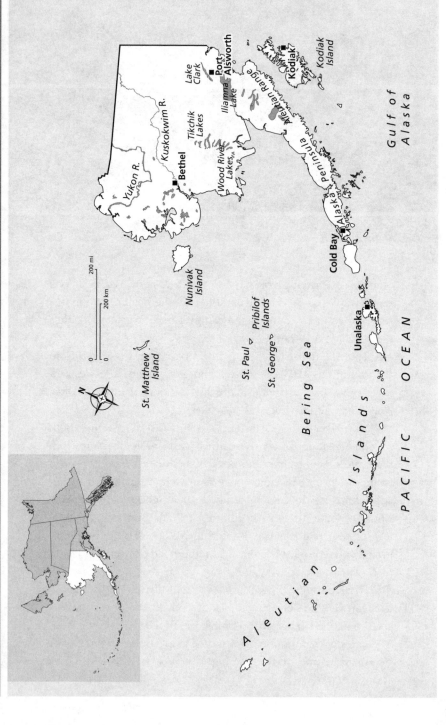

SOUTHWESTERN ALASKA

have blown their tops in this area—one of the most awesome, Novarupta, is part of Katmai National Park and Preserve. Through the region flow some of the nation's wildest rivers. And way, way, *way* out in the Bering Sea you'll find two tiny islands on which you'll see more birds of more species than you ever thought possible. Every visitor comes home from the Pribilof Islands a confirmed bird-watcher.

Among Native residents in the region, you'll meet Yu'pik Eskimos on the western mainland, Aleuts on the Aleutian and Pribilof Islands, and Alutiiq Natives on Kodiak Island.

Kodiak Island, in fact, is a good place to start an exploration of the region. The island ranks not only as the largest in Alaska, with a population of about 14,100, it also contains Alaska's earliest continuing European settlement, the city of *Kodiak.*

No roads or bridges connect Kodiak Island to the Alaska mainland, but the Alaska Marine Highway System (800–642–0066; www.ferryalaska.com) offers regular, dependable passenger and vehicle ferry service from Homer and Seward on the Kenai Peninsula several times each week. Alaska Airlines and ERA Aviation provide daily flights from Anchorage. There are visitor accommodations and services aplenty in the community. For information contact the *Kodiak Island Convention and Visitors Bureau* at 100 Marine Way (907–486–4782; www.kodiak.org).

Tourism as a major industry has not yet discovered Kodiak. It's clearly still off the beaten path. The result is that you can come away from a visit with a genuine feel for the way Alaskans live and work and play in this part of the Last Frontier. It's fun simply to wander along the boat docks and cannery sites, watching the frantic, frenzied busyness of salmon, crab, halibut, shrimp, and other fisheries landings. More than 3,000 commercial vessels—some quite

TOP 10 PLACES IN SOUTHWEST ALASKA

Dimitri's Greek restaurant	Kodiak Island Winery Cottages
Fort Abercrombie State Historical Park	Lake Clark National Park and Preserve
Galley Gourmet Dinner Cruises	Margaret Bay
Katmai National Park and Preserve	Raspberry Island Remote Camps
Kodiak Game Ranch	Shuyak Island

large—utilize Kodiak's two harbors, St. Paul and St. Herman, each year, making the area one of the busiest in the world. While you're at St. Paul harbor downtown checking out the fleet, make sure to stop in at **Harborside Coffee and Goods** (216 Shelikof Avenue; 907–486–5862), a friendly, comfortable coffeehouse with a water view. My husband and I once passed an entire afternoon there, just watching the boats come and go, the fishermen tend to their chores, and the seabirds ride the wind.

A great deal of Alaska's early European history resides in Kodiak. The first Russian settlement, established in 1784, was at Three Saints Bay, but the Russian trader and manager Alexander Baranov relocated his headquarters to present Kodiak in 1792. Originally Baranov's warehouse for precious sea otter pelts, and now the **Baranov Museum,** it was constructed about 1808 and is the oldest Russian building in Alaska. It's at 101 Marine Way and contains antiques and artifacts of the Russian and pre-Russian era, including grand samovars, handcrafted silver jewelry, and fine-woven Alutiiq basketry. Admission is $3. Phone (907) 486–5920 for information or visit www.baranov.us.

southwest alaskatrivia

Mishap Creek, also known as Big Loss Creek, on Unimak Island in the Aleutians, derived its name from an unfortunate incident. A lightkeeper, attempting to cross the creek after finding the bridge washed out, bundled up his clothes and tried to throw them across. Misjudging the distance, his clothes fell short of the far bank and were washed away.

—*Source:* U.S. Coast and Geodetic Survey

Kodiak's **Holy Resurrection Russian Orthodox Church,** the oldest parish in North America, stands in the city's downtown district at Kashaveroff Street and Mission Avenue. For information on tours call (907) 486–3854 or visit www .dioceseofalaska.org. You'll see colorful religious trappings of the Orthodox faith, including icons that date from Russia's czarist period. At **Saint Herman Theological Seminary,** on Mission Road north of the church, you can visit a replica of the first Russian Orthodox church on the island; the original was built in 1796. Father Herman was one of the early Orthodox monks who arrived to evangelize, educate, and provide medical attention to Alaska Natives. On August 9, 1970, he became the first North American religious figure to be canonized by the Russian Orthodox Church. The seminary's students are primarily Native Alaskans, including Yup'iks, Aleuts, and Tlingits.

Of course, before the Americans and before the Russians, there were the Native residents of Kodiak, the Alutiiq (pronounced Al-LOO-tig) people. In Kodiak you can learn a lot of indigenous history simply by attending the dances

Holy Resurrection Russian Orthodox Church, Kodiak

performed by a talented group called the **Kodiak Alutiiq Dancers.** And these Alutiiq performers are truly one of a kind in their stories and music and in their unique "snow falling" attire, with tassels of brilliant white arctic fox descending over black parkas. Three dozen or so dancers perform regularly in the afternoons when cruise ships are docked. Performers range from small children to elders, and their dances run the gamut from an ancestral kayaking dance to more contemporary, enacted stories of rich humor, such as the tale of a little boy who eats pudding as fast as his frantic parents can make it. For information call (907) 486–6740.

The **Alutiiq Museum and Archaeological Repository,** at 215 Mission Road, houses artifacts from numerous archaeological sites around the Kodiak Island Archipelago, and plans are under way to repatriate additional artifacts and artwork that are now scattered in museums around the world. The facility features a display gallery, state-of-the-art storage for sensitive artifacts, and a research laboratory. There's also a museum store that showcases the work of local artists. Hours are 9:00 A.M. to 5:00 P.M. Monday through Friday, 10:00 A.M. to 5:00 P.M. Saturday, Sunday by appointment. Admission is $3 (907–486–7004; www.alutiiqmuseum.com).

For some close-to-town hiking or exploring, walk across the bridge to **Near Island.** An easy walking path that circles the north end of the island starts on the north side of the road, just beyond the end of the bridge. Continue down the hill and you'll find **St. Herman's Harbor,** where during the summer you'll see the island's salmon fleet, if they aren't out fishing.

To view recent history, visitors can take a 4-mile drive out the Rezanof–Monashka Road to **Fort Abercrombie State Historical Park** to see the remains of World War II gun emplacements, restored bunkers, and other such

Celebrating a Saint's Life

If you're in Kodiak in early August, you can take part in a unique celebration of a unique man. On August 9, pilgrims from around the world gather in Kodiak to celebrate the canonization of Saint Herman by the Russian Orthodox Church.

Father Herman came to Kodiak in 1794 to convert the Natives of Alaska to Christianity and protect them from abuse by the fur traders of the Russian American Company. He helped build the first church in Kodiak and eventually moved to a nearby island, which he named New Valaam, now called Spruce Island.

There, at Monk's Lagoon, he started an orphanage and school for Native children and developed what was probably the first experimental agriculture station. Father Herman is credited with miraculous powers, including healings, averting a tsunami, and befriending Kodiak brown bears. He died on the island in 1837.

Father Herman was canonized Saint Herman on August 9, 1970, and each year on that date a flotilla of boats, all volunteer, line up at St. Paul Harbor in Kodiak to ferry pilgrims to Monk's Lagoon for a short service commemorating Herman's elevation to sainthood. The trip takes most of the day, so bring a lunch. There is no charge, and all who want to visit this holy place are welcomed.

For information on the pilgrimage, call the Holy Resurrection Russian Orthodox Church at (907) 486–3854.

artifacts. It's a toss-up what you'll find the more interesting—the massive concrete bunkers and fortifications that once protected Kodiak from a Japanese invasion or the breathtaking, panoramic view from rugged cliffsides and gentle shores. The area is thickly forested with Sitka spruce, berry plants, and wildflowers. Included in this 183-acre park are thirteen campsites for tenters and RVers, hiking trails, picnicking facilities, and good fishing and swimming spots. Call (907) 486–6339.

Several roads are worth exploring, including the *Chiniak Highway* that runs southwest from town then southeast. Particularly scenic points and beaches can be found from about mile 35 to the end of the 42-mile road. It's great for picnics, photography, and viewing more World War II gun battery emplacements. If you do your beach exploring at low tide, you'll be amazed at the sealife left behind in small pools after the tide has receded—tiny crabs, anemones, starfish, sea dollars, snails, itty-bitty fish, seaweeds, and all manner of other creepy-crawlies.

The Anton Larsen Bay Road, which begins about 5 miles from downtown at a junction with the Chiniak Highway, leads to Anton Larsen Bay. Along the way you just may spot a brown bear. They don't call the golf course at mile 3 (from the junction) Bear Valley Golf Course for nothing.

The road to **Pasagshak Bay** and Narrow Cape begins at mile 30.6 on the Chiniak Highway. The 16½-mile road brings you through scenic Pasagshak Pass to **Pasagshak River State Recreation Site,** which has restroom facilities, a picnic area, and camping. Beyond the river's mouth, visit Pasagshak Beach, where diehard, neoprene-clad surfers often can be seen catching the relentless waves. At mile 14.6 you'll pass the entrance to the Kodiak Game Ranch (more on them later in the chapter). You may encounter the ranch's buffalo wandering the hillsides, but don't give in to any strange temptation to approach them. They are livestock yet essentially live as wild animals. The road ends at **Fossil Beach.** Be careful when approaching the cliffs: They're unstable and falling rocks are a hazard.

If Kodiak has been, until recently, a lesser-known visitor destination, it has nonetheless been one of North America's best-known hunting areas for decades. The reason is *Ursus arctos middendorffi,* the Kodiak brown bear, which can weigh in at 1,500 pounds or more. Around 2,700 or more of the big bruins live on Kodiak Island, according to biologists. Most reside in the 2,491-square-mile **Kodiak National Wildlife Refuge** on Kodiak and nearby Uganik, Ban, and Afognak Islands. Visitors can dwell among these critters if they like by renting one of several backcountry recreation cabins constructed by the U.S. Fish and Wildlife Service. Access, incidentally, is only by float-equipped airplanes or boats. For

TOP ANNUAL EVENTS IN SOUTHWEST ALASKA

Camai Native Dance Festival:
Held in Bethel each spring to celebrate, well, just to celebrate. Features Native crafts, dance, food, and other activities. For information call (907) 543–2835 or visit www.bethelarts.com.

Kodiak Crab Festival:
Held each May in Kodiak to celebrate spring. Lots of rides, crafts, entertainment, and a survival-suit race challenging those brave enough to swim in the cold. Call (907) 486–5557 or visit www.kodiak.org

Unalaska World Record Halibut Derby:
Held each year in Unalaska. See if you can beat Jack Tragis's world-record 459-pound halibut and win $100,000. For information call (907) 581–2612 or visit www.unalaska.info/derby.htm.

information contact the Kodiak National Wildlife Refuge Manager, 1390 Buskin Road, Kodiak 99615 (907–487–2600), or stop by the ***U.S. Fish and Wildlife Service Visitor Center,*** about 4½ miles from downtown on Chiniak Highway.

Another place to bask in Kodiak's unforgettable beauty is to take a trip to ***Shuyak Island State Park.*** The 47,000-acre park, incidentally, encompasses part of a coastal forest system unique to the Kodiak Archipelago that contains only one tree species: the Sitka spruce. The 12-mile-long, 11-mile-wide island is 54 air miles north of Kodiak and has more sheltered interior waterways than anywhere in the Kodiak Archipelago. That's what makes it a great kayaking destination. Access to Shuyak Island is via water or air, and camping is by tent or public-use cabins, four of which are available for $75 a night. Contact the Kodiak District Office for current information (1400 Abercrombie Drive in Kodiak; 907–486–6339; www.alaskastateparks.org).

Kodiak's Waterfront

I walked with my husband along the docks of Kodiak's St. Paul Harbor on an unusually sunny morning in the middle of the week. Everyone was hard at work doing their day-to-day thing. For us it was a vacation, a getaway from our Kenai Peninsula home. My husband lived here once, before we met, and he was serving as something of a tour guide. As we neared the ferry dock at the Near Island channel, I saw nothing out of the ordinary. A commercial fishing boat was tied up, and a fisherman hosed off the decks. The Near Island bridge loomed above, a sharp concrete contrast to the beauty of this mostly green place.

"Why are we stopping here?" I asked. I was anxious to check out the historic-looking church I had seen earlier in the morning.

"You'll see," Andy replied, and he led me closer to the edge of the dock.

I peered into the inky blue water and looked. Nothing.

"Just give it a minute," Andy said, and he continued to stare into the water.

In a moment I saw a brown blur appear from the depths of the water, then, just as quickly, disappear again. Within seconds it returned, and then, as my eyes adjusted to this maritime setting, I saw them: sea lions. Not just one, or two, or even a handful, but more than a dozen of them—diving low, surfacing, racing one another around the fishing boat vying for the scraps of fish being hosed off the deck. They swarmed the place like so many ants on a picnic blanket.

Take advantage of this close-up—and free—glimpse of the North Pacific's wildlife. These thousand-pound-plus sea mammals may seem plentiful here, but elsewhere in Southwest Alaska their numbers are on the decline. Scientists are currently trying to figure out why they are disappearing.

—Melissa DeVaughn

If you don't want to arrange your own sightseeing, fishing, or hiking expeditions, there are several Kodiak outfitters that can get you set up. *South Kodiak Adventures* offers sportfishing packages for halibut, ling cod, and several species of salmon as well as wildlife viewing and photography tours. They offer years of experience with local wildlife, particularly the famous Kodiak brown bears. In addition to bears, you'll see all sorts of other land and marine mammals plus ancient petroglyphs while cruising in their 33-foot boat. For more information call (907) 836–2846 in the summer, (907) 929–4935 in the winter, or visit www.kodiak adventures.com.

southwest alaskatrivia

The Aleuts are known for producing beautiful handwoven baskets. The baskets come in all shapes but are most often cylindrical with a small knob as a handle. They are made from rye grass and can be ornately woven. The three most common styles of Aleut baskets are named after their islands of origin: Atka, Unalaska, and Attu.

Kodiak Sports & Tour is operated by Scott and Sonja Phelps in nearby Port Lions. The Phelpses offer sightseeing and photography trips, fishing charters, and hiking tours. For a really "out-there" experience, try a guided fly-in float trip on the Uganik River. Call (907) 454–2419 or visit www.kstkodiak.com.

Saltery Lake Lodge offers fishing, photography, and (in season) hunting adventures on Saltery Lake, near Ugak Bay on the eastern side of Kodiak Island. The lodge operates a floatplane and fishing vessel to aid guests in their quests for sockeye, pink, chum, and silver salmon as well as Dolly Varden, rainbow, and steelhead. A canoe is available for exploring the lake. Prices begin at $440 a day and decrease as length of stay increases. Call (800) 770–5037 or visit www.salterylake.com.

No trip to Kodiak is complete without exploring the many bays, inlets, and coves that are home to Alaska's diverse wildlife. And what a safe place from which to view an occasional Kodiak brown bear! In town try *Mythos Expeditions Kodiak* (907–486–5536; www.ptialaska.net/~mythosdk/mythos/index .html). Operating year-round and specializing in small groups, Mytho owner Dave Kubiak will help plan all sorts of expeditions, from close to town to far-off islands. In season you can also tag along to see how commercial cod jig fishing and halibut longline fishing are done. This is the only company to rent kayaks at Shuyak Island, which will save the trouble of flying one in.

A little farther out is *Spirit of Alaska Wilderness Adventures,* a business located on the south end of the already remote Amook Island in Uyak Bay. This company is designed with the independent traveler in mind. Getting there—usually by floatplane then by boat—will cost the most, and it'll cost you $245 per person per day for all the kayaking, wildlife viewing, fishing, beachcombing, or whatever else you choose to do, as well as lodging. Bring your own food. Call (866) 910–2327 or visit www.spiritofalaska.com.

For a completely different experience, try horseback riding at Bill Burton's 21,000-acre **Kodiak Game Ranch,** where you'll see not only ranch cattle but also huge buffalo wandering over the range. Burton's been in Kodiak since the sixties and has tried raising just about every breed of cattle known. But a rather large problem, the Kodiak brown bear, kept killing off the cattle. It wasn't until Burton began raising buffalo that he found success. Even a Kodiak brown won't mess with these big creatures. This is a working ranch, to be sure, but there are enough horses there to borrow one for a few hours. The rate is $60 for three hours. Phone (907) 486–3705 or visit http://chiniak.net/buffalo.

For charter fishing try **Kodiak Kingfisher Enterprises** (907–481–2803; www.kodiakkingfisher.com). They offer eight-hour charters departing at 8:00 A.M. from the St. Paul Boat Harbor as well as half-day and group-combo packages. Tackle, bait, gear, beverages, and snacks are included.

southwest alaskafacts

Wood-Tikchik State Park is the largest park in Alaska. It encompasses 1.6 million acres of wilderness in Southwest Alaska, near Dillingham.

The Aleutian Chain extends more than 1,100 miles and consists of more than one hundred islands.

And for a truly Kodiak experience, how about a dinner cruise upon the 42-foot yacht *Sea Breeze*? The **Galley Gourmet Dinner Cruise** features wonderful gourmet meals and locally roasted coffee, all while you enjoy the scenery of sea life and ocean. Marty Owen is your skipper, while wife Marion is the creator of the masterful dishes featuring fresh organic produce and award-winning seafood as available. Call (800) 253–6331 or (907) 486–5079 or visit www .kodiak-alaska-dinner-cruises.com.

If by horse and by boat isn't enough, yet another option is by bike. Kodiak is a great place for cycling. Bike rentals are available at **58 Degrees North,** located at 1231 Mill Bay Road (907–486–6249; 58north@ak.net). Rates begin at $35 for twenty-four hours for a mountain bike, and a printed mountain biking guide is available. Bikes also may be rented hourly for $5 per hour.

For a unique lodging alternative, try **Kodiak Island Winery Cottages** (907–486–4848; www.kodiakwinery.com). On the grounds of the winery, located on a tidal lagoon surrounded by towering alder and spruce, are three fully furnished cottages, with rates starting at $125 for the first bed, plus $25 per extra bed. The cottages are one hour from town and a short walk from ocean beaches and salmon streams. Make time to sample some of the winery's award-winning wines crafted from locally grown berries and fruits. The cellar and gift shop are open for tasting from 1:00 to 6:00 P.M. daily.

A unique stay is offered at the remote *Zachar Bay Lodge,* a cannery turned vacation destination 50 air miles southwest of Kodiak. This family-run business offers fishing and wildlife viewing, modern accommodations, and great meals. Package rates include round-trip airfare from Kodiak and four days' lodging for $2,500 per person. Call (800) 693–2333 or (907) 486–4120 or visit www .zacharbay.com.

A truly remote destination is *Raspberry Island Remote Camps,* operated by Lee and Cilla Robbins. The camp is situated amid an ancient spruce forest that prompts wide-eyed gawking. At the Robbinses' camp, you'll enjoy fishing, sightseeing, hiking, boating—you name it. Then, at the end of the day, you're on your own to lounge in the camp's hot spa or sauna, relax on the sundeck, or just retreat to your room to relax. Phone (907) 486–1781 or visit www.raspberry island.com.

southwest alaskafacts

Lake Iliamna, on the Alaska Peninsula in Southwest Alaska, is the state's largest lake. It covers 1,000 square miles and is 70 miles long, 20 miles wide, and 1,000 feet deep.

Kodiak became the first capital of Russian America in the late 1700s and was a major fur-trading center for many years.

Kayak Island in the Gulf of Alaska was the site of the first landing of Europeans in Alaska, on July 20, 1741.

Katmai National Park

During the morning of June 1, 1912, a volcanic mountain in what is now *Katmai National Park and Preserve* began a series of violent quakes and eruptions, the likes of which had seldom been recorded in earth's history. A full foot of volcanic ash fell on Kodiak, 100 miles distant, and darkened the sky to inky blackness. When the eruptions subsided, a valley at the site lay buried under 700 feet of ash. In 1916 when the first expedition entered the area, thousands of still-steaming fumeroles inspired the name Valley of 10,000 Smokes. That valley, curiously, remains stark and desolate to this day, though the surrounding area now thrives with lush growth and beautiful lakes and rivers teeming with salmon and other fish. You can visit the park easily, though no roads lead to it. Propeller-equipped aircraft offer daily access from King Salmon (accessible by jet from Anchorage) and less frequent flights are also available from Kodiak.

If you're a photographer you may want to join an annual *Joseph Van Os Photo Safari* in Katmai. Air transportation from Anchorage, hotel accommodations, meals, tours, and the expertise of a professional wildlife photographer are included in the weeklong tour. Call (206) 463–5383 or visit www.photo safaris.com for more information. Trips are in the $3,200 range.

Incidentally, if you want to bring a tent and camp in the park service *Brooks Campground* near the Brooks Lodge, be advised that reservations are required, as space is limited to sixty campers. For more details call the superintendent's office at (800) 365–2267. The phone is often busy, so you can also request information by mail from Katmai National Park, P.O. Box 7, King Salmon 99613 or by visiting www.katmainationalpark.com.

Katmai Wilderness Lodge, headquartered in Kodiak and located on Kukak Bay on the eastern coast of Katmai National Park, limits its guest list to twelve visitors a day. The company offers abundant wildlife viewing both ashore and from the water, including brown bears, whales, fox, eagles, seals, sea lions, and sea otters. There are also glacier treks, nature hikes, and kayak trips. The area is especially rich in archaeological resources. A four-day bear-viewing package from Kodiak costs $2,500; five days and four nights in a comfortable log cabin, with cook and guide, cost $2,950. Prices include a floatplane trip from Kodiak. For details call (800) 488–8767 or visit www.katmai-wilderness.com.

Unalaska and Dutch Harbor

If you look just at location, *Unalaska* and its adjacent neighbor, *Dutch Harbor,* would seem the most unlikely of tourist destinations, situated as they are out on the Aleutian chain. The two towns (functionally they're really just one; only a small bridge separates them) lie 800 air miles from Anchorage, about midway along the 1,000-mile Aleutian Islands chain that extends westerly from the Alaska Peninsula almost to Japan.

If you're a true fan of out-of-the-way travel, don't overlook this destination. Unalaska and Dutch Harbor offer a surprising number of pleasurable places to see, lots of things to do, and an amazing comfort level. Although no roads or surface highways lead there, the towns enjoy excellent daily air service from Anchorage (via PenAir) as well as a monthly schedule of calls by the Alaska Marine Highway System's passenger and auto ferry **Tustumena.** Traveling aboard the stateroom-equipped *Trusty Tusty,* as she's called, is in fact a terrific way to see this part of Alaska. The vessel leaves Homer twice a month, April through September, en route to Kodiak, Chignik, Sand Point, King Cove, Cold Bay, False Pass, and Unalaska. She leaves Unalaska twice monthly, arriving back in Homer two days later. One-way

Margaret Bay, a Land Rich in History

There's a place in Unalaska that tells much of the story of life in the Aleutians before the white man arrived. The site, in Margaret Bay, is being studied by scientists from around the country. But if you're interested in archaeology yourself, you can study it, too. Excavation of the site has revealed the tools and implements used by the Unangan people who inhabited this village more than 6,000 years ago.

Excavations at the site began in May 1996. It revealed remains of several stone-walled semisubterranean houses, as well as tools made of chipped stone, blades, stone lamps, bowls, lebrets, grinders, and pendants. The researchers even uncovered miniature carved masks.

The Grand Aleutian Hotel offers an adventure package that includes digging alongside professional archaeologists by day and relaxing in the comfort of Unalaska's nicest hotel by night. Call (800) 891–1194 or (907) 581–5150.

fare costs $325 from Homer, meals not included. Call (800) 382–9229 or visit www.ferryalaska.com.

Now for some geography: Unalaska is located on Unalaska Island and Dutch Harbor is situated on Amaknak Island. The bridge that connects them is called the Bridge to the Other Side. Incidentally, construction on a new Bridge to the Other Side is under way, so be prepared for delays.

Rich in Aleut, early Russian, and World War II history, Unalaska and Dutch Harbor have become a major bustling seafood landing and processing center in recent years. Together the two towns are in effect the number-one port in the United States in terms of pounds and value of fish and crab landed. The year-round population totals more than 4,300 residents, and there are thousands of additional commercial fishermen coming and going at all times. Recently the community has enjoyed a small but growing visitor influx, particularly World War II veterans who served in this theater in the 1940s. Many return to see the site of Japanese bombing attacks and the defensive fortifications the U.S. troops built and manned along shorelines and on mountainsides.

Birders come from around the world to see the rare whiskered auklet and other species, and anglers journey here to land world-class halibut and three kinds of salmon.

Accommodations here are much more plush than you might imagine. The wonderfully named *Grand Aleutian Hotel* (498 Salmon Way), in fact, offers uncompromising luxury in its 112 rooms, public areas, and gourmet restaurant, the *Chart Room,* where the chefs make innovative use of locally abundant seafood. The hotel offers rooms starting at $164 for doubles as well as tour packages for sightseers, birders, and sportfishers. Call (800) 891–1194 or visit www.grandaleutian.com for information and reservations.

The **Unalaska/Port of Dutch Harbor Visitor Bureau** can help with other activities in the area. Call (877) 581–2612 or visit www.unalaska.info.

With such excellent commercial fishing in this region, it goes without saying that those who enjoy recreational fishing will have a fine time here. **Shure-good Adventures** is one of several outfits offering halibut fishing and sightseeing excursions out of Dutch Harbor. Phone (907) 581–2378 or (877) 374–4386.

Surely the most compelling cultural and historical site is **Holy Ascension Russian Orthodox Cathedral**, constructed 1894–96. It contains an astonishing 697 documented icons, artifacts, and significant works of art, one of the largest and richest such collections in Alaska. Within the structure, too, are remnants of earlier churches and chapels used in 1808, 1826, and 1853. Most ground tours offer a visit to this historic landmark. Call the visitor bureau at (907) 581–2612 for details, or visit www.unalaska.info.

southwest alaskatrivia

Lake Iliamna, the state's largest lake, is reported to be inhabited by a sea monster. There's speculation that it is either a whale that somehow made its way into the lake in pursuit of salmon (the lake, by the way, supports the world's largest sockeye salmon run) or an oversized sturgeon.

Other possibilities in Unalaska and Dutch Harbor include nature excursions that focus on wildlife and geological features, marine adventures including World War II shipwrecks, gold-mining claims, sportfishing aboard charter vessels, and visits to a state-of-the-art processing plant. Again, contact the visitor bureau.

Bobbie Lekanoff is the person to call for a personalized tour of the area. Her **The Extra Mile Tours** specializes in off-the-beaten-path tours. Lekanoff has lived in Unalaska for over twenty years, so she knows these islands well. Choose from either standard or customized tours, including historic World War II sites, wildflower identification, bird-watching, and hiking. Her Ferry/Cruise Ship Special for $65 per person includes admission to the Museum of the Aleutians, the World War II Visitor Center, and the Holy Ascension Russian Orthodox Cathedral (if open). Two- and four-hour tours are available. Call (907) 581–6171 or visit www.unalaskadutchharbortour.com.

Greg Hawthorne offers an option even farther afield. His **Volcano Bay Adventures** tour starts with a fifteen-minute floatplane ride around the end of Unalaska Island to a lake at the foot of Mount Makushin. The camp there consists of five large wall tents, complete with kitchen-dining facilities, where a chef prepares hot meals daily. The main attraction, however, is stellar salmon fishing. Call (907) 581–3414 or visit www.volcano-bay.com.

Much of the land on Unalaska, Amaknak, and Sedanka Islands is privately owned by the **Ounalashka Corporation,** an Alaska Native corporation. It asks visitors who want to hike, ski, bike, or camp on this land to first obtain a permit from the corporate office. Permits may be requested by phone at (907) 581–1276 or from the office between 8:00 A.M. and 5:00 P.M., Monday through Friday. The office is located at 400 Salmon Way.

The Pribilof Islands

If you think the Aleutians are "far out," wait until you hear about *St. Paul* and *St. George* Islands in the lonesome middle of the Bering Sea. Located about 800 air miles west-southwest of Anchorage and more than 200 miles north of the Aleutian chain, the Pribilof Islands are home to fewer than 1,000 people, but—in the summer at least—the islands provide a hauling-out place for an estimated one and a quarter million howling, barking, fighting, breeding, birthing fur seals. In addition, the islands' craggy sea cliffs provide a summer nesting sanctuary for more than two million seabirds (211 species), some of which you'll see nowhere else in this hemisphere. Add domestic reindeer and fascinating Native Aleut cultures and history, and you have a superb, offbeat travel destination.

It's surprisingly easy to visit the Pribilofs. Many hundreds do each year. *St. Paul Island Tours* (877–424–5637) offers three- to eight-day excursions that include round-trip airfare from Anchorage, accommodations at the new King Eider Inn, and daily forays to beaches and cliffs. From behind protective blinds at various beaches, you'll view thousands of fur seals, including bellowing "beachmasters," their "harems," and pups. A three-day, two-night tour is $1,406. Tours do not include meals or gratuities. Meals are served buffet-style and typically cost between $10 to $17, or around $39 dollars a day. At numerous cliffs you can easily photograph superabundant bird species. You'll also visit the ornate Russian Orthodox church and the new TDX Corporation museum, and you'll meet members of the largest population of Aleuts anywhere. The eight-day option goes for $2,420. Meals are extra and average $30 to $36 daily for breakfast, lunch, and dinner.

Dedicated offbeat travelers—especially birders—will want to extend their trips to St. George, about 40 air miles south of St. Paul. Travelers (or their travel agents) will have to make more of their own arrangements, but the opportunity here is to view not only fur seals (250,000 come to the island each year) but the largest seabird colony in the Northern Hemisphere. On its precipitous cliffs, St. George hosts the largest colony of thick-billed murres in the North Pacific as well as 98 percent of the world's population of red-legged kittiwakes. It's also the the largest breeding colony for parakeet auklets . . . and the list goes on.

southwest alaskatrivia

Unimak, the first island in the Aleutian Chain, is home to Shishaldin Volcano. Shishaldin has erupted several times over the last two centuries, earning the local name of Smoking Moses and, before that, Pogromni, Russian for "desolation."

PenAir (800–448–4226; www.pen air.com) operates between St. George and St. Paul (round-trip fare, $176) and also provides regular service between Anchorage, St. George, St. Paul, and back for $894. Tours that include accommodations and meals unfortunately aren't available. The single hotel on St. George is the ten-room *St. George Hotel,* which can accommodate a total of eighteen guests, and although the hotel offers no meal service, guests have free use of the kitchen and dining-room facilities. A grocery store is located about a block away. The rate is $169 per person per night. Call (907) 859–2255 or (907) 859–9222.

Lake Clark National Park

It's probably one of the National Park System's least known and visited parks—but that's one of the things that makes *Lake Clark National Park and Preserve* across Cook Inlet from the Kenai Peninsula special. Access is only by air (or water, on the shores of Cook Inlet); you certainly won't find Yellowstone- or Yosemite-type roads and trails within the park boundaries. This is some of the wildest and most breathtakingly beautiful country on earth, with saltwater shores, turquoise blue lakes, steaming volcanoes, and cascading waterfalls that drop from towering mountainsides. Three rivers in the park have been designated National Wild Rivers. You travel in this country by foot, by boat, or by air. Accommodations in the backcountry are tents; either you bring your own or book with an outdoor guiding service that provides everything from fly-in charters to shelter, food, and expertise.

To access Lake Clark you can hop a one- to two-hour charter flight from either Anchorage, Soldotna, or Homer. Check with *Rust's Flying Service* out of Anchorage (907–243–1595; www.flyrusts.com), *High Adventure Air Charter* (907–262–5237; www.highadventureair.com) out of Soldotna, or *Bald Mountain Air Service* out of Homer (907–235–7969; www.baldmountainair .com). Expect to pay about $350 to fly round-trip from Anchorage. Another option is to take a commercial flight from Anchorage to Iliamna and then book a charter from there on *Iliamna Air Taxi* (907–571–1248; www.iliamna air.com).

Port Alsworth is the primary jumping-off point for the park. There you'll find the *Lake Clark National Park Visitor Center* and the *Tanalian Falls Trail Head,* along with a number of lodges and private airstrips. At *Island Lodge* (877–349–3195; www .islandlodge.com), longtime Alaskans Richard and Alison Lausten offer three-, five-, and seven-day packages that include lodging, meals, and your choice of activities. Located on a forty-five-acre island in Lake Clark, the lodge

Food cache at Lake Clark National Park and Preserve

offers great views of the lake and the Chigmit Mountains. From there you can fish, kayak, hike, walk along the beach, or take a sightseeing cruise. Package prices begin at $1,816 for three days and four nights and meals are included, with complimentary beer and wine at dinner.

If a lodge stay sounds too cushy, the Laustens also offer river rafting on the Mulchatna and Chilikadrotna Rivers. Trips start at $2,200 per person for four days and include transportation from Island Lodge, food, gear, guides, and lodging at the beginning or end of the journey.

Another lodging and outfitting option is *Alaska's Lake Clark Inn & Air* (907–781–2224; www.lakeclark.com), also operated out of Port Alsworth. Hosts Mark and Sandy Lang are experts in planning and providing outdoor recreational opportunities. From the lodge you can hunt, fish, sightsee, hike, take a river trip, or just relax in one of the guest cabins. They offer a la carte services that include cabin rentals, meal packages, boat rentals, raft rentals, and floatplane charters, or you can request a custom package. Both guided and unguided fly-out fishing are available, too.

For bear viewing you can't beat Carl and Kirsten Dixon's first-class operation at *Redoubt Bay Lodge* through the *Within the Wild Adventure Company* (907–274–2710; www.withinthewild.com). Located only 50 air miles southwest of Anchorage, the lodge is the only five-acre privately owned property in the area, and it is home to one of the densest bear populations in the state. From the handcrafted lodge and cabins, you can also enjoy hiking, sportfishing, kayaking, and flight-seeing adventures. Choose from one- to four-day trip options starting at $1,025. Their Evening with the Bears package is $985. Unlike many of the other Lake Clark options, Within the Wild includes airfare from Anchorage in its rates.

Bethel

The city of *Bethel* and the surrounding Yukon-Kuskokwim delta country really doesn't come readily to mind when one compiles a list of Alaska's better known visitor destinations. Located 400 air miles from Anchorage on the banks of the mighty Kuskokwim River, this city of 5,500 mostly Yu'pik Eskimo residents is primarily a commercial fishing, trading, and government center. None of the Goliaths of the travel industry have offices here. Fact is, there aren't many Davids either.

But of course that's what attracts a good number of us. That and the community's location about 90 miles inland from the Bering Sea and the mouth of the Kuskokwim River. Bethel sits in the midst of the United States' largest game refuge, the twenty-million-acre *Yukon Delta National Wildlife Range.*

southwest alaskatrivia

Bethel is one of the western-most communities in Alaska. It began as a mission in 1889 when Moravian missionaries came to "tame" the people. In keeping with its Godly ambitions, the community became known as "Bethel," which comes from the biblical passage Genesis 35:1, "Arise, go up to Bethel, and dwell there."

The range, incidentally, is one of those places where you really ought not to venture on your own—not, at least, without knowledgeable local advice. Fortunately, such information is readily available. *Kuskokwim Wilderness Adventures* (owned by long-time Alaskans John McDonald, Beverly Hoffman, Mike Hoffman, and Jill Hoffman) rents outdoor equipment, including rafts, life jackets, tents, cooking gear, and Coleman stoves. They can arrange custom tours. Contact them at (907) 543–3900 or visit www.kuskofish.com

Whether you take a package tour or not, don't fail to include the city's *Yugtarvik Regional Museum* in your itinerary. (*Yugtarvik,* in Yu'pik, means "place for peoples' things.") Located in the city's cultural center, the museum is chock-full of Eskimo art, artifacts, tools, and household items from the past and present. There's a full-size kayak, complete with a realistic paddler in it, paddle, grass mat, ice pick, and other accessories. You also will find a mounted musk ox head and cape on the wall, mounted birds of the region, dolls, grass baskets, ivory work, and beaded items. Many of the craft items are for sale. Call (907) 543–1819.

There are several hotel and B&B accommodations in Bethel, among them ***Allanivik Hotel*** (1220 State Highway), operated by the Association of Village Council Presidents (AVCP, Inc.). Summer room rates start at $97 for a single and $108 for doubles. In addition to the guesthouse, there is a separate building featuring suites with private baths starting at $145. For those staying long term, Allanivik offers a bunkhouse with kitchenette. Prices vary depending on length of stay. Phone (907) 543–4305.

There are three places worth mentioning for excellent meals. At Allanivik Hotel (formerly Pacifica Guest House), there's the ***VIP Restaurant*** (907–543–4305) a local favorite featuring great sushi, among other menu items. Another popular choice is the ***Shogun Restaurant*** at 320 Tundra Street (907–543–2272), which despite its Japanese name serves authentic Mexican and Chinese cuisine. ***Dimitri's*** (281 Fourth Avenue; 907–543–3434), features Greek specialties—be sure to try the gyro.

Places to Stay in Southwestern Alaska

BETHEL

Allanivik Hotel,
1220 State Highway;
(907) 543–4305.

KATMAI NATIONAL PARK AND PRESERVE

Brooks Campground,
near Brooks Lodge;
(800) 365–2267.

Katmai Wilderness Lodge,
eastern coast of Katmai
National Park;
(800) 488–8767,
www.katmai-wilderness.com

KODIAK

Best Western Kodiak Inn,
236 Rezanof Drive;
(888) 563–4254.

Buskin River Inn,
1395 Airport Way;
(907) 487–2700.

Kodiak Island Winery Cottages;
(907) 486–4848.
Three fully furnished cottages
adjacent to an award-
winning winery.

Raspberry Island Remote Camps;
(907) 486–1781,
www.raspberryisland.com
On Raspberry Island outside
Kodiak.

Saltery Lake Lodge,
1516 Larch Street;
(800) 770–5037.

Zachar Bay Lodge,
50 miles southwest of
Kodiak;
(800) 693–2333, (907)
486–4120,
www.zacharbay.com

LAKE CLARK

Island Lodge;
(877) 349–3195.
On a forty-five acre island in
Lake Clark.

Redoubt Bay Lodge;
(907) 274–2710.
Handcrafted lodge and
cabins near the eastern end
of the park; great bear-
viewing opportunities.

UNALASKA

Grand Aleutian Hotel,
498 Salmon Way;
(800) 891–1194,
www.grandaleutian.com
Upscale accommodations.

Places to Eat in Southwestern Alaska

BETHEL

Dimitri's,
281 Fourth Avenue;
(907) 543–3434.
Great Greek food,
including superb gyros.

KODIAK

Buskin River Inn,
1395 Airport Way;
(907) 487–2700.
Excellent steak and seafood.

El Chicano,
103 Center Avenue;
(907) 486–6116.
Tasty Mexican food.

**Harborside Coffee
and Goods,**
216 Shelikof Avenue;
(907) 486–5862.
Friendly, comfortable
coffeehouse.

UNALASKA

**Chart Room at the Grand
Aleutian Hotel,**
498 Salmon Way;
(800) 891–1194.
Freshly caught, local
seafood.

Indexes

Entries for museums and national and state parks appear also in the special indexes on pages 212 and 213.

GENERAL INDEX

Wiseman Museum, 175
Within the Wild Adventure Company,
87, 195–96
Wonder Lake, 143
World Championship Sled Dog
Race, 88
Worthington Glacier State Recreation
Site, 122
WP&YR Depot, 42
Wrangell, 11–15
Wrangell Chamber of Commerce
Visitor Information Center, 12
Wrangell Garnet Ledge, 13
Wrangell Hostel, 14
Wrangell Mountain Air, 124
Wrangell Museum, 12
Wrangell Ranger District, 15
Wrangell–St. Elias National Park, 122
Wrangell–St. Elias National Park and
Preserve Headquarters and Visitor
Center, 125, 148

XYZ Center, 166

Yugtarvik Regional Museum,
196–97
Yukon Arts Centre, 63
Yukon–Charley Rivers National
Preserve, 73
Yukon Conservation Society, 63
Yukon Delta National Wildlife
Range, 196
Yukon Permanent Art Collection, 63
Yukon Queen, 74
Yukon Riverboat Tours, 65
Yukon River Camps, 174
Yukon Transportation Museum, 62
Yukon Visitor Reception Centre,
61–62
Yukon Wildlife Preserve, 62–63

Zachar Bay Lodge, 189

MUSEUMS INDEX

Alaska Aviation Heritage Museum, 84
Alaska Railroad Museum, 146
Alaska State Museum, 25–26
Alutiiq Museum and Archaeological
Repository, 183
Anchorage Museum of History
and Art, 84
Atlin Historical Museum, 58
Baranov Museum, 182
Carrie McLain Museum, 166
Clausen Memorial Museum, 18
Corrington Museum of
Alaska History, 42
Dorothy G. Page Museum, 112
Elmendorf Wildlife Museum, 85
George Ashby Memorial Museum,
124–25
George Johnston Museum, 61
Juneau–Douglas City Museum, 25
Kluane Museum of Natural History, 76

Knik Museum and Sled Dog Mushers'
Hall of Fame, 113
MacBride Museum, 62
McCarthy Museum, 123
Mining Museum, 66
Museum of Alaska Transportation
and Industry, 113–14
Museum of Yukon Natural
History, 58–59
Pratt Museum, 109
Sheldon Jackson Museum, 20, 22
Sheldon Museum and Cultural
Center, 36
Skagway Museum and Archives, 44
Soldotna Historical Society
Museum, 106
Stewart Historical Society
Museum, 11
Talkeetna Historical Society
Museum, 114